LITTLE SHIPS

a novel

SANDRA SCOFIELD

Print ISBN: 978-1-93083-531-3
eBook ISBN: 979-8-35093-875-3

WELLSTONE PRESS
Wellstonepress.com
4364 Wolff St.
Denver CO 80212
www.sandrajscofield.com

Excerpts from the novel appeared in *Narrative Magazine* and *StorySouth*

BOOKS BY SANDRA SCOFIELD

FICTION

This Is Not a Novel (ebook)

Swim: Stories of the Sixties (Wellstone Press)

Plain Seeing (HarperColllins)

A Chance to See Egypt (HarperCollins)

Opal On Dry Ground (HarperCollins)

More Than Allies (Plume)

Walking Dunes (Plume)

Beyond Deserving (Plume)

Gringa (Plume)

MEMOIR

Mysteries of Love and Grief:
Reflections on a Plainswoman's Life
(Texas Tech University Press)

Occasions of Sin: A Memoir (W W Norton)

CRAFT

The Scene Book: A Primer for the Fiction Writer (Penguin)

The Last Draft: A Novelist's Guide to Revision (Penguin)

SOME PRAISE FOR SANDRA SCOFIELD'S PREVIOUS WORKS

"Scofield constructs her usual rich tapestry of family interaction, showing how both heartbreak and bad patterns are endlessly repeated."

—*Publishers Weekly*

"A memorable family ballad, in tune with the times."

— *Kirkus Reviews*

"An intelligent, wickedly observant novel."

New York Times Book Review

"Few writers capture feelings of yearning and disappointment as palpably as Scofield."

Newsday

"Wonderfully evocative."

The Los Angeles Times

"A novel whose plot, like a vast open sky, is enlivened with a fireworks display of colorful, twisting, brilliantly rendered emotions...."

—*New York Times Book Review*

For Bill

Nothing is so easy
when you might come apart
in the middle at any moment—

Tove Jansson, *The Summer Book*

BLOOM

First is love.

Nick Becker was in his first job out of pharmacy school, working in a grocery store in Frost, a small town in southern Oregon, forty minutes from Lupine, where he grew up. Customers liked Nick. He was tall and thin, he looked serious, and he spoke in an authoritative, patient manner. Now and then somebody told him he looked like a young Abraham Lincoln. He remembered names.

His mother had wanted him to be a doctor. "With all you know about drugs," she told him, "you'd be a hell of a psychiatrist." His father, who owned the hardware store in Lupine, had wanted to help him buy his own drugstore. Nick had earned excellent grades and had passed his state license exams without a blink, but he didn't want to own a business, and he didn't want to go to any more school. He was grateful to his parents, but he was ready to be on his own. He had a PharmD degree from Oregon State University—three years of undergrad prerequisites and four years of training—and no debt. He had an apartment over a leather goods store right in town, a sound system, a little TV, a 1993 Plymouth Colt, and two weeks' supply of long-sleeved light blue shirts. He had had a steady girlfriend through his last two years of school, but she got a job in Seattle that was too good to refuse—she was a physical education teacher—and they parted with no drama. They had spoken cheerfully on the phone a few times, then let their relationship fade like an old letter. She was a great girl, but not *the* girl.

At night Nick smoked a couple joints and stayed in; he liked to listen to Townes Van Zandt, The Band, Johnny Cash, old blues. His girlfriend used to tease him, saying he was an old fogey. He liked music he already knew, a steady rhythm. Sometimes he read a mystery, but he almost always thumbed through the middle to get to the end. He went to sleep around midnight and woke up in time for coffee, toast, and two strips of bacon at the cafe on the Wellen highway.

Then he met Karin Sundersson. She looked like a Norse goddess. She was as tall as he was, with limp pale hair. She had lived her whole life in one house. Her Swedish immigrant parents, Henry and Helve, co-owned a berry farm in Frost Valley above the town with Henry's brother, Karl. The daughters Karin and Elin had grown up like Swedish farm girls, with ponies and long blond pigtails, modest clothes, good manners, endless hours in the outdoors. Elin graduated from high school and moved to Malmo to visit her mother's sister, Anna, for a year while she explored the country and improved her Swedish. She stayed. She married a policeman and was living in Uppsala, working in a preschool. She had acquired Swedish citizenship and had never returned to the United States. She wrote Karin and told her Sweden was beautiful and she could stay with her as long as she wanted if she came, but Karin didn't know why anyone would want to live so far from her parents. She put Elin out of her mind. She was close to her mother, and at twenty still lived at home and worked as a cashier in the store where Nick was a pharmacist. Recently, for no good reason that she could name, she had been suffering from insomnia. Nights were interminable. Lights stung her eyes; darkness frightened her. She staggered to work and pulled herself together, shift to shift.

One night the store was closing. Lights had been dimmed, there was the shuffle and clank of boxes and registers, calls of "G'night!" Nick had work to do before he could go home. He liked this time, when the store was dark except for the strip of light above his counter. He was filling the last of the call-in refills. He put prescriptions into plastic baggies that had attached tabs with holes, so he could hang them alphabetically on horizontal poles in rows. He was thinking that it was a tried and true but old-fashioned way to organize orders, when he looked up and saw a young woman standing in front of him; the gate was shut and she looked like someone looking out of a jail cell. She said, "I need something, Nick."

He couldn't remember her name or whether he ever knew it. He snapped his fingers.

"Karin," she said. She pointed toward the front of the store, and he remembered who she was. He opened the gate on his window.

"How can I help you, Karin?"

"I can't sleep." She raised her cupped hands. From the pharmacy nonprescription shelves she had collected bottles and tins of syrups and tinctures and pastilles and lozenges and tablets: herbs and painkillers and antihistamines. "I'm strong," she said. "Healthy. But I wonder if I'm going crazy. I can't sleep."

"None of that will help," he said. "It takes either real drugs—your doctor has to prescribe them, and they mess you up; or you get so tired you fall over—or—" She blinked and said, "Or what?" almost demanding, and he loved her right then and of course ever after. He said, "If you will go out with me, I will explain sleep hygiene to you. I will share my secret and you will sleep."

She called her mother, who would otherwise be worried and call all around, maybe the sheriff; she babbled a lie about an old friend whose house was in Wellen. Then she and Nick went to the Alehouse nearby, and they had bottles of beer and long salty fried sweet potatoes, and began slowly to catch up on the little they needed to know about one another, before they went to Nick's apartment to smoke and sleep. They didn't bother to make love, because they knew there would be time for that. There was no talk of sleep hygiene, but he did teach her how to roll a joint and how to inhale and not cough. He taught her to sip water and hold it on her tongue before she swallowed. He taught her to bat away the giddy feeling, so that she would fall into sleep like a feather through humid air. He didn't let her smoke very much, because it was new for her, but he saw right away that she understood what was happening. He didn't have to ask if she would come back.

She had never liked anyone, never dated in school, hardly noticed men. Her father worried that she would never get married. Her mother wanted her to take her time. She was very private. She had a girlfriend from high school, Jenny, who still lived in the area, but she was married and had children, and Karin only saw her when she came in the store. Her cousin Collin, two years younger, still lived at home nearby and the two of them sometimes went to movies, but all they had in common was the familiarity of cousins. She helped her mother with household chores, and read romances and cozy mysteries, but recently something had happened that turned time around, so that there were hours and hours in the night to wonder if this was her life.

Nick had thought he loved the woman he lived with in school, but when he would wake from a long doze and see her so sturdy and bouncing and earnest, he would know they were only waiting for an easy stopping place, which came when she got her job and he got his.

He hadn't thought of her in a long time. He had no notions about love, he could not have said what he wanted, but when he and Karin stretched out on his bed, smoking in the dark, he was content. Some things are outside of thought. The smoke glides snake-like toward the open window, the hot place in your throat relaxes, your chest blooms.

MARCH

1

The Beckers—Nick, Karin, and their adolescent daughters Tilde and Juni—had been living in a two-bedroom apartment half an hour south of Portland, Oregon for four months, since Nick got a job installing new computer software in the pharmacies of a chain of drugstores all over Oregon. He enjoyed the challenge and the break from being cooped up in a pharmacy kiosk counting pills and advising customers. It meant he did a lot of driving and once or twice a week stayed over out of town. He had rented their apartment in a two-story complex right off the I-5 freeway, promising they would get a house as soon as the job settled down, but he hadn't mentioned moving again. He and Karin talked about putting the girls in public school so they could join some sports teams, but he drove away in their only car every day, and the middle school was across the freeway and another two miles after that, so the girls didn't go. At their age, they should have been in seventh and eighth grades, but their mother said they were good readers, and what else mattered? They had both taken required state tests for fifth graders two years earlier (to keep the state off their backs), and though Juni was behind in math, the state did no more than send a form letter urging attention to the deficient skills. The girls had a big carton of homeschooling books and workbooks and a laptop computer that had been sent to them from the state education offices in September, when they were living in Salem; and there were certified teachers who could have helped the girls online, but the internet had

been cut off because Karin didn't pay the bill. She had lost interest in
school stuff, so the girls dipped in the box when they wanted to. Juni
read the language arts books—anthologies, novels—and any parts of
the science texts that were about animals. Tilde read a lot, too, and
worked through the mathematics books—hers and Juni's; her mother
said she was like a caterpillar chewing through parsley. Sometimes the
girls drilled one another on spelling science vocabulary, easy words
like muscle and environment and savanna and terrestrial. The state
materials included fabric-bound journals for both girls. Juni wrote
poems in hers, and lists of places she wanted to go in the world, and
designs of clothes she would buy if she could, and sometimes, cats with
large paws. Tilde copied her favorite (hardest) mathematics exercises
into her journal, and drew sketches of trees, plants, and fish. Neither
girl ever wrote about what was going on or not going on in their lives,
any more than they spoke about such things. Each had memories they
didn't talk about. They had no friends—they never had had—but they
had each other and the open promise of the future.

If there was a library, they hadn't found it, but they knew where
all the fast food places were on their side of the freeway, and there
was a discount mall where they spent hours looking at things like
tennis shoes, camping equipment, stuffed animals and baseball caps.
Once in a while they shoplifted something cheap and useless, but they
seemed to be invisible and it wasn't a thrill. Whatever they took they
threw behind a bush on their way home. There was a pocket park
nearby with two swings and a shabby backboard with a basketball
hoop. Homeless people had tents and sheets of plastic to sleep under
at the edge of the park, and they hung out in the day; sometimes the
girls stood at the edge and said hi if someone noticed them, then ran
away. Sometimes the girls waited for their mother to nap, and then
they sneaked out and ran across the freeway overpass like vagrant

dogs. There was a cluster of nicer stores over there. If no cops were around, they begged, and they always got a few dollars and coins. Once a lady with gray hair cut short as a man's gave Tilde a five-dollar bill and offered them a ride. They gave her wide-eyed looks and Juni said, We're not allowed!

Nick always stopped at a grocery store on the way home and brought in milk, sacks of cereals, soups, sandwich meat, bread, margarine and candy bars—the sort of things you bought to go stay for a weekend in a cabin in the woods. Karin never left the apartment. She played solitaire, watched TV, looked at magazines, colored intricate designs on pages she tore from the girls' journals, and slept a lot. She had been thin, but now she was fat in the middle, while Nick was skinny like a stick. The girls washed clothes in the basement's coin-operated machines. When Nick got home at night, he ate a sandwich and sometimes played cards or Scrabble with the girls, and then he went in his room and smoked.

If he hadn't lost his job at the big box store in Salem, the family would still be in a house, and the girls might be going to school.

Sometimes the girls wandered along the freeway and talked about what would happen if they hitchhiked—north or south, it didn't matter. They didn't have any real sense of where they were or what was beyond them. Their grandmothers were four hours away, and they knew if they called them, one or both would come get them, but you can't leave your parents like that, just when they are having a hard time. It was understood: the family was a unit. You are my ruby ring, Karin told Tilde; you are my opal brooch, she told Juni. You are my heart, Nick said. You are my girls. Juni and Tilde believed them.

One night, Nick called from Bend to say he was late and they shouldn't wait up for him. A little later he called and said he was going to get a motel. He was too tired to drive.

Karin said, oh well, we can watch TV. She liked QVC. The girls scrambled the last four eggs and watched them congeal in the skillet, then cut them into wedges like pie.

Karin lay on the couch with her swollen leg stretched out, bundled in a blanket because she was chilled. She had a ring on one toe, and she couldn't get it off. She turned on the TV and sent Tilde to get her credit cards from the shoebox under their bed. Tilde brought back bracelets, too. The girls sat on the floor, leaning against the couch. They held their hands up so the bracelets wouldn't fall off.

It was time for jewelry. Karin decided to buy matching necklaces for the three of them. She shuffled a deck of cards for a while, then picked one, held it up as if it had an answer, then called in her order. Her hair was wet around her face and her skin was bruised under her eyes, purple like the swollen toe.

Are you sick? the girls asked. Are you okay, Mommy?

Karin said she was tired and limped off to bed. Her bracelets jangled. The girls watched TV until they were too sleepy to undress, and they crawled into bed together.

Early in the morning, Karin woke them with her howling. They ran in and begged her to stop. What's wrong? what's wrong? they cried. Karin was tossing around on the bed. After a while she got quiet, and the girls couldn't wake her. Their daddy came home soon after and called 911, and off he went with their mother in an ambulance.

The girls watched from the window as they pulled away.

They were hungry. There was cereal but no milk. They found a can of pineapple and one of lima beans. They watched TV. They spread their mother's credit cards out on the kitchen table and they drew their own. Tilde's had fish on hers; Juni's had birds. They slept through the long afternoon. When it was dark they put on pajamas and went to their room.

Juni said, Let's play store.

They took out all the boxes from the ends of their closet and from under the bed. Many boxes were still wrapped in shipping paper and tape, and they had to get a paring knife. They opened all of them and set the boxes around the room, nested in their lids. They lined the walls and the closet doors three deep. They put on all the jewels they could wear: two on every finger, up their arms to the elbows, heavy around their necks. There were tiaras for both of them. They got lamps from other rooms to make theirs bright.

When Nick got home, he came into their room carrying the credit cards from the table. He looked around the room like he had never been there before, then plopped the cards down on their bed. It was low and his skinny knees stuck up. Tilde pulled the shoeboxes full of bills from under the bed and dumped them beside him. He rustled the envelopes with one hand, swish swish, and threw the cards on top. He put his hands out on the bed and wadded the sheet. He was crying without making any sound. In a little while he told them he had brought a pizza. Then he went out again.

The sisters lay down on the floor. They spread their limbs like snow angels. The lamplight shone on their glittering arms.

***

When Nick hadn't come back from the hospital in the morning, the girls looked around the house until they had a few dollars, then walked to McDonald's and split a pancake breakfast and a cup of orange juice. Tilde put a sausage between her teeth and bent toward her sister; Juni bit off half.

Tilde said, "Remember Mormor's pankakkor?" and Juni said, "If we wait a little while, we could have a hamburger." But they were out of money. They filled their juice cup with Coke. They sat away from the service counter, looking out at the traffic, sometimes knocking each other's legs under the table, never changing expression. They didn't talk, but they called out words: aphrodisiac! sentimental! anthropomorphic! indubitable!

The counter clerks watched them; they weren't causing trouble.

They rushed back to the apartment to pee. The door was ajar and the apartment reeked of marijuana. They looked in their parents' bedroom. Nick was asleep on his bed. He was on his back in his boxer shorts and undershirt, his arms straight at his side, his legs open in a long upside-down V, his mouth slack. They stood there a few minutes listening to him snore, and then Nick's cell phone rang. They found it on the floor by his bed.

Juni answered. It was a woman who wanted to speak to Mr. Becker.

"Daddy is so asleep I don't think I can wake him," Juni said. She put the phone on speaker. "He was at the hospital all night."

"Sweetheart, I know, I'm so sorry, I have to talk to him, so I will know what we're supposed to do here."

Tilde flapped her hands: Who? Who?

"I can tell him to call you if you tell me who you are."

"It would be better if you could wake him up. We can't start anything until your father comes down. How old are you, honey?"

"Thirteen."

"Oh dear." There was a silence Juni couldn't fill.

"Do you have a pencil and paper? I'll wait while you find something."

Juni laid the phone down. Tilde picked it up and looked at caller ID. It said, Gateway Abbey.

"Daddy," Tilde said, leaning over him. His breath was hot and horrible. "There's a woman on the phone for you."

Nick grunted and rolled away on his side. The back of his shirt was wet.

"He'll call you in a little while," Tilde told the woman. "He can see your number on his phone." She hung up.

"Who was it?" Tilde asked.

"I think it was about Mom. A nurse, maybe."

"If we wake him up, we can find out," Tilde said.

"Whether she's dead."

"He's been smoking," Tilde said.

"No use trying," Juni said.

Juni got a volleyball from the closet and they went downstairs and practiced serves against the door of one of the garages, standing far back at the driveway entrance. Thump. Thump. The door next to them rose as a gray snub-nosed car approached. A woman drove into the space, got out, and walked towards them. They could see bulging plastic bags in the back seat.

Juni held the ball, twirling it on her fingers. The woman scowled.

"It may not be my business, but I am going to ask anyway. Why aren't the two of you in school? I see you around here, where's your mother?"

Tilde said, "She home-schools us. We have exercise time."

Juni sent the ball flying hard against the garage door right back of where the woman was standing, and she jumped. The woman said, "I have a mind to call the police, young ladies."

The girls watched the woman get her bags, close the garage, and go into her apartment at the top of the near stairs, and then they went up to their own. They turned on the TV, but they hated daytime programs—all the talking, the drama. They sat on the couch staring at the TV, though, because they didn't know what else to do. They kept the sound off. There were five women sitting along a table, talking and gesticulating madly. It didn't seem possible that anyone was listening. You couldn't tell if the women were arguing.

When the girls were little, they used to pretend to be characters in *Days of Our Lives*, but now that would feel stupid. They had a few library books from Salem, months overdue, but they had read them numerous times. Their mother's magazines—gossip, knitting, cooking—were scattered around the apartment.

The woman from Gateway Abbey called again in an hour or so. Tilde answered and said, "You hold on and I'll make him talk to you."

She shook Nick's shoulder and she kicked the bed and then she told the woman, "He says he'll call you as soon as he has a shower."

Then she called their grandmother Eleanor, Nick's mother. Phone numbers were written an inch high with marker ink on the wall by the hallway door. Eleanor was at work—she was an attendance counselor at the high school in Lupine, the last town in Oregon before the mountains into California—and the number of the school was annotated: *Emrgncy only*. There was nothing to do but give her the number of the woman who didn't know what to do with their mother, because Nick was not going to get up any time soon.

2

Eleanor had never liked Helve, but she thought it was surely the hardest thing she had done, telling Helve her daughter was gone.

The call from her granddaughter Tilde had come at work just after lunch. Eleanor had been on the attendance hot line, talking to a chronic truant who was in danger of failing and maybe worse, bringing official attention to his home situation. "Everyone wants to help you, Jason," she was telling him. "We can work with you." She heard the plaintiveness in her voice and straightened her spine. "You can still make your nine-thirty class," she told him, her voice shifted from sympathy to sternness. "Get in gear."

Then the office secretary rushed to her. She had a phone in her hand and was wide-eyed. "Your granddaughter," she said. "I think she's crying."

Eleanor went home and made a cup of tea. She sat on the sofa to drink it and to think of what would happen now, two girls without a mother. She called her daughter, Alison, a teacher, to let her know what was happening. Alison said she would call Walter, but Eleanor said, "There's no use just yet." Then she gathered a few things and washed her face and headed for Frost.

When she went up the long drive to the Sundersson property, Eleanor could see the tiller at the edge of the house and the ground beyond the house where Helve would plant her kitchen garden. Light shimmered on the pine trees farther up the hill. It was a nice day, cool and sunny, a break from the spring drizzle they had had the past week. Helve, dressed in old clothes, came down the steps, holding her hand up to shade her eyes; and when she saw who it was—Eleanor's face flushed and evading—Helve stopped and reached out for a wall that wasn't there, seeking her balance. When Eleanor told her Karin was dead, Helve smacked Eleanor's face with her open hand. Then she shut her eyes and put her hands on top of her head and keened and said, "Forgive me." Eleanor's cheek burned and her stomach roiled. She took Helve's arm and they went indoors.

They drank cool water in Helve's spotless kitchen and talked about what to do. Both of them were crying, wiping their faces with their fingers, snuffling and shaking their heads. Helve had the better reason to cry, but Eleanor felt engulfed with dread. Nick and Karin had been like conjoined twins. He would be worthless without her. Helve would arrange things with the funeral home so that Karin's body would be brought back to the valley immediately. Helve didn't want a funeral; she said her pastor would attend them graveside, just the family. She was a courteous woman, but not sociable. They were Lutherans; Karin had been baptized. Helve believed in eternal blessedness and she would take comfort in thinking of being reunited someday, a family again, with Henry and Karin. She believed God would not let her suffer grief forever. She was not worried about Nick, but the girls, oh the girls would need her.

Eleanor was wondering how much stuff she would have to bring back to her house from Nick's apartment and how they would get rid of the rest of it. There wasn't any doubt in her mind that he would be in a shambles without Karin, unable to cope; that he would come home.

But Nick had always worked. He had always held a job.

"You don't think he will want to cremate her, do you?" Helve asked.

"Oh my, no. None of our family has done that."

"I want to see her. I want to bury her beside her father and the baby at our plot. Do you think Nick will agree?"

Eleanor thought, Nick will be out of his mind, but all she said was, "He knows how close you were, Helve. He knows what Karin would want." She told Helve that she had talked with a woman at the funeral home. Evidently Nick had okayed them to receive Karin's body, but he hadn't followed up. They said they would have to send the body back to the hospital morgue after twenty-four hours. The woman said they had very limited refrigeration, but Eleanor didn't mention that to Helve.

She called the funeral director and made an appointment for six that evening; she would stay with the girls while Nick and Helve went to make the arrangements. Eleanor would take the girls somewhere to eat and then to then to a nearby motel. She and Helve agreed they would try to get everyone to bed by ten, and they wouldn't rush in the morning. Working out details helped both of them calm down.

Helve said right away, "I wouldn't think that Nick can afford the expenses. Not after being out of work."

Eleanor started to say she would help, but Helve was looking somewhere past her, still talking.

"There's no point in him taking on debt, I've got the money. The casket won't be fancy, we Lutherans don't do that." She looked at Eleanor, wide-eyed, as if inspired. "I don't want her to be embalmed."

The plot was Sundersson property. Helve said, "There's room for Nick, too. "It was infuriating to hear her already planning Nick's burial, but nobody stricken with grief is rational, and Eleanor, who dealt with teenagers and their teachers and parents all day, usually had a lot of patience.

She listened while Helve went on talking. Simple casket. Viewing just for the family. Eleanor thought about saying that she would pay for the casket herself on Nick's behalf, but she didn't want to start some kind of struggle with Helve. And Nick wouldn't be insulted if Helve assumed the costs.

While Helve talked to her pastor, Eleanor made sandwiches for them and made coffee and put it in a thermos. They could pull over before Roseburg and eat a bite. Helve changed into clean slacks and a light wool sweater the color of mustard. She pulled her hair into a tight braid and wound and pinned it at the base of her skull. "Ready," she said, and followed Eleanor out the door, locking it behind her.

They went in Helve's Subaru sedan, and Eleanor drove. Eleanor would drive back to Lupine with Nick, in his car, and Helve would bring the girls to Frost. She said she would like to have them with her for a few days. Nick could stay too, she said, but both women knew he wouldn't.

Someone would have to take Eleanor to get her car.

Once they were in the car, they stopped talking. Helve sat most of the way with her eyes closed. Every once in a while, she gasped. In Roseburg they got gas. Neither of them was hungry.

Karin had been ill late last summer and into the fall—it was March now—and Helve had thought she would lose her then. Karin had been bitten by a bat, going out to the trash in the dark, and then she had stumbled and hit her head on the edge of the porch and been concussed. She had had rabies shots and then a series of seizures that the doctors said had nothing to do with the bat (which wasn't found, so no one knew if the shots were necessary), and a few weeks later, she had a cough that turned out to be pneumonia. That was when Helve went and stayed at the house in Salem for two weeks, sleeping on a rented rollaway bed, until Nick told her it was all right for her to go home. He had taken time off from work and he could handle things. He delayed his return to work, and after several calls of sympathy from his supervisor and one of warning from a senior manager, he was fired. In retrospect, it was foolish for Helve not to have stayed on, but none of them had been comfortable with the arrangement.

As they traveled, Helve remembered Karin's pallor and the wracking cough and the vacant look in her eyes; and she remembered how, when Karin took the narcotic syrup prescribed for the cough at night, she slept without moving, even when Helve washed her face and spoke to her. She wondered if the infection that killed Karin had been in her body all this time, lying in wait, or if it was something new and unfair, like an errant arrow through a window. It was terrible that it had been such a quick dying, that there had been no time for goodbyes, but Henry—Helve's husband and Karin's father—had had a long dying, and there had been no comfort to him or to her in being beside him while he suffered.

Helve didn't think about Nick, whom she had never learned to love, because he had his own mother and besides, he was alive. She could not imagine how he would care for his daughters alone; suddenly she realized that she and Eleanor would have to find a way to set aside their mutual jealousy and resentment for the sake of the girls. Nick would need his mother, and where he went, of course the girls would go, too.

She wondered if something had bitten Karin. If there had been much pain.

She pressed her head against the window and groaned. Eleanor touched her arm lightly. When they reached the apartment, everyone was asleep. The door was unlocked, there were dirty dishes and pizza cartons on the counter, clothes in heaps, the television was on, the blinds were up. There was a fetid, ashy smell. Nick was in bed and the girls lay on the couch in pajamas and sweatshirts, feet to feet, their legs tangled. Helve fell to her knees a yard inside the door, and Eleanor went down beside her and put her arms around her, and they wept. The girls woke and came and stood and watched them, neither curious nor upset, only witnessing the end of life as they knew it.

Helve sat on the couch and the girls tumbled down beside her and bent their heads onto her thighs. She laid her hands softly on their crowns. They whispered, "Mormor, Mormor." *Grandmother.*

Eleanor opened the door to Nick's bedroom and was breathless with fury. It was a small room with one window, now shut. Clothes, magazines, ashtrays, and cups and glasses were strewn about on the floor. He lay asleep on his back in his boxers and a faded green T-shirt. He hadn't shaved in days. He smelled of sweat and the closed room. She couldn't think that he was her boy, who had always made straight A's; who had been so kind and gentle to everyone; who as a teenager read about topics from brain science to deep-water marine life to biographies of spies; who loved to play cards and chess, to water-ski; was a ranked high school golfer; who had excelled in pharmacy school and could have been a doctor; who had been deeply loved by his family, by his friends, by a beautiful, athletic, smart young woman he didn't have the sense to marry. And somewhere, sometime, after he started working and married, he became this sad slug of a man. Oh, what would he do without Karin, without her emptiness to fill his own? They had been happy! And then, in a wave of pity for her grieving son, Eleanor knew Helve would find a way to blame him for Karin's death, and she resented her for it.

She put her hand to her mouth and shut her eyes. God help us all, she prayed. Nothing makes sense, we are so weak, all of us. Make us strong, for these children. Let me live as long as I must to see them grown. Maker, Healer, Father, hold me up.

She thought of Catholics and their obsession with Jesus's mother. That was what she needed: a holy mother. A Mother God. Mother, guide me. Like a pinch appeared the memory of her foster mother, who had once whispered to her—she had been Catholic—that a priest could never understand who Mary was; that only a mother would admit that Mary was the true source of a woman's strength. "And you," she had said to motherless Eleanor, "must remember she will look after you if you ask."

She went to the bathroom and rinsed a frayed washcloth in warm water and wrung it out. She looked in the mirror and washed her face. She was fifty-nine years old, barely gray, barely wrinkled; she had planned to work a long while yet, and maybe travel—a cruise or two on little ships. A river through France; the islands of Greece. Blue water, the pleasure of other people's company. Ruins and gardens and monuments to the past. A slow pace, to take it all in. Now she would have two girls to raise, and she had to think about Nick; there was no possibility that he would do more than scrape through his days like a prisoner at hard labor. He would work, though; it would save him—the tedium, the responsibility. And she would have him close, there was that.

She knew she had to call Walter, her husband and Nick's father. He hadn't slept in their house for almost a month. She thought of his absence as a tantrum gone sour, but she wondered if he intended to come back. She didn't know what she would say to him, how she would step over their disaffection to say, Nick's wife is dead.

Thank God it wasn't Nicky?

She rinsed the rag and took it in to Nick. She wanted to sit down and take him in her arms. She wanted to shake him.

She stood at the side of the bed. "Wipe your face and get dressed, Nick. You have to talk to the girls."

He rubbed his eyes and sat up slightly. "Huh?"

"You have to tell Juni and Tilde that their mother is dead."

"They know, Mom. Jesus."

"They think they know. They suppose. Things happened away from them while they were sleeping. They are children. They need for their parent to tell them: Your mother is dead, but I'm here and we will make it. Do you hear me?" She thrust the washrag at him.

"I'll be there in a minute."

Eleanor found a pitcher and a few cloudy ice cubes left in a tray, and ran water and set glasses on the counter. She wondered if anyone had had a drink all day. Next, they would all fall over from dehydration.

Nick came out of his room in jeans and a worn denim shirt, and perched on the coffee table in front of the couch, buttoning the shirt.

SANDRA SCOFIELD

His daughters raised their heads from their grandmother's lap. Helve's skirt was damp where their tears had leaked.

Nick said, "Your mother was asleep when the ambulance came, you remember that. She never woke up again. It was all something strange, a kind of bug in her blood. It was bad luck, like lightning." He paused and swallowed; his Adam's apple bobbed. The girls were bent over slightly, rapt, their eyes wide, their expressions blank. Their arms hung down past their knees. They had drawn on their kneecaps with ballpoint pens: little flowers and hearts and their mother's name.

Nick said, "The doctors and nurses tried really hard to make the infection stop but they couldn't and she never woke up. I said that. She—" He began sobbing. "I don't think she hurt, maybe a little bit of time before she went to sleep here." His girls were sobbing, too. "I love her so much."

"Nick," Eleanor said.

"Your mother died yesterday." Nick pulled up the hem of his shirt and wiped his nose. He closed his eyes and spoke weakly, coldly. "Your mother is dead."

The girls rose up and threw their arms around his neck and shoulders.

Eleanor poured water into glasses. She gave each girl a glass.

She took over. "We have to get through the next few days. Your dad and Grandmother Helve will see about the casket and the transportation while we get your things together here. You will go with your grandmother to Frost Valley in the morning; your dad and I will go to Lupine later in the day; Saturday morning you will go to a funeral home in Wellen to see your mother, and from there the funeral home will take her to the grave site where Papa Henry is buried, and we will all meet there to say goodbye to her."

Eleanor gave water to Nick, who drank it greedily, and to Helve, who thanked her.

Tilde said, "You can have my bed. One of you."

"And mine," Juni said. "We like the couch."

"Oh no, dear, we'll go to a motel," Helve said.

Juni said, "I don't want to stay here, then. I don't want to."

Helve said, "Just tonight, to be with your father."

"I don't want to," Juni said, and Tilde said, "I don't want to, either."

Nick said, "You don't have to stay." He looked at his mother. "It's okay, Mom."

Helve said, "We have adjoining rooms at a motel just up the road. Eleanor and I. You'll stay with us, then. We'll be together." She had buried her parents, and it had not been like this. She had had history, ritual, memory; these girls were like cats at a gate. Their father was weak.

"What about Daddy?" Tilde said.

Helve said, "I think he wants to be here one more night." She looked at him and knew she was cold, but her daughter was gone and she wondered what he might have done to save her.

"You must find something for your mother to wear," she said in a moment.

The girls went into their parents' bedroom and came back with a pair of flannel pajamas. They were midnight blue with yellow stars and crescent moons scattered on them. They appeared to be almost new, though they were crumpled. "They were her birthday present," Tilde said. "Juni and I picked them out at Target." Karin had turned thirty-four on December 29th. Helve took the pajamas and held them against her chest. She folded them and gave them back to Tilde. "Put them by the door, angel, by my purse."

No one wanted to go out to eat. Eleanor remembered the sandwiches in the car and went to get them for the girls. Nick and Helve left for the funeral home.

Eleanor had brought two empty suitcases. She gave one to each girl and said, "Don't take anything you don't think you'll wear. Don't take anything that is too small or too little-girlish. Take some pajamas and underwear and a few things you like. We won't save the old things, unless there's something special to you; put that in. We will shop for new clothes for school. What will you wear to the burial? It's not a funeral in a church, just us at the plot. You don't have to dress up. But you might not want to wear it again, a dress you choose."

It struck her that both of them had grown three or four inches since she last saw them.

The girls looked sick and dazed. Eleanor helped them sort their things. They didn't have anything nice, but it didn't matter. They didn't have much of anything at all, and they didn't seem attached to any of it. They laid out jeans and T-shirts and tattered tennis shoes. There wasn't a single dress or blouse. They stuffed clothes into one of the suitcases and they filled the other with their mother's jewelry boxes. Then Eleanor took them to a Dairy Queen, and they ate fries and chocolate sundaes.

At the motel, they discussed who would sleep where. The girls wanted to sleep together. They stripped to their panties and T-shirts and got in the second bed in Helve's room. They hadn't washed, and Eleanor hoped Helve wouldn't say anything about it.

While Helve was in the bathroom, Eleanor sat on the bed and tried to talk to them.

"It must feel like a storm blowing around you."

"She screamed," Juni said. Both girls had a blank, patient look. They were obviously exhausted. Eleanor took Juni's hand.

"Please don't worry about what is going to happen. Your daddy will be with you. You'll be with us—in our house, or Helve's. You'll have Papa Walt and your Aunt Alison and your cousin, Fiona. We all love you. You'll get in school and catch up. Everything takes time. You'll make friends. Don't worry about anything, let your father work it all out for you. He's very sad, but he is your daddy."

She gave the girls hugs and then she quietly asked Tilde why she had called her and not Helve.

"I didn't want Mormor to know," Tilde said.

Next door again, Eleanor thought about what Tilde had said. Helve's Karin had been alive two hours longer because of the child's tact. It was touching. And it clarified Eleanor's status in the girls' life. She would have a lot of catching up to do.

She called Walter. She was propped against a pillow so fat it resisted her effort to lean back. She kicked the heavy embossed bedspread off the end of the bed, huffing at its recalcitrance, and stretched out on top of a velour blanket.

"I'm in Portland. I have bad news," she said softly, and Walter said, "Oh no, no."

"Not Nick. Karin died yesterday. Helve and I are at the apartment. "

"Was it an accident?"

"It was a sudden illness. Like a lightning strike."

"What should I do?"

"Helve is taking the girls to Frost tomorrow morning. I'm going to help Nick clear out the apartment. I'll bring them home. They can't stay here, Walt."

"I suppose not, with all his traveling."

"I don't think there will be a funeral, just the burial in Frost. Helve will make the arrangements. We'll call you."

"That's it? I wait for an invitation? I should be there." His voice was sharp.

"There is no 'there' right now. I'm in a motel. We're not leaving you out of anything. We'll be home tomorrow evening. We'll know more then."

Walter hung up.

Eleanor slept little. She woke up over and over, afraid for Nick alone in his apartment.

Tilde dreamed of ships and stars and balls in the sky all at once. Juni dreamed of babies' fists and falling, and floating, glowing crowns. Both girls slept easily through the night and woke up startled in the morning.

In the morning they ate waffles and peanut butter at the motel buffet. Eleanor made a mental note that they seemed to like them.

In his apartment, Nick smoked and lay on the couch for hours, listening to Bob Dylan and Gillian Welch. He thought about the time he and Karin went to Brookings and stayed in a damp cabin for two nights. The second night, there was a brief but fierce squall in from the ocean and the wind blew their door open. Karin jumped out of bed and ran outside long enough to get soaked, laughing and calling for Nick, who didn't go out. Back indoors, she took off her pajamas and Nick dried her slowly and they talked about having children. She had been pregnant then; they would know she was, soon after. She wanted girls; Nick didn't care whether they had girls or boys. "Besides, it's out of our control," he said, and she said, "Isn't everything?"

She said she wanted her children to play naked in the back yard in the hot days of summer, as she had when she was small. Then she laughed and said, "Imagine if it wasn't a storm after all. Imagine that people were crying out and there was a great commotion. A UFO had landed on the beach and people were gathering to see, but not going close. And then our door flew open and this thing, this stem of light, spoke and it said, 'We have chosen you to come with us.'"

"Oooh!" she said. "Would you go? Would we take such a leap, to a life utterly unknown to us?" And of course he said he would.

He woke when his mother came in, and for the moment before she spoke, he held his breath, thinking he had forgotten something important; then he thought of his daughters, and got up.

3

In the morning, Eleanor saw a post office near the motel. She picked up a change of address form and wrote in the Lupine address, but she didn't know the apartment address details. She wondered about all the circulars and bills that had piled up behind Nick and Karin. The trash in anyone's life. So little mattered.

It was a tiresome chore to clear the apartment: two small bedrooms, a claustrophobic and unsanitary bathroom, the rest an open space clogged with furnishings and detritus. She had brought boxes of black plastic lawn bags, and smaller trash bags and a few cardboard boxes. Nick had a suitcase; he scooped clothes from his dresser into it, and some things he put in a bag and set by the door. Eleanor made two piles of Karin's clothes: one for Goodwill, a larger one for the trash. She put the rest of the girls' clothes in a bag, too, hesitating, then adding them to the Goodwill heap. There was a box of books, and papers and a laptop computer. Nick said to take the laptop and leave the rest for the trash.

Nick took a shoebox from the closet shelf and gave it to his mother. "Papers, stuff," he said. "Vaccination records, birth certificates, insurance. School photos of the girls when they were little." Eleanor set the box near the door on top of her own overnight bag. She felt a surge of affection for Nick, that the papers and photographs were collected, and then she wondered if Karin had been the one who took care to save them.

They filled trash bags with grimy sheets and pillows and towels. They put dishes and pots into a cardboard box. Nick dismantled the beds and stacked the parts against walls neatly. Against other walls he propped the mattresses. He stopped often, short of breath. Eleanor threw everything from the refrigerator into a trash bag and left the door propped open. They wrapped the flat-screen television in comforters from the girls' beds, and laid it in the trunk of Nick's car.

Eleanor spoke to the complex manager. She explained what had happened, and what they had done. He was a Middle-Eastern immigrant, kinder than she had expected. He would pay a day laborer to take everything else down to the trash bins. Cleaners would scour the empty apartment. Someone would paint the walls white. In no time, another hapless family would move in. He had seen it all many times.

He said, "I saw the ambulance, and prayed it wasn't one of the children. I'm sorry, Missus."

Eleanor gave him five twenties and the change of address form with Nick's name and her address filled in.

The manager looked at it and nodded. "I'll hand it to the postman myself."

She said, "I appreciate your kind assistance. The last thing my son needs is problems with credit." He gave her something that might have been a smile.

Eleanor drove Nick's car while he slept in the back seat. It was dark when she pulled into her driveway in Lupine. Walter's truck was parked to the far right, close to their granddaughter Fiona's bedroom window. They found him in the house, working in a Sudoku book, sitting in his favorite chair. He got up and put his arms around Nick.

He said, "I'm so sorry, Son."

Nick made a gargling sound and pushed his forehead into his father's shoulder. "I can't," he said, and Walter said, "You have to."

Alison came out of her room. She hugged him awkwardly. "I'm sorry, Nicky. It's awful." When Nick didn't say anything, Alison said, "Fiona has gone to bed," and went back to her room. Eleanor thought Alison had probably stashed her daughter with orders to stay out of the way. What did Fiona know about death? She didn't really know Nick or his children, so maybe it was all vague to her, like a whispered secret.

Nick looked around as if he didn't know where he was, then opened the door to the back bedroom. He looked over his shoulder at his mother, his hand on the door.

Eleanor said, "The sheets have been on that bed for years." She hadn't vacuumed in there since Christmas. Nick shrugged. She took towels out of the hall closet and handed them to him. She watched him go into the bathroom and she stood in the hallway until she heard the shower running.

Walter had come up behind her. He put his hand on her arm. "I shopped, and got hamburgers for Alison and Fiona and me. Alison's pretty shaken. Are you hungry?"

"No."

"There's coffee."

"It's late for coffee," Eleanor said, but then she said she could use some.

They sat at the kitchen table, not talking, while she drank her coffee. Walter opened a packet of shortbread cookies and put out a saucer with a pile of them on it. Eleanor nibbled on one.

"I have been waiting for years for something to happen to the two of them," Walter said. "They always seemed vulnerable to me. Careless. And I worried about Nick driving so much."

"I know." Eleanor wanted to explain how Karin died, but she didn't really understand, herself. She remembered Juni saying that her mother had screamed.

Walter took her cup away and brought her a glass of water. She drank it thirstily.

"We got everything out of the apartment. We didn't talk about it, we just started putting stuff in trash bags. They were living like they were waiting for something better to come along. Like they were waiting for a welfare check. Doesn't Nicky make a decent salary, driving all over the state? Wasn't it a step up from the Walmart pharmacy? That was a good job, I never understood how he could let himself lose it."

"That doesn't matter, hon," Walter said. He got up. "Listen, I'm going to leave you to get some rest. I'll be by. Call me when you know about the service."

He sounded like a good friend. Someone who cared about the family.

She looked up at him. "Walter." She was used to folding into his arms when she needed reassurance or comfort. The awkwardness between them was awful. She had been pretending she didn't care that he walked out, but she was lost on her own.

He kissed her forehead perfunctorily. "We'll talk, Ellie," he said at the door.

And then the next day, Friday, came and went and Walter didn't. Twice at work she picked up her phone to call him but stopped. Helve called in the early evening to say the girls had been napping and watching television; they had eaten a good supper. They would go to the funeral home early Saturday morning, and everyone would meet at the plot at 11:00.

What could Eleanor say? "I'll get my car then."

"Oh yes," Helve said. "You locked it, I remember."

It was trifling, talking about a car.

Eleanor washed and dried her hair, then swept the kitchen. She looked at the clock and saw that it was ten o'clock. Everything was rushing by. She was glad she didn't have to see Karin's body.

4

Saturday morning, Nick left early to meet up with Helve and the girls at the funeral home. Eleanor wanted Nick to eat, but he said he didn't have time. His denim-blue twill suit hung on him. His posture reminded her of Johnny Cash at his worst.

He gulped a cup of black coffee and kissed his mother's forehead. "Helve will have food, I'm sure, Mom."

"We'll meet you at the plot," Alison said. "Dad will be there. Mother talked to Helve earlier. I think she's happier with just the four of you at the funeral home." She kissed and hugged him at the door.

"Did I say 'happier'?" Alison said when Nick was gone. "Shit."

Alison and her mother had to drive Fiona to her father's house in Wellen, but they had time, once Nick left, to sit together at the kitchen table and drink coffee and talk. Alison said she thought the girls would want to stay at Helve's for a while, and Eleanor agreed that they could. She was thinking about Nick. If the girls were in Frost, he could rest at the Becker home. He needed solitude. Maybe he needed to see a physician. He was thin, his skin sallow and pocked across his cheeks.

She said, "I don't have enough beds."

"Mother, we can make do," Alison said. "Put Nick in Fiona's room. Fiona can sleep with me, she'll love it. The girls can take the double bed in the spare room. It's just for the time being. Nick will find an apartment in town. We'll do whatever we need to, but it's not like they are going to live here forever." She sighed. "Not like me and Fiona."

Eleanor swallowed with an audible gulp, but before she could respond, Fiona appeared and plucked a piece of cold toast off the counter and took two logs of string cheese from the fridge. She was eager to go. She looked darling in her little girl jeans, a bubble-gum-pink T-shirt and a fuzzy white hoodie. She was all legs, like her cousins. As Fiona ate, Alison brushed her hair and put it in pigtails. Her reddish blond hair was thick and long, and she squirmed and squeaked when Alison hit a snag or pulled too hard, but she didn't dare complain because Alison had warned her: If it's too much trouble, we'll cut it. And her hair was Fiona's favorite thing about herself. Her father had red hair. So did her half-sister. Badges of their father's power, was that recessive-red hair.

Fiona spent every other weekend at her father's house in Wellen—Saturday, Saturday night, then home early Sunday evening. Her father, Ben Corry, and his wife, Jacqueline, had a three-year-old daughter, Polly, and a baby boy, Sydney. Fiona liked being a big sister. She never complained about going to Ben's house for the weekends, a week at Christmas, and several summer weeks, and she never complained about coming back home. Alison had never expressed any jealousy of the family—she had been the one who wanted a divorce, not long after Fiona was born—and Ben's haste in constructing a new life, though somewhat insulting, had, all in all, been a relief. He had taken a position at Providence Wellen Hospital when Fiona was five, though as an anesthesiologist, he had done much better in Portland in salary and prestige. Driving Fiona back and forth to Portland, though, no matter who had had the chore, had been a terrible burden on all of them. Eleanor admired him for the sacrifice, though of course he was still making multiples of what Alison made as a teacher. The important thing was that Fiona had both parents now. And Jacqueline, with three semesters of art school and a year as a nanny in Berlin under her belt, was a nice young woman and a perfect doctor's wife. She was always courteous to Alison, and Fiona loved her. It sometimes worried Eleanor that Alison had so many complaints about Ben: how he was so superior, had a big house, was full of advice. She wanted to tell her, suck it up; there is no payoff for abiding resentment. At least Alison was careful not to criticize Ben in Fiona's presence.

After all, Alison had her own relationship. She usually spent the Saturday night that Fiona was gone with Steve Nichols, an electrician whose sons lived in Texas with their mother. They had been seeing one another exclusively for two years. He was a nice fellow; he and Walter had become good friends despite their age difference, with a lot of common interests, including golf, local politics and craft beer.

"I can stay home tonight, Mother," Alison said. "I'm sure Steve will come over and we'll watch a movie with you. Something frothy, I could use that."

Eleanor said, "I am looking forward to a bath and a book. You go on with your plans."

"Maybe Dad—" Alison began, but Eleanor scowled.

Fiona was making faces, impatient to go. She pressed against her mother, who took her onto her lap and wrapped her arms around her. "Not long now," Alison said, her mouth against her daughter's hair. Eleanor wondered how Alison had explained all the fuss.

Eleanor got up and cleared their cups. "I'll ask Nick: 'What do you want to do, Son? What do you think is the best living arrangement? Is this all right? Or that? I'll try to find a way to say, 'You're the father, make some decisions.' And he'll say, 'Mom, you know best.' After years of their secrecy, their inaccessibility, their goddamn cult existence, you wait, he'll want me to tell him what to do. He's been bent to her will and he has no reserves of his own. You should have seen him hobbling out of that apartment. He looked like a broken stick."

She stared at Alison as if Alison might argue with her. She said, "He was Valedictorian of his pharmacy class! Karin ruined him!" Her outburst seemed to come from nowhere. She sat down and took a long deep breath.

Alison changed position so that Fiona slid off her lap and ran across the room.

Alison spoke quietly. "Not cool, Mom. The love of his life just died, give him some time. He's in shock. Hell, I'm in shock. It's not the time to evaluate his character. Whatever he might have done wrong in his life, don't you think he's being punished enough? He'll have his kids to think of. To live for. He'll work. He'll have all of us to back him up." She put her hand on Eleanor's. "It's not about you, Mom."

They looked at one another. Eleanor flushed, but she was proud of Alison for her defense of Nick.

She sighed. "One thing I do know, working in a school, and you know it, too. It's going to be hard. There must be a quarter of our kids at the high school being raised by relatives or foster parents."

"You're getting ahead of yourself, Mom. You can't assume what your role will be."

"Do you think Nick and Karin——" Eleanor couldn't finish the sentence. She wasn't sure what the question was.

"It doesn't matter now," Alison said. "Analyzing, supposing—it's all gas and dust over the fact that Karin is gone. And it's just plain better to focus on practical things while the universe settles. Nick needs a lot of backup, but he also needs for us to expect him to rise to the challenge. All that love he had for Karin? Don't you think it will go to his children now?"

She said, "Let's just do the day-at-a-time thing. Let's start with this one."

Alison's equanimity was strained when she delivered Fiona to Ben. He was standing at the front door, and Eleanor, waiting in the car, could see he was angry, with his arms out against the door jamb. He said something that set Alison off; she leaned toward him, her head shaking.

"What was that all about?" Eleanor asked Alison when she got in the car.

"They wanted to go out to breakfast, and we're late."

"Ouch."

"He said it's time to redo our schedule. I should try two nights a month, he says."

"Gosh, he was wound up, huh?"

"He said Nick should have insisted on an autopsy. That's when I lost it. My brother's life is none of his business."

"He's a doctor. They always know everything."

"He is working up to something. I think he wants custody."

Eleanor patted Alison's knee and started the car. "That will never happen, darling. You're Fiona's mother, he can never take her away from you." She didn't look at Alison, who leaned her head against the window. She hoped she was right.

They gathered at the grave site. It was a clear day, cool and dry. The plots were on Sundersson property, the far side of Karl's house. They lay at a place on the hill where the rise leveled. A person standing above the graves could see across woods to far hills. Below the gravesite was a sloping bank, and at the bottom the families had buried two ponies and four dogs over the years.

The casket was pine, unadorned. There was a white cloth draped over it. The family was joined by an elderly neighbor—an ex-nun named Elizabeth—and Karin's girlfriend from high school, Jennifer. The minister prayed: "Christ, the Good Shepherd, enfold you with His tender care. May you see your Redeemer face to face and enjoy the sight of God forever."

He reminded the gathered company that Karin was promised eternal life by her baptism and faith in salvation. They would see her again. Death is a portal, he said. There were no songs, no eulogy. Juni and Tilde wore pretty frocks they had found in the closet of their mother and aunt at Helve's house, simple cotton dresses cut modestly, striking them at their knees. Tilde's dress was a pale mottled blue and gray, Juni's was a light plum color with white flowers. Each girl had braided her hair and fastened it across the top of her head like their grandmother did hers. Juni wore a gold-plated crucifix on a silver chain. Tilde wore a silver pendant with a sliver of turquoise in it. They stood next to one another but weren't touching. Their faces shone with tears. Their grandmother and their father stood beside them like bookends. Helve wore an old-fashioned black crepe dress, zipped in the back, striking her legs inches below her knees. Behind her, Karl and Ivy stood, also in proper funeral clothes, held over from the funeral of Helve's husband two years ago. Eleanor and Walter and Alison were on the other side of the cavity in the ground, dressed in dark but not black clothes. Two men from the funeral home stood behind the family, their hands crossed in front of their zippers.

Helve pulled the cloth off the casket and shook it vigorously. Nick stepped toward her, but she shook her head and folded the cloth into a neat packet. The girls had found small wildflowers poking up behind their grandmother's house, and they put them on the bare wood of the casket. The men stepped forward and lowered the casket by straps that girdled it. Walter took his wife's hand and his daughter's. Juni reached out as if to recover her flowers, but Nick touched her elbow and she stepped back. Jennifer was sobbing. The family looked stunned. Nick stepped between his daughters, put his arms through theirs, and turned them from the grave. The minister shook hands with everyone, including the girls. He didn't say anything more before he left in his ancient blue Datsun.

Everyone walked to the house. As they passed Karl's and Ivy's house, Jennifer, Elizabeth, and Ivy stopped to get the trays of food they had prepared earlier.

At the house, Helve opened the front door to the pleasant spring air, and the living room seemed to extend onto the painted porch. There was an old brown velour sofa pushed almost against the windows at the back of the room, two stuffed chairs, each with a small table beside it, folding chairs, and a bench from the kitchen, used as a makeshift table. The wood floor gleamed. Everyone took a small plate and some of the simple food: open-face sandwiches with cheese, ham, or fish paste. A square flat pastry with a dollop of raspberry jam. Coffee or orangeade.

Elizabeth recalled first meeting Karin and Nick and Juni and Tilde when Tilde was a toddler and Elizabeth had recently left the convent to live in her mother's house in the valley. Karin had told

Elizabeth details of the children's lives: little stories about their first words, the books they loved, what good eaters they were.

Karl spoke of the children—he meant Karin and her sister and his own boys—riding their ponies, gorging strawberries, taking their poles up to the stream that fed the Frost River. "Karin never wanted to keep a fish," he said. "She liked to catch one, then she was very careful unhooking it and putting it back in the water. The boys teased her but she didn't care."

Jennifer said, all in a rush, "Karin was my favorite person in the whole world at the very time a friend mattered most, when we were teenagers and we were ugly and we were sure nobody would ever love us." Everyone smiled. Helve, on the couch, asked Jennifer to sit beside her and she took her hand. "You were two princesses," she said. "Elin had gone to Sweden and I worried so about Karin, left behind, but she had you."

Silence fell across the room like a shadow, and before long, the platters, the neighbor, the friend, and Karl's wife were all gone. Karl and Helve went out on the porch to talk for a few minutes. They embraced lightly, and Karl left.

Juni collapsed on the rya rug in front of the couch and pounded the floor. Helve went into the kitchen and stood against the wall, where she was away from the sight of her grandchild's grief. Eleanor stepped forward, but Alison restrained her, and she sat on a kitchen chair that had been pulled in across from the couch. Nick knelt and tugged Juni up from the floor and wrapped her in his arms. Tilde went to Helve in the kitchen alcove and leaned against her. Helve took Tilde's hand and led her to a chair with the others. Tilde sat on Helve's lap and put her arm around her neck. Walter, who had been standing at the edge of the room, went to Nick and squeezed his shoulder, then left. In a little while, Nick and Eleanor moved the bench back to the kitchen and put the folding chairs in a closet, while Helve moved dishes to the kitchen sink.

Nick broke the silence. He told his mother and sister that they should go home, too. He told Helve that she should rest. He was going to take the girls for a ride. He said, "Don't worry about us, I'll have them back before dark. I'll feed them. I'll stay the night, if that's all right." He gestured to the couch. "A pillow is all I need." He hugged his mother and told her he would see her in the morning. Then he sent Juni and Tilde to change into jeans, loaded them into his car and drove away. Alison put the dishes in the dishwasher while Eleanor and Helve stood at the doorway. Alison came behind them and handed her mother her purse. "We should go, Mom."

Eleanor gave Helve an awkward embrace, then exclaimed, "Oh! The obituary!"

"Monday's papers," Helve said.

Nick took the girls to a new miniature golf course on the east side of Wellen. There were a few other families. It was an easy pace and fun. They went around twice. Then they went to a park, where Nick produced a basketball from the trunk of his car. Both girls were great shots and deft guards. They shot baskets for a long time, then played a quick game and lost track of the score. They went to a little diner downtown and the girls ate hamburgers and fries. After that he drove them to the park on the Frost River, a few miles past the Sundersson property, and they sat on the grass near the water, thinking their private thoughts. When Tilde said she was tired, they went back to the car, and there in the parking lot, each of them leaning against a window, all three fell asleep, more deeply than at any time since Karin died. They slept and dreamed and saw her and lost her and slept some more until twilight. Then Nick hurried them home, because he didn't want their grandmother to worry.

5

Nick woke hours before dawn, sweaty and tangled in the sheet he had lain under on the couch. His head was pushed against the arm of the sofa, and the pillow had fallen to the floor. He stood and unwound himself from the sheet, then sat down again and pulled it around his shoulders. He was in his undershorts and T-shirt. He could see the white sheen of his skinny legs down the shins. A night light in the kitchen glowed. He was thirsty, hot, achy. He wanted to smoke.

He let himself out the front door and went to the car. The ground was cold. There was half a bottle of water on the passenger seat. He drank it all, then peed, standing on the far side of the car. He sat in the back seat and closed the door and smoked a joint. He was cold but he didn't care. He put his head back and slept.

Helve tapped on the car window. "You all right in there, Nick?"

He put his hands, fingers spread, on his legs just above his knees and pressed hard to keep from groaning. In the pale light of early morning he felt naked. He didn't know how long he had been asleep.

She tapped again. He nodded and she walked to the house. Sheepishly, he followed well behind her. He quickly picked up his clothes from the floor by the couch and went straight to the little bathroom under the stairs to dress. He wanted to leave as fast as he could, though the girls were surely sound asleep. No way could he wait around, nor would the girls appreciate being wakened.

"I'm going to take the girls to church," Helve said when he sat down at the table. "You are welcome to come." She poured him a cup of coffee. "I'll make you some breakfast when you're ready."

"Thanks, but no need. I'll go to Mom's. She'll have a list of things she wants me to do." His voice croaked and he felt his cheeks burn.

Helve put her hands on the back of a chair and looked somewhere past him. "What I'd like to do is crawl under my bed and never come out."

He stared at her, startled.

"But the list is: What do Juni and Tilde need, to get through today? What do they need, to get ready to go to school? When my mother died, I was Tilde's age. It was a Tuesday. Autumn, cold. We had known she was dying, so there wasn't much fuss. I went back to school on Friday after we buried her, and my aunts and uncles went home. Nobody asked me what I needed. It was my father and me and my little sister, Anna, and we all knew what to do. We had a few small animals and it was my job to feed them. We did what we had done every day, except that at thirteen, I became the cook. A little while later, my aunt came and took Anna away to live with her."

Nick had a crazy urge to laugh. Nobody in his little family had been a cook. "I'll come for the girls this evening."

"I would rather have them here a few days. Please. Take this next move in steps." She was squeezing the chair-back so hard her knuckles were white. "You'll have to get things ready for them at your mother's, won't you? They are a consolation. I'll keep them busy. You can come and go as you like."

He felt outmanned. "I'm going to put them in school."

"They are all I've got now," she said. "I have time——" She was shaking her head back and forth slightly, looking somewhere over his shoulder. He thought she was deranged, and he couldn't fault her for it. He was linked to her by grief, maybe more than he had been linked to her by marriage. Karin's death had stranded him like someone swept to sea, and when he looked back, there was Helve, ready to help, ready to take over, standing on shore.

She didn't go on. He drank his coffee, tepid now, and got up from the table.

"We will do some shopping," Helve said. "I noticed they need shoes."

"All right. A couple days." Nick went upstairs to kiss the girls. When he came back down, he said, "They were sound asleep. Tell them I'll call."

He got to the bottom of the hill and pulled over. He squeezed the steering wheel so hard his hands cramped. "Bitch," he said. His throat hurt, and his chest. He was going to see a lawyer as soon as possible. No way was Helve going to get his daughters. The thought startled him. Why would she? He sped away.

The first thing Eleanor did that morning, still in her robe, was take the sheets off the bed in the back bedroom. She couldn't think how long they had been on, not that Nick would care. She stripped Fiona's bed, too. She put the sheets in to wash and looked in the linen closet in the hall to see if there was another set of full sheets. Her bed was a queen, Fiona's was a twin, Alison's was a queen (she had her own sheets, pricey ones). They hadn't used the back bed in years. She couldn't find a double set and she thought she remembered putting them in the supplies they were accumulating for a contingent of war country refugees who were expected to arrive in the city sometime soon.

That thought sent her to the garage. There was a large bin there, but it contained towels. She stood with her hands on her hips, wondering where was what. She would just have to wait and put the fresh-washed sheets back on the bed and get another set right away— something crisp, maybe a pretty print, something the girls would slide into, not realizing that the sheets made them feel better.

When Nick brought the girls back with him—today? tomorrow? she would put them in the back bedroom and they would have to get something else set up for Nick. She stood in the living room, turned around, and tried to imagine where to put a bed.

She was startled to hear a car in the driveway. She opened the door to find Nick. He was alone. She made biscuits and scrambled eggs, and both of them ate. She moved the sheets to the dryer. Usually she turned on NPR in the morning, and now she missed the familiar voices. She missed the presence of Alison and Fiona. And Walter.

"I woke up so early," Nick said, "I feel like I haven't been to bed."

"Oh dear," she said. "Those sheets are in the dryer. It won't take much longer. Or you can sleep in my bed."

He shrugged. "The sofa. The floor. The bathtub. Just not Helve's couch!" Both of them laughed.

She walked down to the curb in her robe to get the paper. She had another cup of coffee, and read the first page and the comics. She pulled out the dry sheets and went to make the bed. The door to the bedroom was ajar. She saw Nick sprawled on his back across the mattress on top of the old chenille bedspread. He was snoring. She snapped the top sheet open and let it fall over him like a parachute. She felt a burble of happiness in her chest at the sight of him home.

He had been a cheerful baby, a rowdy boy, a gangly teen. Walter taught him to golf early on and he ranked at state meets in high school. They teased him that he was kin to his golf clubs, he was so skinny. In his Junior year he was manager for the basketball team; his senior year it was football. Walter insulated the garage, laid a linoleum floor and bought a ping-pong table and a sound system. After games, the kids gathered at the house, boys and girls both. They seemed to fill the garage and the house with their music and laughter; midnight was the bewitching hour when they knew to go home. Other evenings, she would come home from work and find Nick and his friends spread out on the living room carpet, their books splayed. Some of them called Eleanor "Ellie-Mom," teasing, affectionate. Walter and Eleanor would go to bed late and sigh and one of them would say, "We always know where he is!"

The first year of college, some of the boys came around during Christmas break, but one day it was over, just like that. Alison—she must have been in seventh grade—remarked that it was great that Nicky's friends weren't crowding the house anymore, and Eleanor   for a fraction of a second, that was all   wanted to slap her.

6

While Nick slept, Eleanor showered and washed and dried her hair. There was a long mirror on the bathroom door, and she stood in front of it and thought about how old she was—sixty in a month—and wondered what Walter saw when he looked at her. At 5'9," she was still a bony size ten. Most of her clothes were at least a decade old. She had always favored classic cuts, things that didn't go out of style—maybe because they didn't have style. In warm weather, she liked skirts and blouses for work; in winter, she wore light wool or corduroy pants with shirts and a dark gray cashmere cardigan she had had for thirty years. She wore no jewelry except her wedding rings and occasionally a pendant. She had two such necklaces, one with a lapiz stone, one with an Australian opal. The opal had been a gift from Walter's mother for her twentieth wedding anniversary, a lovely surprise.

She kept her thick dark hair in a loose bob just above her shoulders—long enough to pull into a short messy ponytail. She swam once or twice a week and walked to and from work in nice weather. She had never been seriously ill. Nor had Walter.

They could have many years together yet.

She was keenly aware of how much she missed Walter, missed being touched. He had always been so enthusiastic, so good-natured, in bed; he sometimes said wow! like a boy just discovering pleasure. He liked for her to say what she wanted. His huffy defection was out of character—he a man of good humor and zest—and she needed him now more than ever.

She chose clothes she wore often. The skirt was a light wool wrap in a rich coral color, and the black blouse was a puff sleeve linen jersey knit. The outfit made her feel comfortable and pulled together, and she knew Walter liked it. She hoped he would look at her—really see her; she hoped he would come home. She wondered if he had been going to church without her—they had always attended St James United Methodist, in which Walter had grown up—but since he moved out, Eleanor had gone to the Congregational church with Alison. It had been like a holy vitamin shot for Eleanor; she had been surprised at the enthusiasm she felt, as opposed to the dutiful, familiar boredom of the other church. For a long time, church had been nothing more than habit. Faith had been a habit. If someone had asked her what she believed in, God wouldn't have been her instinctive answer. Her faith had to do with family, work, friends and memory. Faith was optimism and connection, responsibility. It was what kept families together.

She enjoyed going with Alison. She liked the ministers. Madeline Evans was a woman Eleanor's age, plump, cheerful and intellectual, if that was the right word: her talks were always friendly but also challenging, calling on literature and history as well as the Bible. The other minister was a young man, Dan Gordon, probably right out of divinity school, who had the rough good looks of a sportsman, maybe a climber or hiker, but who stuttered and blushed like a newly appointed vicar in a *Masterpiece Theatre* series. He was catching on; the congregation was patient.

Today, he talked about Bishop Spong's idea of "wasteful love." If God is love, and he gives it to all of us, there is no end to love, so why hold it back, even when someone doesn't seem to "deserve" it? Eleanor thought there was something in that to consider, but she wondered if maybe she had spent all she had in her account, with a husband who had walked out on her, a son whose wife was dead, a grown daughter sleeping in her childhood bedroom. If she had any extra love to spend, she thought she would give it to migrants crowding desperately at the border, or maybe to Jason Logan, a boy at the high school who was perennially absent because his mother was too sick to look after Jason's baby sister. What Nick and his daughters were going to need now was common sense, routine, and optimism.

Services were followed by coffee and socializing and a reminder that the annual book sale was coming up, donations still accepted. Soon, most of the congregation had left, but a small group remained to hear from Amy Kenyanjui about the status of the refugee project. Amy, an attorney and the coordinator for nontraditional students at Southern Oregon University, had been the liaison person with the government while they waited for delayed federal funds to hire a coordinator for a refugee resettlement field office. The refugees were all victims of war and persecution, well-vetted and long-waiting. The town had been expecting them by March, but now Amy said a firm date still had not been set. She said, "We are expecting the arrival of a coordinator within the next month, and the first group of immigrants after that, no earlier than May, though. Surely soon after that."

When Eleanor had learned that a group of church members was collecting items to furnish the refugees' homes, she had immediately halved her own household linens and kitchen goods, and made a trip to several thrift shops and a big box store as well. Clean, folded, wrapped items were packed in boxes in her garage. Why she had had so much that she could give half of it away was something to ponder.

First they had been told they would sponsor refugees from the Congo, but they were placed elsewhere. Then they were told they would receive eighty-four Syrian refugees, seventeen families. For various reasons late in the process, some had been unexpectedly rejected by the federal government, and the number who would actually be coming might be as low as a dozen families. They had already spent years in refugee camps; of all the children, only two adolescents had been born outside of a camp. In the present political climate, everyone had been vetted yet again, culling families with so-called "single men:" any son over the age of fourteen; uncles and grandfathers younger than sixty-five.

Amy asked those who had stayed for an update to be patient. She reminded them that the program was part of a large federal one, and that the refugees came with assistance to help them settle, find jobs, make social adjustment, and so on. The nationwide settlement record was excellent.

"One important thing we can be proud of and optimistic about is we do have lots of local support. We have a volunteer list of almost two hundred names, people who are eager to assist the immigrants. We can be proud of our openness and generosity. I know that many of you here today have set aside household furnishings, and I want to thank you for all you have done. Once we have a firm date, we will rent apartments and houses again. For now, we have canceled the rentals we thought we would be using soon; landlords have been very good about returning the deposits.

"I am confident that by summer we will see these wonderful people striding down our streets, shopping in our stores, and worshiping in our churches." She hesitated. "Or starting their own," she added.

Eleanor felt a shiver across her shoulders. She reached for Alison's hand and squeezed it lightly. She hadn't really thought about what it would be like to arrive in a country, so far from one's birthplace, into a culture full of unfamiliar things. She had never been out of the United States. In fact, she had never been farther from Lupine than San Francisco, except for a four-day package trip to Puerto Vallarta one June, when it had rained every afternoon and steamed until dark.

She wondered if the refugees would become disillusioned when they learned what American life was all about: who was who, what you owned and what you owed; us and them. There were few people of color in little Lupine, and few whose first language was not English. Maybe with their fresh eyes the country would be a different experience for the refugees, and at least they would be away from the brutality of war. But it would not be easy for them here or anywhere.

She blinked. Everyone was saying goodbye. She turned to tell Alison she would see her at the house, but Amy put a hand gently on Eleanor's shoulder. "I'm so sorry to hear about your daughter-in-law, Eleanor," she said.

Eleanor was surprised. "But we only buried her yesterday, Amy, how did you know?"

"My husband, John, was in Alison's classroom when she got the news. He is doing his student teaching with her. I believe you know him." She turned and waved.

Eleanor looked at Alison. Why hadn't Alison said anything? The family did know John, a man in his late thirties, a little younger than his wife. He was a carpenter, or had been: he had built the Beckers' back deck a couple of summers ago. Eleanor's friend Barbara had introduced them. Eleanor knew that John was Kenyan by birth; his family had immigrated when he was a boy. He had talked with Walter about playing golf, but nothing came of it. He hadn't mentioned being in college.

John, a tall slender man with a warm smile, approached them.

"I'm so glad to see you again, Mrs. Becker," he said, his voice mellifluous. "It has been so long. And I will tell you about Alison. She is a stern taskmaster, your daughter. She will make me a good teacher, she will." He laughed.

Eleanor smiled, too, but she was still trying to take in the new information.

Alison took Eleanor's purse from a chair and handed it to her, then took her arm. "Let's go, Mom."

As they walked to their cars, she said, "He's going to be a great teacher. He's a natural with the kids."

Eleanor stopped at her car. "She's older, isn't she?"

"Who? Oh, Amy? I guess."

"Do they have kids?"

"A daughter, Jamila. She's twelve. Very smart, I think. We should get the girls together."

Eleanor smiled. "You give him all you've got, Alison."

Eleanor got home ahead of Alison. Alison would stop to buy a cup of coffee at Venti's, a frivolous habit Eleanor did not understand, since there was good coffee at the house. Eleanor drove past the widow Velma Franklin's house at the front of the driveway without looking at it, though she knew Velma would be sitting at the sliding doors, looking out, expecting a visit today. There were three vehicles at the house. One was Nick's car, blocking her garage door; the other two were trucks. Her heart skipped when she saw that one of them was Walter's; it said *Becker Hardware* on the side of the bed. The other one was Steve's, its doors emblazoned with lightning bolts.

She opened the front door and saw Nick and Steve on the couch, one on each end, and Walter in a chair working in one of his puzzle books. He looked up, and for all the sadness in the room, in the flicker of a moment he looked pleased to see her. She wondered if he had gone to church, if anyone had asked, where's Eleanor?

Steve jumped up. "Eleanor. Isn't Alison with you?"

"Coming up behind me."

"No cable, huh, Mom?" Nick said from the couch. He had the TV paddle in his hand.

"Antenna and two streaming subscriptions," she said. She pointed to the television. "What have you there?"

"FOX. We're hoping for a game."

Eleanor gestured broadly. "Sit, for heaven's sake." She walked straight through to the kitchen and sat down at the table. From there she could look out on the living room. Walter was on the end of the sofa, bent forward a little, watching Nick fiddle with the television. She could see across to the door of the bathroom in the line of rooms on that side of the house. Once again she found herself assessing space for the influx of Nick's family. They could move the couch forward toward the front door and put a twin bed behind it for Nick. He could sleep anywhere.

The house was built with a large central space from the back door, with a large closet at that end, to the closed-in entry porch at the other. On one side were three small bedrooms, a bathroom, and a large hall closet and a smaller one with the furnace in it. On the other was the kitchen, its functional area tucked behind a livingroom wall, and the dining area open to the the main room, with a large wide opening and no door. The master bedroom suite was beyond the kitchen, with windows on three sides. It extended past the rest of the house in an ell that cast shade on the deck and yard, welcome in the summer. Eleanor had always loved the floor plan of the house, which had been Walter's design. Her contribution to the house plan had been to say she wanted "flow." She wanted it to be easy for her family to be together. (And she had wanted it to be easy to keep an eye on things.) Nick was a baby when they moved in, and she had imagined the house full of kids. She had not had any idea of how much she would sometimes want a hole to hide in; or how her adolescent daughter would turn her bedroom into a fortress against all of Eleanor's efforts to understand what her problem was.

She sat down and rubbed the surface of the large pine table, a gift from Walter's parents. She thought of all the homework done there, the patterns cut for pajamas; the games and crafts; meals and snacks. A large double pane window looked out on the big stretch of their vacant land to the west.

Walter pulled out a chair and sat down. "Ellie," he said.

She looked up. "Will he be all right? Will he survive this loss?"

Walter put his hand on hers. His palm was dry and warm. "People do. It takes time. He's not alone with it."

"The poor girls."

"We'll pull together. We're a family, Ellie."

She felt sobs knotted in her chest. Her throat burned.

"It must bring up so much for you," he said.

She pulled her hand away. "I'll make some lunch." She got up.

"I stocked sandwich stuff."

"Yes, thank you."

She started pulling things out of the refrigerator. Walter said, "I'll leave you to it, then," and went to join the others.

Alison appeared. "I'm going to Steve's, if that's okay with you."

Eleanor sighed and laid bread slices down on the counter. "You could eat before you run off. You could take a plate; I'm sure Steve is hungry, this time of day."

Alison gave her a gentle hug. "I'll be home before Fiona. Call me if you need me." She hesitated. "If you're by yourself."

"Thanks for meeting me at church."

"Have you talked to Barbara yet?"

"I haven't. I'll call her this evening."

Alison bent down and whispered to Eleanor. "Be nice to Dad. Put your spat to bed, Mom."

Eleanor made a face, but Alison was gone. *Spat?*

She announced lunch. Nick slouched in a chair at the table. Walter sat at the end. They ate sandwiches. Eleanor pulled strips from a slice of cheese and made a pile on her plate. She whispered, "A long time."

Nick said, "Huh?"

"The three of us."

"Better times," Walter said.

Nick belched loudly, then bent his face to his hands. "Shit," he said. Eleanor touched his shoulder. He got up slowly. "I'm going to rest. Just a little while. Okay? " He was looking at his father.

"I'll call you, Son," Walter said. "Pretty soon, don't go to sleep."

They heard him click his door shut. Eleanor said, "Remember when he broke his arm? Ten years old. I thought it was the worst thing ever. I couldn't imagine he would be all right again."

"I'm going to take him out to Hot Springs campground for the afternoon. I've got my camper out there. It's a mild day. We'll get a bite somewhere, you don't need to make anything for us. I'll see if he wants to talk. He just has to get through today and then tomorrow—you know how it goes. It's a heartbreaker, Karin dying, all the way around."

"She just lay down and died, with Juni and Tilde in the next room."

Walter held his chin and cracked his neck, a habit Eleanor despised.

"You should have seen their apartment," she said.

"It doesn't matter now. Nick and the girls will start over in a new place. I hope here in town, where we can be back-up."

"Where else would he go?" she said, then got up and clasped her hands. "I need to rest. Make yourself at home." She choked back a nervous laugh. "Sorry."

He stood. "I always liked that outfit. Remember when we drove to Portland to see Bob Dylan looking old as Methuselah? You wore it then."

He was wrong, of course. She had worn the black blouse with jeans. But his half-right memory touched her.

His arms hung at his sides, his gaze was on her like light. "This is crazy. I miss you."

They could talk right then and she knew they should do so, but she was tired. She stared at him. If she put her arm straight out she could touch him. She waited for him to apologize.

Walter was waiting for her to give. Damn him.

She couldn't stop herself. "You were with her all over town!"

His tender expression evaporated. She thought he would explode, the way he did the night he left. But he didn't say a thing. He looked at her as if he couldn't believe what she said—as if she were the one who had rent their bond. He marched off.

She heard him talking to Nick, and then the front door closing. She sat with her elbows on the table, her scalded face cupped in her hands.

7

Walter was wrong: Karin's death hadn't reminded Eleanor in any way of her own mother's passing, but his mention of it—his ham-handed reference to her orphanhood—certainly had.

Eleanor's mother died when Eleanor was eleven. The pain never went away; it was lodged under her breastbone like a sliver of straw. You don't forget your mother. Marla Dennis. She had thick blond hair that she twisted into a French roll and secured with long sturdy pins. She was tall and slender, her legs were pale, her cheeks freckled. Her favorite blouse had tiny red checks and white buttons shaped like daisies. She did crossword puzzles. She called Eleanor Lulu. She made chocolate pie, and Eleanor whipped the egg whites for meringue. She told Eleanor she had come to Oregon from Oklahoma on a bus, and she stopped in Lupine because someone on the bus offered her a place to stay for a little while. She spoke about her family or why she left Oklahoma once, when Eleanor was eight or nine and asked if she had grandparents. She said, "My parents were old to have a child, and besides me, they took in kin; everyone was old, waiting to die. There wasn't room for me in the house anymore. They couldn't help it." She promised Eleanor her life would be better than her own, because she would have an education. Eleanor thought maybe the person on the bus was her father. She assumed her mother would tell her when she was older. The birth certificate said, "Randall," which might have been a first or last name, or a place-saver.

Her mother had worked in the hospital kitchen for a while and then as a nurse's aide. They lived in a series of small apartments in the railroad district. They never had a car. Eleanor remembered being happy. Before she was old enough for school, she stayed with a line of old ladies in the neighborhood, so early on she was good at keeping herself occupied. By third grade she was on her own; she came home, turned on the TV, read books she brought from school, played paper dolls. Her mother came home tired, but they ate together and read and played dominos and slept in twin beds in the one bedroom. They frequented the beautiful park downtown. Once a year in the summer her mother rented a car and they went to Seaside for two days.

Then her mother died of a brain aneurysm. She was at work right there in the hospital, but they couldn't save her. An elderly neighbor took Eleanor in for the night, and the next day a social worker came for her. Eleanor went into foster care. She had had her first period before her mother died. She remembered how calm and kind her mother had been, teaching her how to take care of herself. She remembered how her breasts seemed to grow overnight, high and plump. She was big for her age. She was already tall, and people thought she was older than she was. Even when they knew she was eleven, they expected her not to be a child, not with her breasts.

Marla would never be thirty.

After Eleanor's mother died, there were houses with bedrooms crammed with bunk beds, and food in large pots on a side table, and plastic dishes. There was a house with two little bratty boys whom Eleanor was expected to watch and pick up after. She spent a year on a farm, with chores every day after school, and she learned to love being outdoors; she learned she was physically strong. For a short while she was in a home where she had her own room and a bed under a two-pane window; she could lie there at night and look at the sky. She was full of dreams. But the father in that family came to her door and watched her, night after night. After a while he was stepping inside, and then one night he shut the door. She got sick, waiting for him to come to her; she had pimples and diarrhea and a constant runny nose. Finally she told his wife, who slapped her and screamed that she was a liar and packed her bag and called the social worker to collect her. Then Connie and Alan Wisdom took her in. They put her in a room with their daughter, Barbara, in June of the summer before the girls started their sophomore year in high school.

A foster child learns how to prosper, when the placement allows. She had chores, but so did Barbara and her younger brothers. The family kept up with Eleanor's work in school, celebrated her birthdays, gave her a small allowance. Her clothes were bought at Goodwill and Sears, but she picked them out. They took her to church—they were Catholic—but they never asked her to convert. And Barbara, their oldest child, became her best friend then and now. She knew how lucky she was. She didn't think of herself as a poor orphan; she thought of herself as the Wisdoms' boarder. But ending her time with the Wisdoms had been surprising. One afternoon, Connie sat her down at the kitchen table and poured Coke for them. "We need to talk about your leaving," she said. It was March. Eleanor would be eighteen on April twenty-sixth. "I have a new girl coming May first," Connie said. She didn't seem to notice when Eleanor gasped. "You'll age out on your birthday, you knew that, of course. I have found a good place for you to go."

Eleanor began to cry. She squeezed her hands together in her lap. She was an adult; she knew that. She knew she was being ridiculous, but she felt her true loss all over again. Connie squeezed her hand and softly said, "There are children waiting for placement, Ellie."

There was a boardinghouse run by a woman from the Catholic church. Mrs. Loughlin. She was looking for a girl to help her with the house—the laundry, washing up after breakfast, that sort of thing. A few hours a day. There were three bedrooms upstairs and another one downstairs, populated by eight college girls. Eleanor would have a wage and her own small room by the back porch. She would share a bath with Mrs. Loughlin.

"You can have another job, at least part-time, in the summer. And then you can take classes in the fall if you want. You will qualify for grants if you apply now. You're a smart girl, you should go to college. Mrs. Loughlin is expecting me to send her a smart, honest young woman with her eye on the future. That's you, Ellie."

Eleanor had been completely surprised, and then felt stupid and babyish. She had always known that the Wisdoms were paid to take care of her and that the pay would stop when she turned eighteen. She knew a boy in school who lived in a disused car because he had nowhere to go. She just hadn't been thinking about it.

The day came when Connie took Eleanor to the boardinghouse and gave her twenty dollars and a big hug. "Have a good life, dear," Connie said.

8

So all of a sudden the house was empty. Eleanor went to the bedroom and sat on the side of the bed, her hands on her knees, not sure what to do next. She felt much like she had when Walter moved out: unsure where her body should lie on the bed, hypersensitive to sounds outside the house; a bit nauseated, like someone standing on moving ground.

She thought Walter would push her to talk soon; the separation had gone on too long. He liked his comforts. If he wanted a divorce— oh, it didn't bear thinking! They hadn't come to that. It wasn't as if they had never argued. When he bought a new pickup though there was nothing wrong with the old one. Whether Alison was old enough for sleepaway camp. How she always expected him to fill the car with gas. Once, it was over a city council election. The dumbest things. They settled them or forgot them; sometimes they laughed about them. Kids, money, stuff. They had never before yelled about anything, though. He had never walked out.

She loved him. She did. She felt sure he loved her. But if he did, why did he storm away and worse, stay away? Why did he spend so much time with another woman? How long would his furlough have gone on if this awful thing with Karin hadn't happened? Did a person stare at a hole in the ground so long, it became inevitable to fall in?

He didn't like her telling him what to do. He didn't like explaining that he was helping Celeste, his best friend's widow, get ready to move out of town. Walter didn't understand why Eleanor was sick of him coming home after supper was put away. His ultimate remark the night he left was, well, why don't you do what *you* want. She had gone over and over the moment he said it, how he was looking at her, the emphasis on *you*, the way he lifted his head as if he had just spotted something high on the wall. Did he mean, do-what-you-want, file for divorce? Or did he maybe mean it was up to her to want something that didn't depend on him? Was he pushing her away from him, or was he pushing her out of something: the house? her loneliness? her expectations of him? He had many friends and activities; she had her family, job, and Barbara. The disparity had never bothered her, but Walter was supposed to put her first, wasn't he?

It would have been sufficient to make his point if he had simply moved to the spare bedroom for a night or two. Both of them could have taken deep breaths and spoken honestly and patched the tear in their marriage. But in his absence their breach had swollen. She had lain in bed night after night, thinking he would appear, until she burrowed down into jealousy and resentment, and told herself he could sleep in a motel for all she cared. Alison told her he was staying at the Tennison house—Jim Tennison worked at Walter's shop—and Eleanor thought, well, that can't go on forever, Patricia's hospitality will wane. He was in and out of the house during the day when she was at work, and she thought he would apologize and come home. Then one day he came for clothes and toiletries, and and he politely told her he had patched up his old travel trailer and he was going to stay a while at the Hot Springs campground where there were toilets and showers. In February!

"Just to collect my thoughts. Call me if you need me," he said.

Alison was disgusted with both of them. Eleanor didn't know what she had said to Walter, but to Eleanor she said, you don't dump a forty-year marriage without some goddamned conversation! After that, Eleanor waited. She certainly hadn't thought it would be a death that brought them back together.

After she had dozed fitfully for a short while, she sat up and called Walter. Her call went to voice mail.

"I am sorry," she said. She was careful to inflect each word exactly the same. The expression had no hidden meaning. She waited for a moment, then hung up. She had been trying to think of the right thing to say, when what she needed to say was, come home.

She changed into jeans and a light sweater, filled a thermos with sweet weak hot tea, and went to see Velma.

Franklin Becker, Walter's father, had bought a large parcel of bare land in 1952, and built a bungalow on the lot at the street ten years later, in front of what would become Walter's property. The bungalow had always been a rental, except for the year after Walter and Eleanor married, when they lived in it while they were building their house. Eleanor managed the letting of the place—to students, mostly, though lately the renters had been young men barely getting by in bad jobs.

Velma's house was on the other side of the driveway. Franklin had taken a chunk out of his property and sold it to his friend, Al Howard, the fire chief, without a word of consultation with Walter, whose home had just been built at the back of the property. Becker property picked up again past the Howard garage; that was where Walter parked his travel trailer, to the east of the house. Eleanor and Walter had dreaded further sales, further houses around them, but his father never sold more of the property, and neither did Walter, his heir. Their house was set well back from the two front houses, with a single bare lot on the east, and on the west side, three acres of vacant land that swept from their street, Cherry, to the next one over and behind them, Hickory, and to the ends of both streets, where bare land met a wall of patchy evergreens, and behind that, a trail that ran along the edge of town—a favorite of local runners who didn't believe or weren't afraid of rumors about wild cats.

Eleanor sat at Velma's big round table in front of the sliding doors and watched her sip the lukewarm tea cautiously. Eleanor looked around, as she always did, to see that nothing was worrisome. Everything was tidy, though where the light hit you could see the surfaces were dusty. Velma was wearing a pilled purple zip-up velour housecoat, and Eleanor realized Velma never dressed in street clothes anymore. Her groceries were delivered, and recently she had begun receiving Meals on Wheels three times a week. Eleanor sometimes did little errands for her and looked in on her often. Her son, Andrew, lived in Klamath Falls, a couple hours away; he or his wife came over every few weeks. Andrew had taken her car away more than a year ago, after she drove onto a sidewalk while trying to park at the grocery store. He always checked in with Eleanor, but never made much of her generosity. He seemed to assume she had some responsibility for his mother simply because she was there.

"How are you?" she asked Velma.

"I'm just fine, but what is going on at your house?"

"My daughter-in-law Karin died unexpectedly. Nick is here; his girls are with their other grandmother for now."

"Oh my lord, Eleanor, oh my."

"Don't you worry. We'll get them through this."

For a minute, Eleanor thought Velma might cry, but then she was looking out the glass doors, her eyes narrowed. "That boy!" she said.

"Oscar? Has he done something?"

"He seems to be there all the time now. I don't think he goes to work anymore. He sits on his porch and smokes. And did you see the beer and wine bottles alongside the house?" She pointed straight across. The yellow glass recycling bin was spilling over, and beside it there was indeed a pile of bottles.

"And I bet I know what he's smoking."

"It's legal, Velma. Times change."

"There's a girl who drives a blue car, spends the night there."

"You think she is living there?"

"No, she just comes and stays."

"I can't really do much about how he lives, Velma. Nor would I want to. The house is single occupancy, but I'm not shocked that he has a girlfriend. As long as he pays his rent, he is meeting his obligation to me. And there are laws, you know; a landlord can't harass a tenant. If he has wild parties or fistfights on the lawn, well, you can call me, or for that matter, you can call the police. But honestly—" Eleanor leaned toward Velma, hesitating to touch her. "Oscar isn't on your property. He isn't breaking any laws. Forget about him, dear."

Velma was clearly offended. She sat up a bit taller, huffed a little, and then fell back into her stooped posture. "I just have this feeling he's in trouble, Eleanor. Where do his parents live?"

"Redmond, I think he told me. He'll be okay. Why don't you give him a friendly wave when you see him? I bet it would cheer him up. I bet he'd be glad to give you a hand some time."

"Eleanor Becker, you think too much of people."

"I try." Eleanor hoped it had helped Velma to complain. "I need to get to the grocery store in a hurry, before Fiona gets home," she said, and stood. "Do you need anything? Milk? Bread?"

Velma shook her head and said, "It's a sad thing, isn't it? That poor boy of yours." She took a breath and sniffed, and took another breath with effort.

"It sure is." Eleanor gave Velma a light embrace and left. She wondered how much longer the woman could get by alone. She had the son's phone number, but what could she say to him?

The lights were on in Oscar's place, so she called him when she got home.

"Oscar, it's Eleanor Becker, how are you?"

"Uh. Okay."

"I couldn't help noticing the glass you've got piled up by the side of the house. Remember Tuesday is recycling. Put your garbage can at the curb by seven, okay?"

"Yeah."

"And I'm going to bring you my recycle bucket so you can clear out *all* the piled-up glass in this next pick up. You get it together, Oscar, okay?"

"Yes ma'am," Oscar said, and hung up. She imagined him kicking a wastebasket across the room. Nobody likes a bossy landlady.

She had started her shopping list when Barbara arrived with two bags of groceries. Her friend seemed to enter on a gust of energy, her frizzy silver hair ruffling.

"Alison called me," Barbara said. "I thought you might not have found time to shop. Since you haven't had time to call me." Barbara seemed to mean just what she said, and it was true. She hadn't had time for anything.

Barbara put the sacks down and embraced Eleanor. "Poor Nick," she said, but Eleanor didn't want to talk about him yet.

She said, "Thank you, love."

They unpacked and put things away: a roasted chicken and a tray of scalloped potatoes, lettuce, bread, milk, eggs, chocolate chip cookies, and a chunk of cheddar cheese. There was a bottle of pinot noir, too, and Barbara opened it and poured a glass for each of them. They sat at the table across from one another and clinked glasses. Eleanor told Barbara about the apartment in Portland. About the burial. Nick. All the coming and going, and the girls off in Frost Valley. She ran out of words, out of energy.

"But what about you, Ellie? And Walter?"

"He's sleeping in his travel trailer. He was here, he was nice as could be, but with nothing to say about us. What does he think? That it's up to me to call a truce?"

"That would be great, wouldn't it?"

"Celeste—"

"Celeste is gone. Her house has a Sale Pending sign in the yard. She is not an issue, El."

"But she was."

"You don't want to hear what I think."

"I overreacted?"

Barbara spoke gently. "You don't like Celeste. She replaced Tom's first wife, who was your friend. I get that. But Diane is long gone, Celeste is Tom's widow—and she's gone now, too. I think Walt overdid it, but a fireman's widow needed help, and the firemen came together for one of their own. They stepped up, just as Tom would have for one of them. They are Walter's fraternity. Cut him some slack."

"He hasn't been a fireman for over twenty years. He's like an old guitarist with his band mates."

"It's called friendship, and civic engagement, too, Ellie. He coaches. He fundraises. It's admirable!" She put her hand lightly on Eleanor's. "Maybe he doesn't stop to think that your childhood made you vulnerable to feeling abandoned."

"Oh, for God's sake, Barbara. Get a license." She pulled her hand away.

They sat in silence for a few moments, and then Barbara got up. "I better go."

They walked to the door. Barbara said, "I'm sorry if I overstepped. I love you. Heck, I love Walter, too. Your marriage is strong. Snap it back into place, Ellie, fast as you can. Walter is a good man. He has never let you down. Like every man I know, though, he is lousy at mind-reading. You're going to have to tell him how you feel—not about Celeste. About your life together now. If he has slid away and doesn't know it, tell him. Tell him what you need from him. "

"I don't know how."

"Try."

"You think I should take the blame, don't you?"

"Oh Eleanor, try no blame. Celeste was a match to your dry wood, but I'd lay my life down that there was no affair. And she's in Boise now anyway. Just let it go as old news and a man's clumsy stumble. Tell Walt you want the family back together, for the sake of his son and his granddaughters, and because you love him. And for God's sake tell him to come home."

Barbara hadn't been gone five minutes when Alison drove up, and Ben arrived with Fiona right behind her.

"Gramma!" Fiona cried, and ran to Eleanor as if she hadn't seen her in a week. God, thank you for the delight of childhood, Eleanor thought.

Ben and Alison stayed on the step, talking. The door slid shut.

"I visited a boo-row!" Fiona said. "On a farm!"

"A boorow? What is that?"

Fiona made a braying noise.

Eleanor laughed. "A burrr-ow. Listen, Aunt Barbara just brought some cookies. Want one?"

Alison appeared a few minutes later and kissed Fiona on her crown. "You've got a little time before you have to bathe and get ready for bed, sweetheart. Do you want to play a board game? Read? Are you hungry?"

"Can I watch TV? *Pokemon?*"

"No *Pokemon* tonight."

"*Spirit?*"

"The horse? Okay. One episode."

"Can I watch on your bed?"

"No shoes," Alison said. "Did you watch TV at your dad's?"

"Oh no," Fiona said vehemently. "Jacqueline hates TV."

Alison and Eleanor looked at one another and rolled their eyes, but then Fiona said, quite seriously, "Polly has an I-Pad," and as she sprinted away, the women laughed.

"Barbara brought all kinds of food," Eleanor said. "Are you hungry?"

"Later, maybe."

"Is something wrong?"

"Oh, is it. Just what I thought. Ben wants to renegotiate custody. He told me to get a lawyer. He said there's no use in us discussing it. But then he says he wants to rotate custody, and he wants his turn starting when school is out. Get ready: for two years!"

"Wow. Maybe he's doing that bargaining thing where you demand something you can't possibly get, so that you get something more than what you have."

"I don't care! She's my little girl. He has two other kids."

Eleanor said, "Honey, they don't make up for not being with Fiona. He loves her too."

Alison glared at her.

"The two year business is ridiculous. Tell him he can have a month in the summer. Two, if he presses. I think he's probably just puffing his chest out to see how scared of him you are."

"What he really wants is to be in charge. He thinks his way of life is better than mine. His perfect little family. Siblings for Fiona. They're getting a puppy. He doesn't approve of me. He doesn't approve of my church, either. He said Fiona is missing important cultural tenets. He means Jesus, that's what he means."

"He said that?"

"He doesn't have to say it. He's using Karin's death against me. He said since the family has so much to deal with, Fiona should stay with them the rest of the school year. I told him he had some nerve."

"It does take nerve to exploit tragedy."

"People die. I said that. And families come together. I said that, too. Fiona didn't know Karin, and she's a child, remote things don't exist for her. What she can see is that her Uncle Nick is sad. She hears us talking, but she's not worried. What does Ben want? A bubble for his kids to live in? Our kid?"

"Do you think he'll—take steps?"

Alison shrugged. "I don't know, Mom. He can afford a hotshot lawyer and I can't. I'm going to go watch *Spirit Riding Free*, and hug Fiona, and not think about it."

Eleanor carried her recycling bucket down the drive and set it alongside the one full of bottles at the bungalow. She had an impulse to put the scattered bottles in it, but she left the task to her tenant. She had been glad for the money for years now, but sometimes she thought how nice it would be to have the cottage empty, at least for a while. Or gone. She imagined a field of wildflowers.

Back in the house she made herself a cold plate from Barbara's provisions and ate alone, thinking about what Barbara had said.

She thought about the night she and Walter argued so terribly until he stormed out. She had demanded to know what he was doing, what he thought he was doing, and when he would be done. He didn't like that. She didn't think his anger had anything to do with the past, his or hers. He did not like Eleanor pulling his chain—he said something like that. He was huffy when she said she was tired of him spending so much time with poor widow Celeste without a thought about what he needed to do at home. (And when he challenged her: *Like what? I'll do it right now!* she couldn't think of what to say.) Oh, it was such a stupid argument. Eleanor put her fork down with a sharp click against the table. She couldn't eat another bite. She wanted to go back and shake both of them. How in the world did it escalate to Walter sleeping in a travel trailer?

She certainly couldn't fault Walter for lack of feeling about her childhood. He had been shocked when he met her—a girl all on her own. He still had grandparents then, besides his mother and father. He had an aunt and an uncle and cousins, and lots of friends. One of the first things he did after they were married was offer to buy a proper stone for her mother's grave. There was only a strip of copper on a brick embedded in the grass, with her mother's name and dates. Eleanor had been deeply moved by the whole process of choosing the stone and having it engraved, then seeing it in place: *Beloved Mother*. No, she had nothing she needed to say about her history that Walter didn't already know and about which he hadn't already expressed his concern and understanding. What he didn't seem to understand was her life right now, forty years on.

Maybe she didn't understand it, either. When had she stopped to think about it? You didn't examine life; you lived it. She had been busy raising the children, especially during the years when Walt was a fireman with an on and off schedule. When Walter left the firehouse to run his father's hardware store, they hardly talked about the change. She had been happy that he had an ordinary schedule, that he was home every night. He was depressed for months, moody and touchy, but she thought it was because of Franklin's death. Oh good Christ, she thought. She felt hot, head to toe, with shame for her stupid stupid blindness, but it had been his decision to leave the firehouse. He hadn't asked her opinion. Nobody made him take over his father's life! Oh, Walter.

Then, very close to that same time, Alison started high school, and so did Eleanor. That was a joke, of course. Eleanor had gone to work at Lupine High as Barbara's part-time library assistant, and when a full-time opening for an attendance counselor occurred the next year, she took the position. Sometimes the job was tedious, and it was often aggravating, but she liked everyone she worked with and she felt part of something that mattered. The hours were great. Summers were free. She carried health insurance for her and also, since his recent birthday, Walter's Medicare supplement; she would have a state pension. Life had always been busy and mostly happy. When something had been wrong, it had come from outside her family. Walter's parents' deaths. Bad presidents. A forest fire close to town. A flood that split a street wide open downtown. None of them had ever been seriously ill. No one had ever had a car accident or surgery or lost a job. How many times had she thanked God for her family, their safety and health? Not us, she had thought, time and time again, with fear and gratitude.

She and Walter used to be active in their church together: various committees, fundraising, welcoming newcomers. She couldn't put her finger on the time or the reason they stopped. They saw fewer people now. Two couples they liked moved away. Tom and Diane divorced and Diane left town. Walt got on the Y board, and chaired fundraisers for the firehouse. He coached Little League. She joined a book group that lasted years, until a member died and in grief the others disbanded. Their things to do evaporated and they never replaced them. They watched TV and read a lot. Then Alison came home with her toddler, and for years the empty social life didn't really matter to Eleanor, because of Fiona. How many times had Eleanor begged off when Walter suggested going out? She was happy in casual clothes, making cookies, cutting paper dolls. Supper, PBS news, a book.

Something clenched just below her breastbone. Maybe it was regret, or embarrassment, or longing. Whatever it was, she knew their lives were being rattled, and she hoped she and Walter could find each other again as they looked to one another for consolation and strategy.

Those poor girls needed the best from them; and Nick, oh Nick—he needed to look around and find a place where he could stand tall, like his dad, because Juni and Tilde needed him most of all.

Fiona was in bed, Alison was in her room, and Eleanor was ironing a blouse in the living room when Nick came home. Eleanor looked up, expecting Walter to come in too, but she heard him back up his truck, turn around and leave.

"Did you eat?" she asked Nick, and he said he had.

"I'm going to go to Portland tomorrow, Mom. I'll call Mr. Gleason as soon as I can get him in the morning, to be sure he's in. I need to spend a day in Beaverton and that pretty much wraps up my project."

"Somebody else can't do it?

He laughed, though nothing was funny. He was scratching the back of his hand.

Eleanor felt her stomach constrict. "You won't go back up there, will you? To live?"

Nick was looking all over the room. He was staring past Eleanor when he said, "I don't know, Mom. Gleason has a lot of businesses. I wouldn't mind being a store pharmacist again."

Nick was talking so fast, she wondered if he was upset and talking to cover up his feelings.

"How would you manage with the girls, alone?"

"With a nine to five job, Mom. Routine. Maybe in one of the suburbs where there are good schools."

"Was this Walter's idea? For you to turn around and go back to Portland, you and your girls?"

"No. Dad thinks I'm daft." He giggled. And it hit Eleanor right between the eyes: her son was high.

9

Nick showed himself the next morning in a T-shirt and boxers as Eleanor was tidying up after breakfast. Alison and Fiona were gone. She had just enough time for a second cup of coffee. But there was Nick with dark bags under his eyes, his shoulders drooping, his knees so bony. Whatever energy he had last night was long gone.

"You look tired, did you not sleep well?" she said, and he cocked his head: Huh. Whatever.

"Are you still going to Portland?"

He pulled a chair out and sat down at the table. "I'm having second thoughts. What's the point? Like Dad said, I'm just a cog in a big wheel. Gleason will already have covered for the end of the month. Lucky, huh? Fuck, I'm out of a job, Mom. No job, no wife, no house." He squeezed his eyes shut and bent his head.

"Maybe it's for the best, Nicky. Be with your girls. Be with your family. You know you can stay here as long as you want. You can find a job here."

"I need to go get my daughters."

"Of course." She was glad to hear him say it.

"Helve will have them thinking Karin's death was my fault."

"Nicky, that's ridiculous. No one blames you."

"She has never liked me. Didn't want Karin to marry me——"

"Helve doesn't have to like you. She was the Queen Grandmother, but now she's not."

"Good one, Mom."

Eleanor was surprised by the mean glee under what she had said. "We're all wound up. I would never say anything to her that wasn't polite, you know that. She has lost her daughter, God help her. And she is your daughters' grandmother, just as I am."

"No, not just, Mom. You're the best."

Eleanor put her hand to her chest. She felt hot tears shimmering in her eyes and blinked them away. "You will get through this, Nicky. All of us—Helve, too—will help. You'll see."

"Maybe. But I'll never be happy again, Mom. I wish I could go to sleep and not wake up. I wish it had been me and not Karin."

"Nicky!"

He had his head down, and he spoke in such a low whisper she strained to hear him. He said, "I should have been home that night she went to bed sick. I could have been. I called and said I was getting a motel because work ran late, but it wasn't true. I was late because I played six holes of golf with the store manager. I told him, I've got to get home, but it was way too late to drive. I'd had three beers and no lunch. What difference will a night make, I thought. I felt a little guilty, but I was tired. I called Karin and went straight to bed. While the infection was roaring through her, while there might have been time for the doctors to save her, I was snoring away in a motel. While she was dying." He looked up at Eleanor. "If I'd been there, I would have taken her to the ER twelve hours earlier, and they would have caught it in time. I don't know if I can live with it, Mom. I don't know if I want to."

Eleanor felt faint. How would her son ever get past that weight of guilt? *You had no way to know.* She pulled out a chair and sat beside him. She put her arm around him.

"Go back to bed," she said quietly. "When you wake up, make breakfast for yourself. That's as far as you need to see the day. Do simple things. Take the trash out. Walk down the hill and get some lunch. Visit the park. When I get home, I'll drive with you to Frost Valley to get Juni and Tilde. Give Helve a call to let her know we're coming."

She had to go. She said she would be home a little before four.

"I'll get cable installed," she said.

"No need." He put his head down on the table.

Eleanor went to work. Nick wandered through the house, looked through a window, opened a closet door, patted the couch. He ate a slice of deli ham standing at the fridge, and went back to bed. Or tried to. He couldn't think of what else to do. He lay flat on his back fully clothed and thought about Karin plunging toward death while he slept in a motel two hours away. He could hear her whimpering, the inexorable whistle of the poison speeding through her body, the slap of God's palm against his sleeping face. He opened his jaws to howl, but snapped them shut so hard his teeth rang. Karin, Karin. His blood burned, his temples buzzed, his eyes blurred.

He got up. He couldn't bring Karin back, but he could take his girls and run. He wouldn't fold like wet paper. He didn't need his mommy and daddy and his fucking mother-in-law to save his ass. Gleason could damned well give him a job.

Standing by the bed, he felt limp and hollow. He scrabbled in his shaving kit and found a pill bottle that held a few Adderall, and swallowed them dry. In the kitchen, he ducked his head under the tap and chased the pills with a slug of water. He went to his car and sped down the driveway onto the street, tires screeching.

By the time he passed Gold Hill he was flying. He was doing the right thing, he was on his way, he was Father of the Year, he was the best man for the job. And he was thirsty. He thought about pulling over at a rest stop, but Grants Pass was not that far ahead, and he could get coffee and a breakfast sandwich there. Fill the tank. He would be in Portland by early afternoon.

He pulled into the second exit; he could see the Golden Arches. When he stepped out of the car he thought for a moment he had lost a shoe; his left foot tingled, and he felt a sharp stabbing between his toes. He went inside and ordered and stood waiting, rolling the foot around and tapping the toe of his shoe against the floor. He was perspiring heavily, he could feel sweat rolling down his neck. He grabbed the paper sack and the cup and backed out of the store door. He was hot and then suddenly cold as the damp air glazed his body. At his car he put the bag on the hood and fumbled for his key. His neck and scalp were on fire and his arm jerked crazily, sending the cup flying out of his hand; coffee splashed on his thighs. He was out of breath, gasping, struggling for air. He was desperate to breathe; he brayed like a donkey. Someone shouted. His back was against the car window, and he pushed hard for support, but a spasm made him lose his connection to the car and he slid to a sitting position, his arm jerking; and someone was yelling, someone was crying, he was falling away.

When Eleanor arrived home, she was surprised to see Walter's truck so early in the afternoon. And the travel trailer, what was that about? It was good that he was there for Nick, she had worried about him alone all day, but had resisted the urge to call him during her lunch hour. What could either of them say? And he might be napping.

Walter came out of the house to meet her. "Let's talk out here," he said.

He had spent the day with Nick, most of it in Grants Pass.

"They called me from the ER. *Dad* on his phone. He fell apart in a McDonald's parking lot. Chester gave me a ride so I could pick up the car. By the time I got to the hospital everything was under control. Nick had had a panic attack, he must have felt he was dying, poor kid. He was dehydrated, he's malnourished, he's using drugs. Jesus, Ellie, he's a mess. They said the attack didn't warrant a full heart workup there just then, but he definitely should have one soon. His low weight, his reflux, I don't know what else, but they said to get him to a doctor. What the hell was he doing in Grants Pass?"

"I guess he was going to Portland."

"We talked about that! He's done with Portland."

"I know, I know. I should have taken the day off. He shouldn't have been alone."

"He's a grown man. With children. He's going to have to get himself together."

"Easy to say. Karin's not been dead a week yet."

"I'm upset too," Walter said.

Both of them sighed and he put his arms around her. She leaned into his chest. It felt good.

In a moment Walter said, "I've got to get down to the shop, but I'll be back around six. Should I pick something up for dinner?'

"We're okay."

"I think you should wake Nick if he doesn't get up pretty soon on his own. For one thing, he needs to call his daughters."

"I could call Helve and say he—what?—has the flu?"

"No, Ellie, don't do that. It's his to do. He needs to go get them. One of us could drive him over. He needs to get them registered in school right away. He could stay out of bed, for chrissake."

"I don't know where we'll put the girls."

"I thought of that." Walter tapped his chin with his fist, an old habit. "I parked my travel trailer. If Nick sleeps out there, the girls can have the double bed. Of course—"

Both of them looked at the floor.

"So, Ellie—" Walter began, and Eleanor interrupted, speaking softly. "That would work."

They looked at one another. "Are you still mad at me?" he asked her.

"No. Are you mad at me?"

"No."

"Okay then." Walter nodded, took a breath, and headed for the door. Eleanor called to him, but he was gone.

She wasn't mad, but she wanted him to tell her what he and Celeste had done together. If he didn't sleep with her, he shouldn't mind reassuring his wife. If he did, she would forgive him. She wanted him to ask how it was for her while he was gone. She wanted him to be sorry. Of course, she wanted him home. And here he was. The other issues were moot now, weren't they?

10

Walter returned with a sheetcake from Albertson's. He took it into the kitchen and set it on the far counter. It had white icing with blue and pink flowers. Fiona said it was pretty.

The family ate a chicken, pasta and peas casserole that Eleanor had made, and Fiona talked between bites. A third-grade boy at school hit another boy on the playground and his tooth fell out! A Chinese woman visited her class and taught them to say *ni hao mah*, how are you? They made collages in art, cutting construction paper up and pasting it back together. She had started reading a library book set in *medieble* times!

Everyone smiled and tried to act interested, but Nick, annoyingly, was tapping his foot on the floor under the table, and Alison moved her food around on her plate instead of eating it. Fiona wanted to cut the cake. Alison got plates and helped her daughter load small squares onto them. Fiona happily gobbled her piece down; everyone else picked at the cake and ate a bite or two.

Walter exclaimed that it was a very nice evening, and asked Fiona if she would like to take a walk down the block. She hopped up eagerly, took his hand, and off they went. Nick headed straight for his bedroom.

"So what's what with you and Dad?" Alison asked as soon as she and Eleanor were alone. They had cleared the table and were standing by the sink. Eleanor covered the cake with plastic wrap. Her back was to Alison.

"Mom?"

"He's back."

"You're okay with that?"

Eleanor turned around, smiling. "Of course."

"And it's none of my business what was said," Alison said, with a fake cough and wide eyes.

"Honestly, we didn't talk," Eleanor said. "It was a practical matter—moving Nick out to the trailer to make room for the girls. Nick and I are going to go to Frost to get them, maybe tomorrow."

"Wow. He's up to that?"

"He's their father."

"Mom, Steve and I are talking about getting married soon."

Eleanor put dishes in the dishwasher deliberately, as if it took all her attention.

"Mom."

"He's a nice man. You should know by now what you want to do."

"Not educated. That's what you are thinking: he didn't go to damned college."

"I certainly was not. I thought about what it would be like for me with Fiona out of the house."

"Fiona likes him."

"I should hope so." Eleanor rinsed and dried her hands and faced Alison. "Look, having you and Fiona here these years has been a great gift to me—to your father, too, and I hope to you and Fiona. But

I can imagine you want your own place. If you want to buy a house, Walt and I would help you with the down payment."

"Mom! You think I'd marry Steve to get his house?"

"It didn't come out right. Choose what will make you happy, darling."

"I'll never be far away. I promise."

Eleanor smiled and patted her daughter's shoulder, then went on through the house and opened the door to see if Walter and Fiona were in view. Her heart was pounding. She had seen this day coming and she knew it was right, but she would miss Fiona like the sky would miss stars.

She did wonder what Alison and Steve had in common. He was athletic—he and Walter often met up at the Y or golfed together—while Alison had no interest in sports as spectator or participant. Eleanor didn't know what interests Steve shared with Alison, who read fiction and loved foreign movies. On the other hand, Eleanor was sure Walter's family had been upset with his choice of Eleanor, the slightly-educated orphan, and Walter hadn't cared what they thought. And when you got right down to it, what interests did she and Walter share? Their family. It all came back to having someone to love. Alison deserved that.

Alison caught up with Eleanor and linked their arms. "It would have been wonderful to have loved Ben," she said. "The father of my child. As tall as me. He's so smart. I was awed by him, and I was swept off my feet by the experience of sex—until he told me I was no good at it. He also told me I had shallow interests. And I didn't eat right while I was pregnant. But he married me and would have stayed with me, for Fiona. He would have suffered me for her. He's happy as a clam with Jacqueline, but he still can't forgive me for leaving him."

"I am not comfortable hearing all that, sweetheart."

"You are my mother. You wiped my bottom. Can't you be the one person I can talk frankly to? Steve and I could go on like we are now, but marriage will make me appear more stable if I have to go to court with Ben. It's also my chance to be happy. Steve thinks I'm wonderful. He admires me for being a teacher. He thinks Fiona is an angel. He's a good person, Mom. He goes through his days whistling."

Eleanor put her arms around Alison. "Then hold fast, my love."

Eleanor told Walter about the conversation with Alison later that evening, after Alison and Fiona had gone to bed. Nick was holed up in his room.

They were in the kitchen drinking the last of the wine Barbara had brought on Sunday.

"Steve's solid. It's time for her to make a life of her own," Walter said.

Eleanor wanted to ask him what he thought Alison had been living all along, but didn't. Instead, she said, "Nick did call Helve. I know, because she called me when I was making supper. She talked in that I'm-being-courteous voice she has. She said the girls were busy. Karl lent them his son Collin's keyboard, as if they would know what to do with it. She said they slept all right last night. Like a report from camp. I said that was all good to hear. I feel for her, truly I do, but Nick and his girls should be together. I think Helve wants them to stay with her."

"Don't catastrophize, things are already bad enough." Walter swirled the last drops in his glass and drained it. "It's dumb to buy wine by the bottle, isn't it? We should get a case."

Eleanor took a deep breath. "I hope the girls don't find themselves in a tug of war."

"Eleanor, no way is the perfect way. Let's get them over here and see how we can be most helpful. The girls need all of us, don't you think?"

She got up and opened the refrigerator. "I better go pick up some milk and bread."

"You need me?"

"No. Why don't you get Nick to watch some TV with you."

"Get beer."

They stood and both of them laughed. "What's funny?" Walter said.

"You tell me."

"It's a relief to laugh. All this sorrow and worry. And us—"

"I won't be long," Eleanor said. "The trash barrel is still at the curb—"

"I'll get it."

In the car, Eleanor took a long draft of air. She felt as if they were all dancing on ice floes.

When she got back from the store, the men were watching an old Seinfeld stand-up performance, chuckling and sipping from juice glasses. Walter had found a bottle of whiskey on a shelf with dishes they never used. Eleanor passed them, carrying old pajamas, and went to the hall bathroom where there was a tub. She lay in hot water with the light off, a wash rag draped over her face, and she prayed. She seldom prayed, not because she did not believe in God—she had never questioned whether she did or not—but because she didn't think who she was or what she wanted was important enough to merit heavenly intervention. Now here she was, though, fiercely thinking: keep us all steady and together. She was anxious about being with Walter after the past weeks of separation, but she didn't think God would want to hear about that.

She dressed in her pajamas, shy as afterwards she walked in front of Walter and her son on her way to the bedroom. She turned on her bedside lamp and took up the novel she had been reading, but after some minutes she realized she hadn't read anything at all. The novel, *Across the Garden*, was British, and she was finding its description of domestic life in suburban London arch and overly concocted, but it made her feel ignorant to dislike it, because the writer was much acclaimed. *Exquisite, dangerous,* and *beguiling*: reviews from the likes of *The Guardian* were quoted on the back. She did wonder what it would be like to have a life like the one in the book, in which dailiness had weight and people spoke to one another in complex sentences. Barbara had lent her the book, teasing her, saying she needed to "broaden her horizon." Eleanor wasn't going to argue the matter, but it did pinch that Barbara thought historical novels like *Pope Joan* and *The Heretic's Daughter* were somehow inferior to the latest British literary sensation.

She had turned out the light when Walter came through the bedroom to the bathroom. She was facing away from him when he got in bed naked. The bedcovers were still turned down, and she lay exposed. Her whole body prickled with anticipation, but it wasn't sexy; it was self-conscious and perturbed. She had been sleeping with Walter for forty years, and she wondered if she knew anything at all about how his male mind worked. She had said she was sorry, albeit to to voice mail, but he had not. She thought it might help her anxiety to be held, but she was so tense she felt cold and brittle. When he scooted over to her and said her name, she startled.

"Ellie," he whispered. "You are beautiful." He undid the buttons of her pajama top and moved his hand across her breasts lightly, then down onto her belly. He kissed her neck and pressed himself against her. Gently, he turned her to face him. She smelled his toothpaste. He tugged her pajama bottoms down awkwardly until she wriggled them off. Then he pushed his hand between her legs, stroked her inner thigh, and opened her labia with his thumb.

She twisted away.

There was one moment when they were silent, and then there was the next moment when they spoke, both at once, he to say, "Well shit," and she to say, "I'm sorry." He rolled away. She said, "It's just—I don't know how I feel. I'm nervous." She began to cry, and then she hiccupped. By now Walter was on the far edge of the bed. There was long silence and the sound of their breathing, until Walter said, his voice utterly without inflection, "It's all right, we haven't had good sex in a long time."

She gasped and lay perfectly still. She willed him to disappear from the bed, not out to his trailer, but far, far away. It couldn't be worse if he had slapped her. She lay there and felt him rearrange himself farther away from her, heard his breathing slow as he fell into sleep. Only then could she curl up and stop burning with embarrassment. It was a long time before she slept.

In the morning, while she was making toast and tea and hurrying to get out of the house, he came into the kitchen and stood a yard away from her and said, "Last night is all on me, and what I said, if it's true, that's on me, too."

She despised that expression, "on me." She said, "Honestly, Walt, it is not even seven in the morning and I'm buttering bread."

"I'm not myself. I'm under a lot of pressure." He waited, she supposed for her to inquire as to the nature of his pressure, but she did not, so he went on. "The business has gone under and I've ignored the inevitability of closing it for far too long. I haven't turned a profit in years."

He took a breath, she supposed he was waiting for her to say something. He had said sex with her was no good! And now he was talking about his store!

"I made a fatal mistake when I didn't co-op with Ace. I missed the window, and a big box store opened on the highway. I dawdled and now I've got to clean up the mess I've made. I'm sorry I haven't told you—"

"I'm your wife."

"I never wanted it. It's always been Dad's store, even now, when he's been dead so long."

"Oh please."

"When you want, I'll explain how things are."

She looked at him straight on. "I don't care about the hardware store, do you understand? I have a dependable job with a salary, the house is paid for, there's the rental income; we are not going to starve."

"It isn't that, it's the hassle—the damned waste of years. Honestly, Ellie? I'm embarrassed."

"So I'll go to work, and you come home and help me help our son and grandchildren, and for that matter, Alison has problems, too. Your father is dead, Walt—" and here her anger subsided all at once. "He doesn't care that the business failed. Who needs a hardware store when there's a Home Depot five miles up the road?"

"Exactly!"

"Later, we can sit down and you can explain it all to me." She tried to speak mildly. "You can let me in. But right now, I'm wondering why you let me think you were having an affair if you weren't, and why you haven't confided in me about the store—for years! Do you think I'm too stupid to understand a business failure, or too grasping to love you when—now that I think about it for a quarter of a second—when you've got what you have wanted all along! You are out from under your father at last."

"I'm not sure what you want me to say."

"Maybe you should just tell me what you think I wouldn't like to hear, and get it over."

"There's nothing like that."

"Good. I have to go." She grabbed her lunch and left without looking back.

11

Wednesday morning, Helve told the girls at breakfast that they would be going to Lupine later that day. Neither said anything. She took them into Wellen to a big box store and bought them athletic shoes and socks, underwear, jeans, pajamas, two T-shirts and a zip-up sweatshirt apiece, and rain jackets. It didn't take long, because they hardly looked at items before putting their selections in the cart. She let them choose whatever they wanted and was surprised at their lassitude, as if in selecting goods they were doing her a favor.

She bought flip phones, one for each of them, so that they could call her any time they wanted. "They're just for us," she said. "Pay-as-you-go, I'll take care of that. I have your numbers."

From there they went to eat hamburgers at a diner, and as they ate, she reminded them that school didn't start for almost two weeks, and they would surely have some time in Frost with her again before it did.

Juni said, "If I don't like school, could we do homeschooling instead?"

Tilde said, "Not me."

Helve said, "Let's take it a step at a time, dear. Maybe you will like it fine."

When they got to the house, she suggested they walk to the graves to visit their family. She said it like that, "—to visit our family."

Of course, she meant their mother, though others lay there, too. When they started out, the sun was shining, but by the time they arrived, clouds had moved in and the day was dreary.

"Where is Peter?" Juni said.

Helve reached across Juni, bent, and pointed to a stone set flush in the ground. It was inscribed with the baby's name.

Juni knelt and touched the stone. She started crying. Tilde took her hand.

Helve touched the girls' arms, beckoning them to her.

The girls moved closer and stared at the ground.

"We will always remember our precious Karin," Helve said after a moment. "We will talk about her. She won't be a subject we tiptoe around though it hurts to bring her up. I think about my mother every day. I think about your grandfather. You want to remember specific things. I can still see my mother rolling towels to put in the cupboard; that's what she did instead of folding them. And Henry, putting his teeth in a cup of water on top of the dresser before bed, then giving me a big grin.

"Listen, I'll tell you something about your mother as a child. Ivy took her to shop for a Christmas present for me. They went to the drugstore and a gift shop, and then Ivy took her to a second-hand store, and Karin found the perfect thing. A tea cup with fluted edges gilded gold at the lip. I can show it to you, I have it to this day. It's on the shelf by the pantry."

The girls looked at her.

"I want you to think of something about your mother that you won't forget. Something about who she was, who she will always be to you."

It took them a little while. Helve waited patiently.

Then Tilde said, "Once there was a tiny spider on my pillow. Mom put it in the palm of her hand and took it outside and set it on the ground." Her eyes widened: Was that what Helve had in mind? Helve nodded.

Juni said, "One time on my birthday she made S'mores instead of a cake."

Tilde laughed. "She had forgotten the cake. She had forgotten your birthday!"

"You don't know that!" Juni said. She wailed, "She did it special for me!" She cried, and her sister and her grandmother waited silently for her to stop. When she quieted, Helve handed her a tissue. She said, "We'll stop and have tea with Ivy before we go home. You can meet her chickens." She took Juni's hand and pulled her close. Tilde walked ahead.

"She knew I like S'mores," Juni whispered fiercely. "Better than cake."

"Of course she did," Helve said. "Even I knew that."

Eleanor drove alone to pick up Tilde and Juni, arriving a little before five o'clock. She noted that the girls' shoes were sitting just inside the door, lined up by Helve's. Helve was wearing socks and woolen slippers. There was no sign of the girls, but after a few minutes, Eleanor heard their voices; they were in the attic bedroom.

She accepted a cup of tea from Helve, though she was anxious to get the girls home. That morning, Nick had urgently begged not to go, to have time to get himself together. He said he would move his things to the trailer and tidy the bedroom for Juni and Tilde, though he was still in bed when Eleanor left. She knew he hadn't wanted to deal with Helve, and she relented, but as she sat with Helve, drinking the coffee, she thought Nick should have come and he should have come alone. She couldn't let him pass everything to her.

The living room had been rearranged since the day of the funeral, with pillows on the couch, and the seating facing a television mounted on the wall. On a narrow table in front of the couch was a pack of cards. The old wooden dollhouse that had belonged to Karin and Elin had been brought downstairs and was on a table by the back window; and there were books in a small pile on the floor in front of the sofa. A standing electric keyboard was against the wall. Clearly, Helve had occupied the girls, and Eleanor felt a dart of accord with her. Both of them were mothers and grandmothers, but Helve had lost her husband and her daughter, and for all practical purposes, her first daughter, too.

"Are you okay, Helve?" she asked.

Helve smiled politely, accepting Eleanor's courtesy, and nodded. Eleanor thought her rather cool, but after a moment, she went on to ask after Helve's brother-in-law and his wife, Karl and Ivy, who lived close by, across the berry field, and Helve launched a long account. Helve said that her nephew Collin had moved in with Karl and Ivy for the duration and that his girlfriend, Lily—he called her his partner, Helve amended—would be coming for the summer to help with the farm. (Lily was a crop and soil science doctoral student at Washington State.) They would work with Karl for the season, at the least; Ivy had said she and Karl hoped they would decide to stay on. The young ones had been campaigning for new crops after this next round of marionberries. Probably wine grapes. And Karl had bought acreage on his far side, past the grave site, for lavender. (He had informed her, rather than consulted her, but Helve hadn't felt like saying anything.) Collin had already asked Eleanor if he could plant a variety of greens in her kitchen garden now. He thought he could sell them directly to local restaurants. Helve said of course they could, as long as she got a salad out of it.

Eleanor listened politely.

The girls came downstairs. They were in new jeans and T-shirts, and each wore a pendant set with a blue topaz bead. They were such pretty girls, and Eleanor wondered if they knew it or cared. They looked wary, and she could hardly blame them.

She said, "Let's go, girls, we'll be missed in Lupine." The girls each carried a big plastic shopping bag. They slipped their shoes on, then hugged and kissed Helve. Helve shut the door after them, but as the car pulled away, they waved, just in case.

Eleanor turned on the car radio a little loud—NPR chatter, in case the girls wanted to talk and not let her hear. She thought about her stilted conversation with Helve, and wondered if Helve thought her rude. The resentment about seeing so little of Nick, let alone his family, over the years, was a shard in her civility. She was certain it had been Karin who decided it should be that way, and Nick had not cared to stand up to her; there was no good in blaming Helve. But Eleanor didn't like Helve, plain as that. She didn't like the superior attachment Helve had with the girls, and the obvious conviction that it gave her authority. And after what—fifty years in America—she still expected people to take their shoes off?

Everyone was waiting at home. Walter had gone for pizzas, four different kinds, and had invited Steve. Fiona was by the door jumping up and down when they drove up, though she was shy when the girls came inside. Tilde engaged with Fiona right away, but Juni stood near the door. Alison took the pizzas out of the warm oven.

The men pulled the table from the kitchen into the living room and everyone gathered around on chairs and stools. Nick, looking pale and tired, had a daughter on each side, and Fiona was directly across from Tilde, watching her every move.

When they had settled, Eleanor asked Fiona to say a prayer.

Fiona folded her hands, bent her head and said, "Bless our food and all our kin. Save our souls and save our skin." Everyone laughed and the mood of the group lightened.

After supper, Nick and Walter went outside to shoot baskets. Eleanor showed the girls the back bedroom and bathroom, gave them towels, told them to feel free to help themselves to snacks and drinks any time, and finally just stood there with nothing else to say. The girls stared at her for a few moments, then broke and scattered like loosened kittens. She heard them in the bedroom giggling, and like a snubbed schoolgirl, she felt a flood of embarrassment so hot, she had to go splash her face at the kitchen faucet. She didn't know what the girls would do all day, but they would have to look after themselves, except when Nick bothered to get up. Walter could see to lunch for them. She had an idea they had done a lot of looking after themselves, and it made her chest ache to think of it.

Nick found a movie to watch with the girls and they got through the evening, though Eleanor lamented that they would be sleeping on Nick's sheets; there had been no time to wash them.

After Eleanor and the girls left, Helve went to Karl and Ivy's house. She drove, in case it was dark when she went home. She helped Ivy with supper, chatting about the chickens and the weather and the humor of farming as a college subject. Collin spent a few minutes chatting with her and left to "catch a movie," as he described it. Ivy remarked, once he was out of the house, that he was a lucky young fellow to have Lily. The young woman was healthy, educated, mild-mannered, and had a Norwegian grandmother! Helve asked after their older son, Anson, who lived in Massachusetts and taught high school science and had not been home in over a year.

At dinner, Helve mentioned casually that she needed a workman for a few days, to do minor repairs in the house. She could ask at the church for a recommendation, but she thought Karl might know someone dependable. He said he did, and looked for the man's name and number in his business-drawer, as he called it, at the bottom of a cabinet near the front door. When he had given Helve the information, he excused himself and went outdoors.

Ivy put her hand on Helve's arm and said, "You could have just asked Karl to help you. He will wonder why you didn't."

Helve said, "Karl is busy enough. I have a long list of small things I've overlooked for too long: loose hinges, warped boards, snagged screens, a shelf that's cracked. The porches need painting, and I'm thinking I should replace both toilets with something more up to date."

She knew she was disturbing Ivy, but it was a way to turn the conversation—now or later—to the future. She hadn't intended to speak her mind just yet, but when she saw Ivy's concern, she couldn't pretend a bit of home repair amounted to nothing.

"I'm redundant, Ivy," she said, and Ivy blinked. "There is nothing I need to do anymore. I'm certainly not going to get out in the field, and I'm not going to stand at a register taking sales. I can't leave right now, because the girls need me, but they'll get their sea legs soon enough. I want to go home, Ivy."

Ivy burst into tears.

"Now don't do that," Helve said, taking Ivy's hands in her own. "It might be next year before I can get away. But I need to get the house ready to sell, and I must soon talk to Karl about my share of the farm. And don't tell me he isn't wanting to talk to me, too, with Collin back home with a wife on the horizon, and the pair of them with a bucketful of notions about how to better what we've been doing for fifty years."

Ivy wiped her eyes and chuckled. "Collin is full of himself. It's college does that, don't you know?" She reached for Helve's hand and squeezed it. "It's Karin dying, isn't it? It'll be easier if you start fresh away from all this sorrow."

Helve got up. "There's no hurry about any of this, Ivy. But I'm not one to carry an intention around in secret. It's time to go home, and I want to get on with it. Elin says she's been patient a damned long time now." She smiled. "Her words, not mine."

12

On Thursday, Nick took the girls to register and see where they would
be going to school after spring break. LMS—Lupine Middle School,
situated at the south end of the city—was a handsome two-year-old
single-story building with long side wings and a curve at the back,
where there was a pleasant patio that faced a mown grassy field; and
beyond that were four long rows of fast-growing poplar trees, harvested
for pulp that provided income to the district. One side of the building
faced a rocky hillside, essentially the end of town; the opposite side
faced a recent development of multi-family homes whose backs were
to the school, their trash cans lined up along a gravel alley running
by the school fence. Behind the school were ochre hills and blue sky.
Across the street were a small park and more houses.

"The start of the day is always pleasant," the principal, Mrs.
Kenton, told the girls and their father. Her hair was brushed out in an
airy halo around her head. She was wearing a red sweater and black
pants. They were in the hall just outside her office. "The teachers stand
at the classroom doors to greet you. The halls are clean and brightly
lit." From somewhere out of sight, there were shrieks of laughter and
the sound of running. She chuckled. "We aren't the quietest school;
we encourage collaboration in learning."

The building, new or not, was intimidating, and the sound of
collaborative learning was a din.

A small girl with short dark hair hurried to meet them. She was wearing a blue print (ice-cream cones) cotton dress that struck her legs mid-thigh, black tights that were cut off just below the knees, and a long lacy white sweater. She arrived so hurriedly she seemed to skid to a stop.

"This is Amanda, one of our eighth graders. Amanda, meet Juni and Tilde Becker, our new eighth and seventh graders. Girls, Amanda will show you around today and she can answer questions, too. I'm going to chat with your dad and we'll see you here in fifteen minutes. I'll send you home with a short list of supplies you'll need and a student handbook that will fill you in on rules about cell phones and campus restrictions, what to do if you're absent, and so on. One of the adults at your home should be familiar with the rules, too."

Amanda was cheerful. She moved between Juni and Tilde, both of whom stepped away from her, and took off quickly. "School is school, right? You come, they tell you what to do, you mostly do it. The teachers are pretty nice."

Juni and Tilde saw the large library, the art studio, and the music room. It was all new, clean and bright, nothing like they had expected a school to look. They peeked in windows at ongoing classes. The teachers, young and old, looked a little sloppy, their arms up and busy, their heads poking forward. In some rooms, kids were talking to one another in little groups, hunched over tables. In other rooms, they sat with their legs stretched out, slouched in their chairs. Everything appeared and disappeared like video as they moved quickly down the halls. Amanda chattered all the while. They stepped into the gym, where boys were bounding across the floor, their silky shorts fluttering around their thighs. They looked into clean bright bathrooms. When they reached the main office again, Nick was waiting, ready to go.

"Are we in?" Tilde asked as soon as they left the building.

He said, "All good." They were quiet on the drive home.

That evening, at supper, everyone wanted the girls to report on their visit to LMS. Both girls shrugged.

Eleanor had made chicken strips, mashed potatoes, and salad, hoping to please the girls, but they moved their food around on their plates and ate little. She asked Nick, "Was there any problem enrolling them?"

"I think the principal was caught off-guard, that there were no records for the girls, but she seemed relieved that their vaccinations are up to date. I explained that they had been homeschooled with their mother, and Mrs. Kenton said she could get in touch with the state about that."

"Hmm," Eleanor said. Nick grinned. "By the time they realize the girls have been off the grid, they'll have learned how smart they are. Right, Juni?"

"Right, Dad," Juni said, and excused herself. Fiona asked Tilde if her school had a band. "I don't know," Tilde said. "Why?"

"I'm going to be in a band when I'm bigger."

"Really!" Alison said. "I hadn't heard about this."

"Oh yes," Fiona said. "Ginger told me her big sister blows a horn and marches at the football games. She wears a hat.""Well, that does sound like fun," Eleanor said.

Juni and Tilde disappeared into the bedroom and shut the door.

Nick and Walter turned on television and Eleanor went into the kitchen. Alison and Fiona were doing a jigsaw puzzle at the end of the table by the window. Eleanor sat with them a while and watched, and then cleaned up the supper dishes. Afterwards, she sat on the couch and looked at a kids' science magazine with Fiona, an issue on octopuses, until Alison said it was time to get ready for bed. Fiona gave Eleanor a fierce hug, as if she might not see her for ages. Eleanor pulled her onto her legs and exclaimed, "Oof! You are getting to be a giant girl, Fiona!"

She went into the kitchen and cut a sliver of lemon pie and ate it slowly, trying to remember Alison at Fiona's age. She could remember Nicky's long gangly legs and his habit of bouncing his leg while he sat in his chair at the table. He liked to eat and get away to play. Alison was the quiet one; she used to hang her head while she sat at the table, as if she were waiting for a scolding; she would look up and give everyone a tight-face look, as if accused. Whatever made her so tricky certainly hadn't passed on to Fiona. Alison was raising a confident child, she had to be doing something right. But then, what had she, Eleanor, done wrong, that Alison had been and was still so tetchy?

Later, Eleanor and Walter got into bed, each with a book. She was feeling nervous with him, and she couldn't think of a thing to say. He held his book, and looked over at her several times, but didn't speak. Though she was glad he was home, they hadn't settled things between them. "I'm not mad" hadn't quite done the trick. Their freeze-up sexual encounter certainly hadn't. She didn't want to quarrel anymore about his time-out, but she realized they never talked about their feelings. Sweet talk, sexy talk, silly talk: all were things of the past.

She wasn't angry anymore, only apprehensive, like someone on the wrong side of the front door. In a while she put her book on the floor and slid down under the covers, facing away from Walter. He turned off the lamp and lay on his back, close to her, not quite touching. He put his hand on her hip and held it there briefly, then patted it and turned over.

She wanted to say the right thing but she didn't know what it was. Actually, she wanted him to say the right thing. The longer she lay there, the more awake and anxious she was, so she got up. Walter was asleep, snoring softly.

She decided she would see what books she might give to the church drive. It had been several years since she culled them. Both she and Walter read a lot and then piled books on shelves, in corners, in boxes. Certainly she could donate the many novels she had read, mostly historical novels, and some she had bought because the bookseller, Lauren, insisted she would love them, though she was sometimes left wondering how books got chosen for acclaim.

She pulled on a robe and went out to the garage and turned on the lights. There were boxes stored in a deep cupboard along the wall past the washer and dryer. Immediately she spotted one that said ALISON, and pulled it out and carried it back in the house, put it on the floor in front of a chair, and sat down and opened it. She was flooded with nostalgia the moment she pulled back the flaps of the box.

These were books her daughter had loved and saved. Alison might want them, in time, for Fiona, but right now Eleanor could see they would be suitable for Juni and Tilde. *A Tree Grows in Brooklyn*. *The Bean Trees*. *The Summer of My German Soldier*. *The Bluest Eye*. Jane Austen. *Dragonsong*.

She carried the box into the house and put it on the floor by the doorway onto the hall, near the bedroom where the girls were sleeping. She hoped Juni and Tilde liked to read.

13

Saturday morning, Fiona's father picked her up. He and Eleanor exchanged friendly words about the weather. Alison had left for the airport; she and Steve were going to spend a few days in Las Vegas.

Eleanor took the girls to Target, though Juni insisted that Helve had already bought everything they needed. They didn't have shorts for gym, and they had a list of school supplies to buy. Eleanor bought a few staples for the house. The girls picked up notebooks, pens, and so on, and then, with an awkwardness that brought home to Eleanor just how little she knew the girls or they knew her, she consulted with them to buy personal items, including toothbrushes, tampons, hairbrushes, shampoo. Neither girl selected deodorant, so Eleanor added several kinds to the cart. At the last minute, she remembered they would need backpacks. Then Juni asked if she could have a pair of slippers. Tilde said she needed slippers, too.

When they were done shopping, they sat in the Starbucks section. Eleanor and Tilde had iced coffees. Juni had a caramel coffee concoction and asked for a pastry.

"I haven't had a teenager in the house in an awfully long time," Eleanor said. "You have to help me. If there are things you like to eat, just let me know, snacks, too. I want you to feel at home. The most important thing is to get settled in school. I think you'll find it easy to do what is expected. You just have to speak up if you need something."

"We will," Tilde said. Juni kicked her under the table.

"You should talk to your dad about an allowance, but really, anything you need, you just have to ask." Eleanor took a long slow breath. "You haven't spent much time with us, so I understand that you might be trying to figure out what's expected of you. You are our guests, but more, you are family, and we want you to feel at home. The way I see it, we'll all be polite for a while, and then one day when you aren't thinking about it, you'll realize you know where everything goes and you don't have to ask."

Juni looked away, obviously bored.

"Juni?" Eleanor wanted to take her in her arms. Or slap her.

In a moment, Juni asked, in a faltering voice, "When can we go back to Mormor's house? We aren't in school yet, and there's nothing to do at yours."

Eleanor said, "Ask your dad about that. I expect you can spend some time there next week. But let's try to settle in here a bit first, okay?" She stood, anxious to move on.

Juni threw her cup in the trash. Standing a couple yards away from the bussing station, she threw the cup in a high arc, and it went in perfectly, not even grazing the sides of the can. Someone whistled. Eleanor and Tilde walked over and deposited their cups. As they walked out to the car, Eleanor mentioned that she would be going to the grocery store shortly, and she asked if they wanted to go with her to pick out snacks they liked, or if they might make a list.

Juni spoke in a monotone, looking down, "We like sandwiches. We like sliced ham and yellow cheese and peanut butter and white bread."

"I can remember that," Eleanor said.

"And chips," Juni added. "All kinds. And Oreo cookies."

When they got home, they discovered that Nick and Walter had put up a basketball hoop on the garage and had bought a new ball. Eleanor went to the grocery store, and when she got back, there was some kind of game going on. It made her smile to look at the four of them, with their long legs and arms, and the swing of the girls' pale hair. She thought: we are a family of Amazons. Then she wondered how they could ever make things right for Juni and Tilde.

She changed her bed and went to put a load in the washing machine in the garage. She noticed an unused plastic garbage can and took it inside to the girls' bedroom for them to use as a laundry hamper. She wanted to stop fussing.

When everything had settled down—the girls in their bedroom with the doors closed, Walter in a chair with his Sudoku book—she went out to the trailer and knocked on the door. It took a few minutes for Nick to answer, and she realized he probably had been lying down.

He looked distressed, and she asked him why. He told her to come and see.

A forwarded package from QVC had arrived. He explained that it was something Karin had ordered. He opened the box for Eleanor to see its contents. There were three smaller boxes. Each held a pendant necklace with an aquamarine stone surrounded by tiny diamonds set in gold. The chains were gold. They looked soft and warm.

Eleanor couldn't think what to say. She thought the necklaces were vulgar and surely expensive. She picked one up and laid it in the palm of her hand. "What will you do?" she asked.

Nick handed the receipt from the package to her, and when she looked at it, she blew her breath and handed him the necklace she had been holding.

Nick spoke. "You saw the boxes in the girls' closet at the apartment, didn't you? All jewelry. She had been ordering it for months. I never paid any attention; I thought she was buying junk costume stuff. I thought, well, it amuses her. Then, the night she died, the girls showed me a box of bills under their bed. Karin hadn't opened them. "They're—they're staggering." He shook his head.

"Is it all worth a lot, Nick?"

" I can't pay for them. I don't want to pay for them. What the jewelry is actually worth, I don't know, because who else would want it?"

"The girls must surely think it is theirs to keep."

"They do. So what do I say to them?"

"You say you can't afford to keep it. You say you're sorry. Don't criticize Karin, of course."

Nick sighed. "We don't talk. Not a word about Karin, nothing. I have no idea how to reach them."

"You have to try," she said, hoarse with pity.

He doubled over, clutching his chest. He burped loudly and groaned.

"Nick!"

"It's okay," he gasped. "I just get these pains. It's stress, since Karin. It passes." He was shockingly pale.

"Nicky, you have to see a doctor."

He was bent over, his head almost touching his knees. Eleanor hesitated, and then she knelt and put her arms around him. He started to cry convulsively. The sounds were awful. She held onto him as if she were keeping him in a boat on swelling seas. Her boy, and nothing she could do for his pain.

She sat with him, not talking. In a while, he said he would be all right. "I'll send this stuff back," he said. She left.

Walter had set up a folding table and started a jigsaw puzzle. Eleanor could not bring herself to tell him the state Nick was in. He would see it soon enough for himself.

Better to stay busy. She told Walter about the book sale coming up at the Congregational Church, and he suggested they look at what they had, together. He pulled the chair and table away from the bookcase on the west wall of the living room. The bottom shelf held paperback mysteries in stacks. Walter said he thought Nick would want them. The two top shelves, he said, held treasured books he didn't want to give away. They sat on the floor and he told her about some of them: *A People's History of the United States, Stamped From the Beginning, The Warmth of Other Suns, The Worst Hard Time, 1491:New Revelations of the Americas Before Columbus.* Eleanor was excited, looking at them. She wondered where she had been when he was reading them, why she hadn't read them, too. She skimmed the review quotes on the back of *The Warmth of Other Suns:* the story of the migration of six million Black people from the south to northern and western cities in 1915 to 1970. Her mother had been a migrant, too—white, and later, but transplanted south to north, seeking a better life.

"Oh, we can't part with any of these," she said. Someday soon she would read them. They put the books back on the bookcase and brought in a box from the garage. Though he had something to say about every volume he picked up from the box, Walter said he thought the books could go to the sale. They took that box and the one with her novels, and put them in the trunk of the car.

"I'll take them over there for you," Walter said.

"Why don't we do it together now? Someone will be there."

Two women at the church were sorting books, and they were delighted to take the Beckers' contribution. After that chore was done, Eleanor and Walter stopped at a tiny trailer where tacos were for sale, over on the edge of a parking lot near the church. They were served by a pretty, dark-eyed girl, ten or eleven years old; a woman, probably her mother, was cooking behind her. A little boy on the floor at one end of the trailer was drawing with a fat crayon in a coloring book. He looked up at them and grinned.

The food was spicy and delicious. Eleanor and Walter ate, standing on the sidewalk, leaning forward to let drips fall to the walk. They shared a bottle of water. Eleanor stepped back to the stand and leaned in to say, "Muy sabroso," hoping that was right. The girl smiled, and the little boy waved.

They put their trash in a bin by the trailer. Eleanor stepped close to Walter and wiped a bit of grease off his cheek. He took hold of her hand.

"Remember?" he said.

Eleanor's chest felt hot, and the warmth rushed up her neck and made her blush. He had asked her out for the first time when they happened to meet at a taco kiosk near the park.

She looked down at the sidewalk.

"Look at you," Walter said, leaning close to her. He lifted her chin and put his palms against her cheeks. She put her own hands over his for a moment and said, "We better get back and see about the girls' lunch."

That night in their bedroom, she decided to talk to Walter about the residue of bad feeling that she still had about Celeste. Maybe if she expressed it, she could shed it.

"You went out and I didn't know what you were doing." She said this out of nowhere, sitting up in bed, rubbing lotion on her arms. She tried to sound neutral, unaccusing.

"I did try to tell you, Eleanor." Walt put his book face down on his bedside table.

"I can't help the little spasms of pain I feel when I think about you coming in this house, gathering clothes and exiting."

"I have feelings, too."

Suddenly she knew she didn't want to talk after all. "Oh, it's over, isn't it? It isn't worth talking about."

He turned out the lamp. "If you say so."

She thought he would touch her, but he lay still and soon he was asleep. It's just as well, she thought, but there was something chilly about her relief. Maybe it would be better if they had separate beds, she thought, but of course there were no beds to spare.

14

On Sunday morning, when no one wanted to go to church with Eleanor, Walter offered to make waffles for the girls, but all they wanted was toast and juice. He coaxed them into taking a walk with him through the north blocks of downtown Lupine while Nick stayed sleeping in the trailer. A tour, he called it. The streets were empty, the shops not yet open. They were easy together, the girls and their grandfather. He wasn't one to talk much, especially about how someone was feeling. (He knew that was a problem with Eleanor.) He didn't have plans for the girls, he had nothing in mind to instruct them. Though he was sad and a little worried, especially about his son, he was happy to be with his granddaughters. They had missed so much time together, but they could make up for it now. The girls were were young and vigorous, they were his son's children, and he loved them far better than he knew them.

He hoped that the news that everything was walkable from where they lived would give Juni and Tilde a boost of independent feeling. There was the ninety-acre park designed by a famous landscape architect—a jewel, a wonder, he emphasized. It had a story, and he would tell it to them sometime. "It always lifts my spirits just to be in it," he said. The library was new and "snazzy," he said. He pointed out a clothing thrift store, ice cream and coffee shops, and bookstores new and used. On their way back, he showed them where the school bus would pick them up at the foot of Cherry Street; and he suggested that on nice days they might prefer to walk home, straight up the avenue, stopping for a snack or to browse. The bookstore was always good for an hour, he said. "Just let one of us know if you go out—we'll get you phones; but you can feel free to explore town, go to the library, all of it." When they didn't respond, he added, "If you like, we could go to the Y one day next week. The two of you are natural athletes." He grinned. "Runs in the family." Neither girl reacted. He picked up the pace and headed home.

Just as they reached the driveway, Walter noticed that Juni was crying, and he stopped. The girls stood near him, looking at the ground. Juni's face was stony, and rivulets of tears ran down her cheeks. He took out his handkerchief and held it out to her, but she ignored it. He put it away. "Did I say something to upset you?" He put his hand on her shoulder lightly. "What can I do?"

Tilde spoke politely. "We want to see our grandmother Helve. We want to stay with her instead of here. There's no school yet. Why can't we?"

Walter nodded his head; he understood. "Okay. Sure."

They walked up the drive.

"Come in and have something to eat first," he said. "I'll let your dad know."

He reappeared and made sandwiches with butter and deli ham, cut them into quarters, and stacked them in a clumsy tower on a plate. He laid the plate on the table with a bit of a flourish. He put out milk and chocolate chip cookies, and bowed. Juni looked at him, startled. Tilde giggled.

"Eat and wash up, and I'll take you to Frost."

Nick didn't come in the house, but he met his daughters at the car. He hugged them and said, "I'll see you in a few days."

When Walter and the girls arrived at Helve's house, she had just returned from church. She stood on the porch and the girls ran to her and wrapped their arms around her waist.

"What a nice surprise," Helve said. "Come in, Walter, and have a cup of coffee with me."

"Oh, I can't   "

"Of course you can. Please do."

They sat at the table and talked about the weather for a little while, how it was pleasant now, and how it would get so hot before they knew it; how you had to get out early in the day and relish the smells of spring. The coffee was very strong. Walter said, "Helve, is there anything I can do to help you? A chore? An errand?"

She smiled. "There's naught to do, but thank you."

Walter nodded and said he had to go. "I'll have Nick give you a call later." They got up from the table and headed to the door.

"It was good of you to bring the girls, Walter," Helve said.

The girls were beside her. "Bye," they said, smiling. "Bye bye." They watched him leave, and waved as he drove away.

It was a beautiful day, a beautiful drive back to Lupine. Walter caught himself whistling. He hoped Eleanor wouldn't make a fuss. She could use the break to get some rest and arrange the house to her satisfaction. She could swim at the Y, she hadn't done that since she got back from Portland. They would have some time together; there were things they should discuss.

Helve had put dough to rise before she went to church. She had planned to make bread loaves, but she told the girls the dough was meant for cinnamon rolls, and they could help make them. Of course they said they would. They washed and dried their hands and put on aprons. They held their hands over the bin while Helve sprinkled them with flour. Already they were giggling with anticipation.

Helve cut the dough down the middle and had each girl punch her share down. She powdered part of the counter, where they stretched and rolled the dough into two long logs.

"Now we'll brush with melted butter, sprinkle with brown sugar and cinnamon—not too much—and roll them up." This took quite a bit of time, as the girls took such small portions of sugar at a time. The next step was to slice the logs so that they could unroll the dough in strips. "Cut a strip this long—" Helve held up her hands—"and do it all the way up." Soon they had two big pans of curled buns set in paper cups. Helve put them aside with floured towels across them, and told the girls to wash up. There would be more rising of the dough while they went next door to visit Karl and Ivy. And the chickens.

Ivy was in the kitchen, as she always seemed to be. Karl was napping, and Collin had gone to visit Lily in Seattle and bring back some of her belongings. Ivy picked up two small folding stools from the porch and led the girls to the coop. She had eight chickens—"my barnyard bunch," she called them. Most had names associated with their appearance: Red, Spotty, Gray Girl, and so on. A few of them liked to go out and forage, and the others liked the coop. The girls had learned to open the stools and sit quietly, and in a little while, the chickens came to visit, peeping and gurgling. Tilde favored the smaller hens, while Juni loved the one big Rhode Island Red, called Barbro, which jumped onto her lap right away. Juni was quite attentive as some of the chickens cooed and clucked and settled down. Meanwhile, other chickens were scurrying about. Tilde asked where the rooster was, and Ivy pointed. It was foraging behind the coop.

The girls sat for a while, each with a chicken on her lap, and then went inside to have cheese and bread and juice with Ivy, Karl, and Helve. Afterwards, back at their grandmother's house, they both fell asleep on the couch, settled in their old way, their legs entwined. Helve baked the rolls.

She brought a small box down from the attic that contained furniture for the old dollhouse. After some discussion, it was decided that the girls would clean the dollhouse the next day and arrange the furniture. That evening, after they had cups of soup, the girls ate rolls and watched old cartoons on TV until Helve sent them to bed. Then she took a chair out onto the front porch and sat a long while, studying the sky.

15

Monday morning, Walter suggested to Eleanor that they have breakfast on the plaza, to celebrate spring break. Eleanor protested mildly, but he insisted that it was a nice day for a walk, and she could have something she wouldn't cook at home. She liked the blintzes at Caffe Giotto. He liked the sourdough pancakes. And it was a nice day.

What breakfast at the plaza was really about became clear once they ordered their food. Walter poured cream into his coffee and stirred, and stirred some more.

"What?" she asked. She smiled. She would rather hear it sooner than later.

"I just don't want you worrying."

"I have things to worry about," she said, with a little shake of her head.

"Oh, I know you do; we do. But the store—our finances—you don't need to worry about those things."

"No?"

"We're going to have an auction. Clear out what we can and give the rest away. I've talked to a real estate agent about selling the building—"

"What does she say?"

"She says downtown real estate is moribund."

"Hmm. And Jim?"

"This is Patricia's last year of teaching, and Jim is nearly seventy. Do you realize he started working for my dad forty years ago?"

"He's been your rock, hasn't he?"

"He has. I think he's invested all his salary, and Patricia has forty years in the system; they're going to have a good retirement."

"And you? Do you have a retirement?"

"That's what I wanted to talk about. Yes, I've put whatever profits there have been straight into our funds, except when there was a big purchase—a car, the solar panels. I can start Social Security anytime, though I'll get more if I wait."

"If you've thought about all this, why don't you just tell me what we're going to do?"

"I thought we could live on your salary for now, and there's the bungalow rent if we need it. Let our money continue to grow. There'll be college for the girls. Maybe we'll live to be a hundred and need care." His parents had lived their last few years in a beautiful facility at the edge of town, new the year they moved in. Expensive. His mother had dressed up practically to her last day. His father had slacked off, favoring pants with elastic waists.

Walter had recently turned sixty-five. Eleanor would be sixty soon. "Isn't that how we've lived all along—on my salary?"

"Mostly. The tenant rent has gone to savings. We have a lot of money, Ellie. I mean, you could quit, too, if that's what you want to do."

"You sound doubtful."

"What would you do if you retired?"

"What will *you* do?"

They stared at one another.

They finished eating in silence.

While they were waiting for the check, Walter said, "I didn't want you worrying."

"I'm worrying about other things now."

"Well, sure. Things will settle down. The girls will get in school and make friends. Nick will get a job."

"I think Nick is really sick."

"He's grieving."

"He coughs, he has chest pain, he's underweight. He smokes constantly. I think he's a heart attack waiting to happen; I want you to lean on him to see a doctor."

"I can talk to him."

"You didn't answer me. What will you do now?"

"There are a lot of things to do around the house and property."

"Sure, but not enough to occupy you very long."

Walter leaned back, tipping his chair. "I'm looking around, Eleanor. First I have to get out from under the store, and then I'll find a project. Steve and I have been tossing some ideas around. Summer, I'll do some coaching."

They walked in silence on the way home. As they neared the house, Walter stood in front of Eleanor and held her shoulders and said, "We've lived modestly, saved regularly, and never touched the funds from my inheritance. We've got our home and a million dollars, Eleanor."

"Oh, stop," she said. She thought she might faint, or giggle. On second thought, she said, "You're serious."

He saw her expression. "You sign tax returns every year, Eleanor. You put money in savings every month."

"I had no idea," she said. "I never think about money. I left everything to you." She put her head back and closed her eyes. "The idiot wife."

Walter put his arm around her. "You okay?"

She heard birds chirping. Some kids playing on the street behind their house. Her ears buzzing. She walked fast up the drive and went into the house and straight to the bathroom, where she threw up her breakfast, washed her face and brushed her teeth, and sat on the toilet to consider what it meant to have more money than she could ever spend.

That evening, after a supper of leftovers, while Walter and Nick shot baskets outside, she made herself comfortable in a chair and read from the British novel. She was glad she had stayed with it. Secrets were festering, and Eleanor anticipated the couple's relationship would soon detonate. Ugly things were going to be said—in impeccable English, of course.

Later, Walter came in and sat in a chair with his Sudoku book on his knee. He worked a puzzle for a while, then arose and said, "I'm ready for bed, how about you?"

Eleanor said, "I'm not sleepy."

Walter shifted on his feet, sighed audibly, and went out of the room. She felt her face get hot; she realized he had expected her to follow him, but she had been preoccupied with her reading and had missed his subtle invitation. She thought about getting up, but the moment had passed.

She turned the book over on her lap and thought about what Walter had told her that morning. She had been a 1950's wife where money was concerned, but she trusted him, and she hadn't ever been very interested in money, because she knew she didn't have to be. For Walter, work had ultimately been about doing what his father wanted him to do. Had Walter promised? He never told Eleanor. She couldn't begin to understand the dynamics of that relationship. When Franklin went into assisted living, Walter took over the store as if he had been waiting for it all his life. What kept him from offloading the store when his father died? *It was just a dumb business;* being a fireman had been a vocation. She had tried to believe he was ready for a nice quiet business life after the physical challenge and risks of being a fireman.. At least he had never tried to mold his son, though he would have liked to see Nick become a doctor. He wasn't the kind of person who spent a lot of time thinking about what other people ought to do. She thought that was admirable, though right now Nick could stand some direction.

He told her once long ago that he had considered going to graduate school to study History—he had earned his bachelor's degree with Honors at the University of Oregon—but his father had asked him to wait a year or two to see if the impulse was still there. Soon he became a fireman, a job he loved, and he didn't care about his studies anymore.

She remembered him saying, "It's just as well, I'd probably have ended up teaching high school and coaching baseball." As if that would have been a bad life. As if that wouldn't have suited him a whole lot better than running a business.

It was ridiculous to think about what-if now. What mattered was that she and Walter had had a life together. Children. A home.

She met Walter a few weeks before she began her second year at the college. She was in the park, sitting above him on the gently sloping hillside above the bandstand where the Lupine City Band was playing Ralph Vaughn Williams's *The Folk Song Suite*. She had an open thermos of iced tea tucked against her hip. Then a yellow Lab bounded away from its owner and loped past her toward the path; she recoiled and turned over her thermos, and the tea splashed onto the grass and ran straight down to Walter Becker's blue-jeaned backside. He leaped, she leaped, she was sorry, he said it was okay, and she fled in embarrassment.

Months later she was standing in line at a pop-up taco stand on the plaza, and he recognized her and introduced himself and bought her a taco, and that was that. To the moment, she could still remember the flutter in her throat when he came to the boarding house for the first time to take her on a date. He was tall and handsome, he was courteous, and he made her laugh. Being with him completed something in her. She wasn't going to be alone anymore. They married at city hall in the early summer, after the semester was over; she was pregnant with Nicky. She had earned sixty-one college credits, straight A's except for a B in Algebra II. She had decided to major in History. She had been thinking about being a teacher, or going into Civil Service. Then that part of her life was over.

That's my story, Eleanor thought.

She put her hands on her cheeks. My God, she thought: all these characters, these problems. Family. Tinsel chattering in the wind. My God, she thought again. She looked at the British novel, still on her lap, and laughed.

16

Early Tuesday afternoon, Alison and Steve returned from Las Vegas.
They came straight from the airport to the Beckers' house, except for
a stop to buy a bottle of champagne. They came in the door laughing.
Alison announced, "Surprise! surprise! Ta da da da, we give you Mr.
and Mrs!" She would never change her Becker name. She kissed her
mother's cheek and whispered, "Wish us luck, Mom." Walter shook
Steve's hand, and then on second thought, gave him a hug.

Alison said, "We were out walking that first evening and we
saw a boutique chapel, and we turned to each other, both of us saying
the same thing at the same time: let's just do it! So we did, yesterday."

Nick came in the house to see what was going on. Steve filled
him in, and Nick hugged his sister and shook Steve's hand.

They all stood around for a moment, then broke into chatter.
Alison had brought gifts for Tilde and Juni. Eleanor put them on their
bed. Eleanor took Alison aside and said it might be a good idea to
bring Fiona back to the house for the night after she picked her up at
Ben's. "You and Steve can settle in, and we can explain things to her
tomorrow. We can assure her she'll still be here a lot, but now she'll
have her own house. I can bring her over after breakfast. This is going
to be a shock to her." Alison was indignant. She said, "*I* will explain
things to her tonight. Maybe this will make Fiona remember who her
mother is."

Eleanor wanted to shake her and tell her there was no insult in the suggestion. She had to swallow the who-is-the-mother comment, but swallow she did. She thought Alison was tired and anxious, in need of sleep; it would take a while for everyone to adjust to her marriage. Including Eleanor.

Alison and Steve left, and without saying anything, Nick disappeared, too.

Walter and Eleanor weren't surprised by the marriage. They sat a while and had a glass of wine and talked about it. Alison and Steve were ready to make a home together. Walter liked Steve, spoke of him as "solid." Eleanor nodded; she hadn't actually spent enough time with Steve to know him very well, but he was a respected tradesman, and he obviously loved Alison. He was easy-going. She just wondered what Alison expected from marriage. What she brought to it.

Later that same day, Walter and Steve moved Fiona's Princess desk and accoutrements, along with all of her and her mother's clothes, to Steve's house. Eleanor offered to make dinner for everyone, Walter said they could go out, but Steve said Alison—who hadn't come over—was going to pick up Fiona and get her to bed early. They would celebrate another day soon.

Eleanor and Walter had just gone to bed that night when Alison called. Eleanor sat up in bed. " Is something wrong?"

Alison said something, but Eleanor couldn't hear her. "Speak up," she said. "What is it?"

"It's Fiona. She had a big fit, Mom. When we got here, I explained that we lived here now, that we had brought all her things for her, and she jumped up and rattled the front door, screaming, until she ran out of steam. She kept saying, 'I want to go *home*!'"

"Oh poor darling."

"It really threw her that her furniture is here. She said she was going back to your house. I should have prepared her for this. I feel awful."

"How is she now? Is she there by you?"

"She's asleep in her clothes on top of the covers. I feel so bad for Steve. What must he think?"

"Is he there?"

"No, he went to his cousin's for a while. I didn't tell Ben in front of Fiona, by the way. I don't know that it's his business."

"It isn't, except that drop-off will be there instead of here."

"I told her she would see you lots."

"Of course."

"Steve is such a nice man, Mom."

"I know. Why don't you take a hot bath and have a cup of chamomile tea—-"

Alison laughed, not convincingly. "And sweat the worry away. I'll try."

When Eleanor hung up, she broke into sobs. Walter said, "Is someone hurt? What's happened?" She waved her hand and shook her head and cried more, thinking of Fiona torn away from the home she had known almost all of her life—away from *her*— and without any warning. When she told Walter what had happened, he put his arms around her and hushed her, his face in her hair. He said, "I'm not sure what the right way would have been, Ellie."

Alison called after breakfast to say that the three of them had gone out for breakfast, and that Fiona was doing better. Eleanor relayed the information to Walter and then said, "I don't believe her."

The next morning, Eleanor found a daybed and a skinny chest with two deep drawers at Home Depot, and arranged for them to be delivered the following day. She went to Target and bought two twin sheet sets and a couple of pillows. Then she went home and mopped the front and middle bedroom floors and scrubbed the windows. When she was done, she plopped on the floor in the hall and leaned against the wall, her legs stuck out, her eyes shut. She thought of how nice it would be to have a study—a private space where she could read and think and be alone. Time enough for that. And what did she need a study for, anyway?

Juni should have first choice, as the older girl. One would have a twin bed, but also the wonderful windows and light; the other would get the TV and the queen-sized bed.

Walter walked by and saw her on the floor. He gave her a hand to get up.

She said, "It's going to be different around here, isn't it? Having Tilde and Juni here all week. Not having Fiona."

"They'll all be fine," he said. "Kids are resilient."

"And us?"

"We're resilient, too," Walter said. "We just have to be steady, you know? They have to know they can depend on us." He put his arms around her and gave her a squeeze. "It's a gift, in a way. Their presence. Nick." She was shocked to hear him say that—that he saw past Karin's death and everyone's grief to the simple fact of this opportunity to be with their grandchildren and their son.

She wondered if he remembered any more why he had moved out of the house. Why he had wanted to be somewhere she wasn't.

17

Nick picked up his daughters in Frost early Sunday afternoon, the end of spring break. Tilde seemed fine, but Juni shuffled into the Becker house with her head down. Eleanor explained the change in bedrooms to them. Juni said she wanted the front room. She immediately moved the bed across the room away from the door. Tilde asked if Alison had left her TV for good, and indeed she had. Once the move from the back bedroom was done, the girls went to Tilde's room to watch a movie on the TV. That evening, Alison, Fiona, and Steve came for dinner. The adults tried to encourage the girls about school, which started the next day. They just had to hang in there. Lupine kids were nice, and so on. The girls sat quietly. Juni looked across the table, through the window onto the expanse of empty land. Walter blew his nose. Alison said they needed to get Fiona home.

Alison said, "Some kids don't know how to be nice, so you have to be nice first. Smile and say hi and introduce yourself."

Steve said, "Good luck to you." Tilde smiled, but Juni had turned her back to the room.

Eleanor and Walter walked Alison and Steve to the front door. Fiona, trying to lag behind, gripped Eleanor's hand so hard it hurt. Eleanor walked her to the car, ignoring Alison's scowl. Fiona started to cry, but Eleanor gave her a quick kiss and shut the car door before Alison had time to say anything. Then she hurried into the house and she cried, too.

Nick sat down with his daughters on the couch. He said, "Get a good night's sleep, that's my advice." He touched Juni's shoulder and she looked at him. He said, "It might help if we had a little ice cream," and though Juni rolled her eyes, they did.

The next morning, he was up as soon as his daughters were moving around. He sat drinking coffee while they ate toast and cereal. Eleanor appeared and reminded them she had made lunches for them.

When Eleanor was gone, Nick reached across the table to squeeze each girl's hand. "You'll be fine. Don't rush, I'll drive you." The girls told him "no way," and said goodbye.

Juni was wearing new jeans, washed twice, and a flower-printed voile blouse from the Frost house attic. Tilde wore a short black pleated skirt that Alison had bought for her in Las Vegas. She wore a white cotton T shirt and Karin's yellow cardigan. Off they went down Cherry Street to catch the bus. Nick went back to bed.

Juni and Tilde reported to the office and the clerk gave them the codes for their lockers. They had different schedules for different rooms; they stood at their lockers for a minute, looking at one another. Then Tilde said, "It can't be that hard, everybody does it." They went in opposite directions.

———————

Juni remembered very little about school. She and Tilde had been in fourth and third grades when their mother didn't send them back after spring break. Juni remembered desks and chalkboards, but not where she sat. The teachers were women. She remembered fire drills. One day Karin had said, "I've decided to teach you myself." She bought board games, lined paper, new pens and crayons. She cleared the dining table and wiped it down. After that, they all slept in every morning. Mornings, they watched cartoons and then sat at the table and read. Karin signed them up with the state for homeschooling, and boxes appeared, full of books. The second year, the state sent a laptop computer. Karin said they were big enough to study on their own, and in their own way, they had done so.

In Juni's first class, language arts, the teacher put her at a table with another girl, Sam. She took the folder the teacher gave her— vocabulary exercises—and tried to concentrate and do the work. There was a group of girls, five of them at two tables, who seemed to find everything funny. She caught them looking at her quite brazenly, and she tucked her chin and pretended to be absorbed in work. Sam noticed and leaned close to whisper, "Melanie, the one with all the hair, is the queen of those bees. She hates me, so the others shun me. My mother turned her mother in for embezzling student activities funds at the high school. Her story is my mother lied to hide her own guilt. Everybody knows Melanie is full of it, but somehow she's got her gang."

Juni didn't know what to say. Melanie caught her staring and gave her the finger. Juni moved her chair so her back was to Melanie's view. In math class, there was a test. A short review, the teacher said. Not for a grade. Juni was lost by the middle of the first page. She drew hearts and X's along the margins. Her face burned. Things were a little better in science, where they sat at counters, because the teacher, talking about food webs, didn't ask any questions at all, and never looked at Juni even once.

Then it was lunchtime. She had her sandwich and a quarter for milk. She got in line, looking at her feet. At first she didn't notice that a boy had come behind her and was standing close. He lifted the curtain of her hair and tucked his head under it. She felt his hot breath on her spine. Kids noticed and called out: Yo, Jasper!

She jerked around and put her palms against the boy's chest and sent him sprawling. There was a whoop and cheer from onlookers. An adult came running over and sternly asked Juni what was going on. She was short and had to look up at Juni. She had a bright white streak in her hair, like a skunk.

Juni was shaky, but she had a steady stance.

Someone said, "Dodo fell down," and someone else said, "It was his fault!" Then a girl stepped forward. She said, "Ms. Dee, Jasper slipped and grabbed her hair to keep from falling."

The boy giggled and muttered sorry to Ms. Dee, but not to Juni.

Mrs. Dee crooked her finger and led Juni away to the wall.

"You're new, aren't you? What's your name?"

Juni told her. Mrs. Dee wrote it on a little pad.

"First day, Juni Becker. This won't happen again." Mrs. Dee left.

Juni turned and went out the back door, her face on fire. She went past the kids on the deck and sat on the patchy grass with her back against the fence. She had dropped her sandwich and she hadn't had a chance to buy milk. Her stomach was growling.

The sunshine was warm on her arms.

She had the phone Helve had given her in her pocket. They were supposed to leave phones in their lockers, but what good would that do? She called Helve.

"Why dear, what a surprise. Aren't you in school?"

"It's lunch, Mormie, and I wanted to say hello."

Helve told Juni she was making a pastry from leftover roast in the freezer, with potatoes and onions and parsnips. Juni said it sounded good. She didn't cry until she had hung up.

She was in social studies when a woman came to the classroom door and asked for her.

She said she was Ms. Gregory, the counselor. "When you have a problem, you can come to me," she said.

"Who said I had a problem?"

"You did knock a boy down in the cafeteria."

"He put—his mouth—under my hair—on my back."

"I know. I talked to him. But we don't hit one another here. We don't get in fights."

Juni asked, "Am I done?" She was staring at the floor.

"There is one other thing. Ms. Dee said she saw you on the field talking on a cell phone."

"I called my grandmother."

"Lunch is considered part of the academic program. This is all explained in the student handbook. Students don't have access to their phones until the end of the day."

Juni looked at Ms. Gregory. "Okay. Bye." She turned and went back in the classroom, her heart pounding.

Then she had gym. Juni felt exposed and gawky in her shorts and T-shirt, but when she looked around, nobody looked any better. There were stations: light weights, jump ropes, stilts, basketballs. The students were practically hysterical, yelling and jumping around. A pretty, tall Black girl ran past Juni, and Juni wondered if she felt exposed, too. She found a basketball and stood at the free throw line and shot basket after basket. A couple of girls stood near her, watching.

When she stopped, one of them said, "Amanda, remember? I showed you around?"

Juni said sure, but she was glad that the teacher called for their attention just then, and sent them around the room conga style, bouncing basketballs.

At the end of class the teacher, Ms. Leydon, pulled her aside. She asked her if she was interested in playing basketball or volleyball or both. Juni didn't know what to say. She had never played either.

"I'm moving to the high school next year. I'm looking ahead. You move well, you look strong. What sports do you play?"

"You mean, like on a team?" Juni shrugged. "I've been homeschooled." She felt her face flush.

"Don't worry, you can learn rules and strategies. It's talent and sweat that make an athlete. I know it's hard coming in late in the year, but high school will be a fresh start." The teacher leaned closer to Juni. "Being on a team is sort of like having a family at school. Girls on teams are tight, you won't be lonely."

Juni's face felt scalded. This was about her mother. She imagined a teacher meeting, someone saying, "Look after those two Becker girls. Their mother is dead. You'll notice them because they are tall."

In the locker room, the Black girl said hi. Juni said, "Juni. Hi."

"Safi." They both smiled. Juni thought they were about the same height, and that made her feel better.

While Juni was in Spanish class, the math teacher came to the door asking for her. She had gone over her tests from the morning. She wanted Juni to know that math class was divided into groups, and that Juni would be able to make good progress with students at the same proficiency level. She didn't want her to be discouraged because of the test that morning.

The teacher had seen her distress; it was humiliating. Juni's ears were buzzing. *Proficiency level.* That meant stupid, but there were other stupid kids, so she would have them to be stupid with.

She went back to class, where she had no idea what was going on.

She was angry at the math teacher for calling her out like that. And at Tilde, for being so happy about school, probably having a great day. At her mother, for saying school was no big deal. At her father, for not knowing that Juni hadn't learned anything, staying home.

What would she know if she had been in school all along? She didn't know if she would ever catch up. Maybe it didn't matter. She could read and write. She knew how to make change.

On her way to her locker after class, she stopped to get a drink of water. She was surprised that the fountain was so clean and the water so cool. She realized that everyone carried water bottles around. The fountain was all hers. She drank and drank.

18

Juni and Tilde trudged up Cherry Street from the bus. The ride from school had been noisy and they hadn't talked. They had almost reached the driveway when a horn beeped, startling them. It beeped again and they looked around.

Helve was parked across the street from the bungalow. They ran over as she got out of the car.

"I had to see how your first day went," she said. She kissed each of them.

By then, Eleanor had arrived. She turned into the drive, parked, and got out.

"Girls. Helve," she said from across the street. Helve and the girls walked to her.

"I had an errand in Wellen," Helve said. "So I thought—"

Eleanor said, "Come to the house." She didn't wait for an answer, but got in her car and drove up the driveway. She was at the door, her hand against it as if it might shut on her, when Helve and the girls reached the house. "Welcome, Helve. Have a seat. I'll make coffee."

"Please," Helve said. "Don't trouble yourself. A glass of water would be fine."

Eleanor waved her hand above her shoulder as she went into the kitchen.

Helve looked around the room. The house was bigger than her own, with a comfortable feeling to it.

Juni took her arm and tugged her to the couch, where she and Tilde sat close on each side of her. Helve put her arms around them.

Eleanor appeared. "Come into the kitchen, we will be more comfortable at the table." She had cooled down from her annoyance.

She had made coffee and also set out Cokes and a carton of orange juice, cups and glasses, cream and sugar, and store-bought butter cookies on a saucer. She gave Helve a glass of ice water as well.

"It's nice that you are off early," Helve said.

"I have school hours," Eleanor said stiffly. "I go in at 7:30."

"Oh, of course."

Eleanor poured coffee for her and Helve, and Tilde poured a Coke, half for her, half for Juni. Everyone sipped politely, the girls watching their grandmothers warily.

"We want to hear about your day," Eleanor said. She glanced at Helve, who nodded.

Tilde said, "The school looks brand new, Mormor."

Juni said, "I don't see why we have to be there, so late in the year."

Eleanor said, "Because you belong in school. It's the law."

Juni was sullen. "It is so boring."

"Juni," Eleanor said.

"I see you're fine." Helve stood. "I must go before traffic thickens."

Eleanor said," It's good you were able to find the house. Girls, why don't you show your grandmother your rooms?"

Alone in the kitchen, Eleanor looked at the cookies on the saucer, the coffee in cups, the soda in the glasses, barely sipped. She wanted to throw something against a wall. What was that woman thinking? Had she come to give the Becker home a once-over? Or did she believe the girls could not go a week without her? She went into the living room.

This is where they live now, she wanted to say. But as Helve appeared with Tilde and Juni, she said instead, "You must stay for supper."

Helve, who was squeezing a hand of each girl, declined politely. "I never drive in the dark anymore," she said, and added, "I will pick them up Friday after school."

Eleanor stiffened. "We already have plans for Friday night," she lied.

Juni said, chin up, "I would rather go to Mormor's."

Tilde looked to Eleanor and then Helve and said, "Maybe we could go Saturday?"

Eleanor said, "I'll ask Nick to call you, Helve, about the girls' next visit. Thank you for coming by." She walked behind them to the door. She was ashamed of her rude stiffness, but she had been caught off guard, and Helve intimidated her.

Juni and Tilde went with Helve to her car. Through the window of the porch, Eleanor watched them go down the driveway. Her heart was pounding. *What kind of tug of war is this going to be?* It's early days, she reminded herself. Mormor. What a funny word.

She heard a door open and shut, and turned around. Nick emerged from the back bedroom, a smirk on his face. "You were here!" she said.

"I wouldn't have been any help, Mom."

The girls came back and shut themselves in the middle bedroom. While Eleanor made supper, Nick sat at the table and turned the pages of a *Harper's Magazine*. She couldn't think of anything to say to him. He was wearing the same checked shirt he had worn the last two days.

"I'll do a load of laundry soon," she said, trying to sound cheery. "Why don't you put what you have in the machine now?" She couldn't help herself: "That shirt, too."

He looked at her for a long moment. What was he thinking? That it was none of her business? He got up, looking burdened. He came back through with a load of clothes in his arms and took them to the garage. He had changed his shirt.

Supper that evening was tense. Eleanor noticed that Juni had broken out in splotches on her cheeks and across her chin. She decided not to say anything, not to offer any advice. She didn't want to embarrass Juni, and besides, she figured Helve could attend to Juni's breakouts when the girls were with her. Wouldn't Helve know just what to say?

———————————

That evening, Helve ate leftover chicken and rice that Ivy had sent home with her, and walked over to to take back the plate. Collin was there and they were playing a card game, something like Crazy Eights, calling out in Swedish and laughing. He blew Helve a kiss and said, "Hey hi, Aunt H!" He was a handsome kid, taller than his dad. Helve poured herself a cup of coffee and pulled up a chair. Soon, Collin got up and declared himself king of the world, gave Helve a hug, and excused himself and went outside. Karl asked Helve how the girls were doing, barely waited for an answer, and went to join Collin.

"You look tired, Helve, are you okay?" Ivy asked. "How were the girls?"

Helve told Ivy about the awkwardness with Eleanor. "I shouldn't have gone. Eleanor must have thought I was checking up on them. I only wanted to hear about their first day. I should have called."

"How well do the girls know her? Maybe it's going to take some time for them to feel at home."

"I don't think they ever spent a night in her house until now. Sometimes when the family was here, Nick would take them over to say hello, that's all."

"They're kids, they'll adjust. I had an aunt who drank bleach and died. Her kids were divided up among relatives. They went on to have their own families, to have lives."

"Ivy, I never heard that. How awful."

Ivy shrugged. She got up and cut two thin slices from a lemon pound cake. Helve wasn't hungry, but she could nibble the cake, to be polite. She said, "Juni can be difficult. She always has been."

"They'll get used to it. School. The Beckers."

Helve sighed. "I called Mr. Hagen. He's coming Thursday."

"Who?"

"The handyman."

"Oh, yes. Is there much to do?"

"Small things, but things I couldn't do. When you think how old the house is, it's not so bad."

Ivy pushed the cake plates aside and reached to take Helve's hands in hers. "I love my house," she said, "and you next door." And then, "Do you miss Henry, still?"

"Not so much. Sometimes I am lonely. There's less to do."

"I never heard him say a single word of criticism about you, in all the years. Never a joke, like some men make about their wives."

Helve said, "Now, what would he have had to complain about?" Both of them laughed.

Later, in bed, she stared at the ceiling and tried to remember Henry beside her. He had been gruff by nature; she thought he had never tried to understand what she was feeling when they made love. Had sex. He would need it, have it, say goodnight, and roll over. But he always thanked her for their meals. He always saw her into their pew at church. He was a good father. He worked hard. She remembered how he stepped up when her father died. He was at the farm, doing whatever he could to help. He took her on long drives, to get away from her sorrow and her relatives. He took her to church. After a couple of months he said, "If you want to keep the farm, my brother and I could work it." She was astonished. She realized she didn't really know what he did with his time. She assumed he worked for his father. As for her father's farm, everything had been decided with barely a nod to her, though she and her sister were the heirs, and at nineteen, Helve should have been included in decisions. Uncle Melker, who was an attorney—he and Aunt Linna had been raising Helve's little sister, Anna, since their mother's death—arranged an auction.

School wasn't compulsory after ninth grade, and she had stopped going a few months into the first semester of tenth grade, a relief to her father, who depended on her help. Later, Aunt Linna suggested she attend a training school, to qualify for work in childcare or the medical field. Then Henry Sundersson told her that his dream was to emigrate to the United States. They could buy land there, he said. He had saved enough for the trip, and she had the proceeds from the farm. He didn't mention his brother, Karl, right away, though Karl would emigrate, too.

Henry kissed her and touched her and said, let's get married, so they did.

19

On Wednesday, Tilde helped Eleanor clean up after supper, then sat down at the table as Eleanor made sandwiches for the next day's lunches. She reported that her math teacher had taken her out of one of her other classes for a test, saying that it would help determine the right placement for her, whatever that meant. Eleanor tried to look interested without making too much of it; obviously, Tilde was either extra low or extra high, out of the range of the class. Sure enough, the next day Tilde came home with a note from her math teacher that said she would move to a small class of other high-achieving kids, starting the next week. It said, "This arrangement will accommodate Tilde's advanced ability in mathematics."

The two of them were standing in the hallway by Tilde's bedroom door when Tilde gave Eleanor the note.

Eleanor, juggling towels, handed the note back to Tilde and said, "And how is Juni doing?" Tilde shrugged and stepped into her room and shut the door. Eleanor shut the closet door and put her forehead against it. Damn. She wanted to call Tilde back and say the right thing: What a wonderful opportunity; I'll want to hear all about it; but she knew that to Tilde it surely must look as if Juni had taken first place in Eleanor's attention, as if Tilde didn't matter. Later, in bed, she told Walter about the conversation, and how bad she felt. He advised her not to analyze every exchange with the girls. As if she had not just said, *I could have cut my tongue out, honest to God!*

He said, "Instead of expecting them to shape up, let's just follow their lead."

She took a deep breath and said, "I'll try," though she had to swallow the urge to ask just what lead he was referring to. If Juni had her way, she would be in Frost. Or in bed.

Long after Walter was asleep, she lay away from him, wishing she hadn't said anything to him at all. He was the one who went outside and shot baskets with Juni and Tilde, and they all came in laughing and punching one another on the biceps. Somehow, already, she had become the one who overthought things and made them worse. In one week, she had become the warden. If she disappeared, how would Walter handle things? Would Juni be cooperative when he told her to put her clothes in the washing machine? Would Nick say, oh sure, Dad, when Walter asked him to get out of bed and do some parenting of his own? And Helve. Would she say, you let me know when you want to bring them over? You let me know how I can help.

She tried to remember her own children, and that took her down another alley. Nick had been a boy, simple as that. He built things and knocked them down. He peed in the bushes. He moved in a squad of boys, and went days without saying a whole sentence to his mother. Then came Alison, who seemed to be born insecure and petulant. The children had grown up living conventional childhoods; neither had any trouble at school. Eleanor and Walter obliged them in their choices of universities, their preference to go away and start separate lives. Being their mother, Eleanor had endured difficult phases and enjoyed easier ones; she had never thought they—the Beckers—were different from any of the families they knew.

Though when Nicky was a baby, there had been a time when Eleanor worried that she wouldn't know what to do with him as he got older. What did she know about families, or boys? From the Wisdoms she had learned routine, self-reliance, compliance, and low expectations. So she organized her own household with an emphasis on economy and efficiency; she established routines so that the children knew what she expected of them; protocol made her confident. She was firm but not rigid. She had to learn how to show affection and she did, largely because Walter was so crazy about the kids and showed it. Nicky sailed along. Alison objected. Everything was, *why?* Tears and pouts. But Alison's bad moods were like dust devils, moving through fast. You could wait them out. You could love them away. Eleanor had thought Juni might be like that, moody, obstinate, but soon enough able to see that nobody was against her. That she was safe and loved. She had lost her mother; God, Eleanor understood that!

She wanted to sit down with Juni and put her arms around her and cry with her until they both were dry of tears. But Juni—who didn't know what it was to have no family at all—wouldn't have it, would she? Maybe she needed someone to hate for what had happened to her. Eleanor could see that it might not be specific to her, might not be personal.

Friday, Nick drove the girls to Frost right after school. He left Eleanor a note on the kitchen table. It said he was going to get a hamburger on the way home. When Walter heard that, he said great, they could go out to dinner. But Eleanor was angry; she felt undermined and humiliated. She had told Helve the girls couldn't come on Friday, right in front of everybody.

"Good Christ, Eleanor," Walter said. He put two wine glasses on the table. "What's the problem? The girls love her. We're still strangers to them. I say give them what they want when there's no reason not to.

We can use some down time, you and me. Let's go out. We can walk down to the plaza, we can have a drink—"

"I'm not hungry," she said. "I'm not thirsty, either."

She went to the Y to swim. She had expected the pool to be crowded, but there was only one other woman in it. Eleanor thought she remembered her name was Laura. She was elderly, perhaps as old as eighty, plump, and she swam like a machine on low. She held onto a paddle board and kicked her legs solemnly. Back and forth she went, her eyes half-open, looking relaxed but determined. Eleanor admired her. Laurel, that was her name. Eleanor swam breast-stroke and tried for a calm rhythm—dictated, perhaps, by the older woman's measured progress.

After she swam, she sat in the sauna until she felt drained and basted and loose.

Walter was right. She wasn't in competition with Helve, and she was too quick to interpret Helve's gestures as presumptuous. She resented her, though, not because the girls loved her, but because they knew her, and Eleanor had never had a chance to earn their affection. That wasn't Helve's fault. Karin hadn't wanted anything to do with the Beckers, it was as simple as that. It was futile to try to understand why now. The girls clung to Helve because they knew her, loved her.

But Eleanor believed that it was best that Nick, Juni, and Tilde live together as Beckers, in the Becker home. Didn't anyone understand how important it was to be together? Didn't they understand that dead mother or not, they had family?

Sunday, early in the afternoon—and meeting protest for his timing—
Nick went back to get the girls. Juni was carrying a small suitcase when
they arrived home.

Eleanor met them at the door and held it open. "What have
you there?" she asked.

"Stuff," Juni said, averting her eyes. She lifted the suitcase
against her chest.

The girls went straight into Juni's bedroom, shut the door, and
opened the suitcase. It was filled with small boxes that held Karin's
jewelry. Eleanor heard them speaking.

"Do you want to divvie it up?" Juni asked. "For our rooms?"

"No," Tilde said. "Keep it all together. You can keep it in here."

Eleanor interrupted them to say they still had their laundry
from last week to do. She wanted them to take care of it right away.
She had shown them how everything worked. She gave them each a
set of clean linens. "Pile your dirty sheets on top of the washer, I'll
take care of them."

She stood in Juni's doorway. Tilde scooted past her.

Eleanor spoke to Juni. "The bag you brought back from Frost—
is it your mother's jewelry?"

"What if it is?"

"We have a safe in our bedroom."

"I want it with me."

"You mustn't wear it to school. It's not appropriate. Kids will
think you are showing off, flashy jewelry like that. Someone could grab
it off your neck, Juni. You must put it away until you are older. It's not
a young girl's collection."

Juni backed away, past her bed. "That's stupid," she said. "It's mine."

Eleanor felt hot; if she spoke, she would be sorry. She kept looking at Juni, though, until Juni turned away toward the window.

"Your father will talk to you," Eleanor said. She closed the door after herself gently.

She cornered Nick after supper while Walter went outside with the girls to shoot baskets. He was in the living room, looking for a book in the bookcase. He was sitting on the floor. She pulled a chair around. He looked up, surprised.

She told him she was concerned about the jewelry. "I thought you were going to return it."

"I never decided that. I sent back that one package. They credited me, but the rest of it is far past their return cut-off."

"Nick, she's a child. You're the parent here. She has no business with a suitcase full of expensive jewelry."

"It's not all that good."

"It cost a lot, didn't it? Is it insured?"

"Juni clings to the jewelry because it was Karin's. How can I take it away from her?"

"You can tell her it must be kept in the safe. You can tell her she isn't old enough to wear it. Say you will keep it for her until she is older. Couldn't they each pick out a piece or two, and you sell the rest?"

Nick looked at the ceiling, then back at his mother. "Mom, you're micro-managing. You want everything to be neat. You don't like that it's Karin's jewelry, so you don't want it around."

"Nick!"

"I can't take it away from Juni."

"What can you do, Nick? What do you do all day?"

He had a paperback in his hand, and he lifted it to show her. A Scandinavian mystery.

"That's a dark story, Nicky."

"You read it?"

"I looked at it. Your father liked it."

He ran his fingers along the row of books. "I'm working my way through these."

"Real life is going on. How are you spending yours?"

"I am awake most of the night. I get up in the morning to see the girls off. I go back to bed after you all leave. I listen to the radio, read, sleep. Sometimes I just stare at the ceiling."

Her chest heaved. She felt deflated.

"Mom, it's really hard for me. I'm trying. I need time. Don't you see that?"

"I see that Juni needs a parent. They both do."

"Here I am!" He threw his arms out and laughed. She thought his eyes looked out of focus. Once again he had deflected her concern.

One day at work, Barbara gave Eleanor two old I-phones for the girls. She said Eleanor should tell Nick to get music subscriptions for them. "Trust me," she said, "it will help a lot."

Eleanor was afraid he would put them in a drawer and forget them, but he didn't. She noticed, not long after, that Juni was often on her bed lying down, earplugs in her ears.

APRIL

20

Helve immediately recognized Mr. Hagen from church. He was a ruddy, solid man with a bald pate and a squint. He shook her hand when she offered it and said he was sure sorry about Mr. Sundersson's passing. He asked her if she had a list. She did. They sat at the kitchen table to go over it.

"I remember when this house was built," he said. "I was just out of sixth grade. My father told me it was a catalog house. I didn't understand that he meant the plans had been ordered; I thought the whole house had come in pieces., like Legos." He laughed heartily. "I got a lot of teasing for that. Later I learned that Sears had sold "kits" that included all the materials, but that was much earlier. There's one of theirs on Main Street in Frost, you know."

He looked at the porches and suggested that it would be better to replace the front one rather than try to repair it. He went down the list. He asked her when the last time was her water heater had been flushed. She showed him the one in the closet by the downstairs bathroom, and he said never mind flushing it, she should replace it. The new ones used so much less electricity. She had him look at the one in the garage, too, that Henry had put in for the washing machine. He said that was fine, then he asked who had wired the garage. When she said Henry had done, he said, "You better get an electrician out here. If you ever want to sell, an inspector will be all over this. You might as well have your heating system checked, too." None of this surprised Helve. The house was old. She and Henry had taken care of it, respected it, but it was made up of parts and systems, and things got rigid or worn.

She made a light lunch for her and Mr. Hagen, who said she could call him Otto, unless she preferred the formality. She said Helve was fine, too.

The list got longer. Helve didn't mind. Mr. Hagen seemed knowledgeable, and he was a courteous man. Karl had recommended him. She would be glad to have him come to work on the house as often as it took. She had enjoyed their time taking an inventory of the house repair needs. She wanted everything to be the way it should be in the house, because she wanted to sell it, she just didn't know how soon.

21

Eleanor waited until the fifth of the month to talk to Oscar about the rent. She dreaded it, but he hadn't bothered to make any excuses for not paying. She went to the bungalow after supper and knocked sharply. She knew he was there, because his car was parked at the curb and she could hear his music. After a few moments, she knocked again, louder.

He opened the door a crack. "Mrs. Becker."

"Oscar, I don't have your rent."

"I'm sorry. My dad was supposed to send me a check but it hasn't come."

"What happened to your job?"

"I lost it. I'm looking for something else. And you have my deposit."

"Yes, I do, and I will keep it if you don't pay this month's rent. But that doesn't mean you can stay. I'm sure you understand how it works."

He glared at her. "I have rights."

"Oscar, what happened?"

"Pilfering. I work at night by myself, and they said I wasn't watching the petty theft. What could I do? I'm not supposed to leave the cash register. And what if someone had a knife? A gun?"

"I'm sorry," Eleanor said. "Truly I am. But I depend on this rent, just like you depend on your salary. What will you do if you don't find a job?"

He hung his head. "Go home, I guess. For a while." He looked up. "You have a cleaning deposit, too."

"Yes, do you want me to look at the place? I pay a professional generously to clean it. You would have to have kept it very clean to cut that cost."

"I don't have anywhere to go."

Eleanor sighed. "You can string this out, but in the end it will be bad for you, Oscar."

Oscar shut the door.

Eleanor had been renting the house out for many years, and she had never had to formally evict anyone, though she had once asked someone to move out because one tenant had turned into four on the floor; and another time because it was obvious there was drug business going on. She had once waited three months for back rent—and that was when she resolved she would never do so again. She didn't know how the eviction process worked. She was pretty sure Oscar could stall while she spent money on fees, and he could play havoc with the place, and the end would be months away. It was too much aggravation to play righteous landlord and it was uncomfortable, besides.

She knocked on the door again an hour later. When Oscar didn't answer, she knocked harder.

He opened the door a crack.

"Here's the deal, Oscar, and there's no negotiating. If you get a job by the fifteenth, you can rebuild your deposit over three months, on top of the rent. If you don't have a job and you move by the fifteenth,

I'll give you a positive recommendation, as opposed to dinging your credit. What works for you, Oscar?"

"Okay," he said. "But I'll go ahead and move out right away, if you'll give me the deposit."

"Half."

"Okay."

"When all your stuff is out, you come knock on my door and we will settle up. Day after tomorrow, latest. I hope things get better for you soon."

"I bet," Oscar said, and this time he slammed the door. Eleanor thought she might have been nicer if he had moved the damned bottles.

She turned and left; Velma waved from across the driveway.

When Oscar appeared at her door the next afternoon with the keys, she gave him his whole deposit, cash. He was surprised, of course.

She told Walter about Oscar.

He said, "You've been renting to the wrong people, Ellie."

"Who else is going to rent this house?"

"A young professional, maybe a nurse or a teacher. Someone quiet and responsible who loves being able to walk to town, who hikes or bikes on the trail. Someone who can pay eight, nine hundred a month rent."

"Dream on." The house was old. It had been taken care of, so it was safe and livable, but it was a long way from modern or striking.

"Why don't you just put it out of your mind for now? I'd like to renovate it. Except for odds and ends to attend to with the auction, I have time."

"I don't know. Is it worth it?"

"You bet."

She was relieved to relinquish the responsibility. "Okay," she said. "I appreciate it."

She came home a few days later to find a dumpster parked at the street.

After supper, she and Walter walked down the driveway. He led her to the yard, where they stood looking at the front of the little house. "So here's my idea. Steve highly recommends Matt Rhimes, who has lately been exclusively building ADUs. I had him over to take a look. He says the bungalow is a sound structure, but it needs rewiring and new plumbing. We'll install a new shower and toilet, and an eco-AC and water heater. We'll get new, compact furnishings. What do you think?"

"Oh my," Eleanor said. "What will all this cost?"

"Don't worry. You'll make it back. Eventually we might sell it. We'll take it down to the studs and make it one big, classy room with a sleeping alcove. We'll put in a skylight. Matt says because it's a small job, he can fit it in around what he's doing, we'll have it sometime late next month. You could rent it for the summer short-term for quite a lot."

"I didn't expect you to make such a big decision, Walt. All on your own."

"I got carried away," he said, grinning. It was hard not to be caught up in his enthusiasm.

"I guess it doesn't hurt to see what it will cost," she said.

So now Walter had a project.

There was a core of heavy-duty bidders happy to get cheap goods, but there were also onlookers—friends, shopkeepers from up and down the street, passersby. There was a festive air—the good feeling of clearing the cupboards. What was left over would go to Habitat Humanity and the high school shop program—-and the dump. Walter and Eleanor met up afterwards with Jim and Patricia Tennison for drinks at the fancy new bar above the Asian fusion restaurant. It was empty, early as it was, except for a guy slumped at the bar. Eleanor had two mojitos and got to giggling. She said maybe she and Walt would move into their bungalow after it was renovated. "For privacy," she whispered. Walter leaned close to her. "Open," he said, and he plucked a speck of mint leaf from one of her front teeth. Then he clucked and said it was time to head on home. Patricia gave her a hug.

"We'll order pizza," Walter told Eleanor in the car. "I don't remember the last time I saw you tipsy."

Eleanor covered her eyes with her hands. "If they had better music, I would have got up and danced."

Walter said, "That's my girl."

At home, Tilde and Juni were sprawled across Tilde's bed, both of them reading. Somehow they had acquired men's boxer shorts—Nick's?—worn now with T-shirts.

"Walter's gone to pick up pizza," Eleanor told them. "I'll go let your dad know."

Juni gave her a limp wave, and rolled over on her belly. She had earplugs in, and Eleanor didn't know if she had heard a word.

Eleanor got some crackers and cheese and a soda and took them to the bedroom. She didn't come out when pizza arrived. She put on her pajamas and read the British novel up to the end. It was a sad story, two people with a long history at cross purposes, though each wanted the love of the other. They had forgiven one another, though. They had started over. Eleanor hadn't expected that. She thought it wasn't very literary; too much had built up that riddled the relationship for her to buy a romantic turnaround at the end.

When Walter came in much later, she was almost asleep, and the book had fallen to the floor. He sat on the bed beside her.

"You sure you don't want something to eat?"

"I'm sure. Are you coming to bed?"

"Yup." He turned his lamp on, and she turned hers off.

He stripped to his underwear. When he got in bed, she said, "Are you okay about the auction?"

"Better than okay. Relieved."

"Now you can do whatever you want."

"I think I know what that is," he said. He scooted close to her and caressed her breast. His breath was hot on her neck.

She closed her eyes and laid her palm on his boxers and gently pressed his penis. He scrambled to take the boxers off. He kissed her sloppily. He ran his hands down her hips, tugging her pajamas down. He grasped her buttocks and pulled her to him, then moaned and ejaculated. "Oh shit, shit," he muttered. He grabbed his shorts and shoved them against his crotch. "I'm sorry, fuck," he mumbled.

Eleanor put her hands on his chest. "It's all right." She went in the bathroom and washed herself. She looked in the mirror and grinned.

They lay on their backs, side by side, for a while. Then Walter said, "About the store. It feels like I graduated from something."

"You're not in business anymore. Your days are your own. You don't have to worry."

"I just want us to be all right."

"Okay," she said. It was a weak reply, but that was what she wanted, too.

22

One warm evening, Nick took the girls out for pizza. He planned to talk to them about their mother's jewelry.

They walked to Ricco's, a casual Italian restaurant on the plaza that had been there since Nick was a teenager. They settled in a booth, ordered family bowls of spaghetti bolognese and salad to share, and sat in silence, as if they were waiting for a bell to ring. Nick laughed.

"You girls look like you are trying to remember who I am."

"That's silly," Tilde said.

"I want to know how things are going at school."

"It's fine," Tilde said. "It's school."

"Do you have a favorite class?"

"Math," Tilde said immediately.

"What about you, Juni?" Nick asked. "You doing okay?"

"Everybody does okay, Dad. You have to be an idiot not to."

"How about you, Dad?" Tilde asked. "What do you do all day?"

Nick said, "I've been helping Dad clean out the bungalow. I checked out some places I might work." He cocked his head sheepishly. "I read mysteries."

Juni said, "As soon you get a job, we'll get an apartment, right?"

Nick was surprised. "We couldn't get anything as nice as where we are right now. We all have our own rooms!"

"In *their* house."

"Juni, *they* are my parents. Your grandparents. We are at home in their house."

She looked at the table top. "Never mind."

It didn't seem like a good time to talk about Karin's crap.

After they ate, they walked in the park a while. They headed back up Cherry Street. Before they reached the Becker driveway, Nick stopped. "Listen," he said. "I'll go back to work, , but we'll still need my folks. I don't worry about you two, living with them. All your needs are taken care of. I don't know how we would get by without them. I couldn't do it alone. You need to give them a chance. You're lucky we're not all crowded in a studio somewhere, eating take-out."

"It's a nice house, I like my room," Tilde said. Juni stomped on ahead.

"Do you know what that's about?" Nick asked Tilde.

"She misses Mormor, and she doesn't like school, and it's worse because I do. And since I went out for track, I'm busy after school and she's by herself. Plus she's just sad."

"What does she do after school?"

"She goes to Alison's and plays video games. Alison said we could hang out in the basement game room. She gave us the key code for its entrance from the yard. There's a little kitchenette down there, with a fridge. Alison stocks drinks and snacks and stuff. It's sort of like having your own apartment."

"Oh," Nick said. "We should all go over some time and play a game." When they got to the house, he went straight to his bedroom. Tilde watched the door close, and turned around. There was a lamp on in the living room; it would soon be dark out. She took a big deep breath and exhaled hard. She was really tired and she wanted to go to bed soon, but she didn't want to leave her sister on her own alone. Juni rushed past her through the living room and outside. Soon Tilde could hear the thump thump of a basketball hitting the garage.

Eleanor looked up from the kitchen table, where she was writing something, and caught Tilde's eye and smiled.

Tilde smiled back, then went out to join Juni for a little while. She suggested they do a fast fifty—shot after shot, basket after basket, like they had done so often in Portland. They could try on jewelry afterwards, Juni almost always liked to do that. Juni shrugged, but right away she gave Tilde the ball.

Later in bed, Tilde thought about her mother and she was sad, though she didn't really miss her. She remembered her lying on the couch that last night, with a ring on her toe. She remembered how she liked to take a piece of pizza and roll it like a fat cigar to eat it. How, when she was resting, you couldn't wake her even if you yelled. Something heavy had lifted for Tilde since Karin died, and she wished she could help her sister feel better, too. It wouldn't mean they didn't love their mother; it would mean they had a right to be happy. She liked living with her grandparents. They were nice people. Eleanor took care of everything. Walter was funny. She liked having clean clothes and a tidy room of her own, and supper at the same time every day. She could open her window at night and it was quiet and dark; and the freeway was far, far away.

Eleanor took the girls to see a pediatrician. Dr. Phoebe. She was nice enough. Before she examined Juni she said, "Is this all right, Juni? (Yes.)

Do you want your grandmother here in the room with you? (No.) Or your sister? (No.) Do you have any questions?" (No.) She gave Juni brochures to read, and her card. She explained the vaccine she was giving her. She told her to eat fresh fruit and vegetables and to cut back on sugar and starch. She encouraged her to play sports.

Later, Juni wished she had told Dr. Phoebe that her periods were changing. She had had about a year of light bleeding, when she could go all day with one or two pads; but now her periods were irregular and heavy, and the cramps were sometimes awful on the first couple days. She worried that something was wrong with her and that she smelled bad. She had always loved to move and play, but now her shoulders rounded forward as she tried not to show her full breasts. She didn't feel strong; she felt like a target too big to miss. She had begun watching what she ate. Usually she skipped lunch, but she ate snacks at Alison's, and she ate supper, and sometimes she ate ice cream while she watched TV.

Helve had picked up on Juni's self-consciousness, and made a point of complimenting her on her hair or something she wore. She insisted that they hike together, the one way Juni seemed to relax about her body. One Saturday they hiked so far, they hitched a ride with a passing neighbor to get home. Helve bought Juni a better pair of shoes for walking, and Juni left them at Helve's house.

"Nature will make you strong and happy, Juni," Helve told her. "You can't stay indoors, you have to be out where God can see you. Some day I'll show you Sweden. I'll show you sea and forest, summer sun and winter snow, and the Swedish people, tall and strong like you."

Juni felt better when Helve talked to her like that, like she was reading from a book; but then Juni always had to go back to Lupine, where she felt like a cow among chickens.

23

Both girls had been avid readers their whole childhood. They had kept journals and had written lots of stories and poems, so they were good at reading and writing, which was most of what they did in school. Lessons were explained and monitored so carefully, you didn't have to know anything coming in, except in math. The teachers tried hard and they never gave homework. There seemed to be an understanding that kids should work in the classroom and then go home and play.

Spring school track events had begun soon after break. On Monday, Tuesday, and Wednesday, there were many events, and then an optional practice on Thursdays for kids who were interested in eventual competition. There were always several coaches, and other teachers came to cheer. Participants did various sprint events, including hurdles. Practice was usually wrapped up with a relay, which was nice, because slower kids could participate and not stand out so much. There was a girl with Downs Syndrome, Audrey, who loved track and tried just about everything except hurdles. Tilde noticed that Audrey seemed to have a lot of friends who stopped to hear what she had to say and made her welcome in the events. After only a few practices, Audrey knew Tilde's name and greeted her happily. The kids who came out for track were really nice.

Running on optional practice days made Tilde realize how much she liked to take off for the distance, like someone flying low to the ground. On the Saturdays she stayed in town, she ran with Jamila, a skinny girl from her math class. Tilde got to know the hills and parks and big creek and neighborhoods of Lupine. Tilde and Jamila ran the trail on the west edge of town, too, the one that was just above the Becker property, and sometimes they stopped at the Becker house for a bathroom break and a snack. Tilde's body grew stronger. Her gym teacher noticed her, and when she heard about the running, told Tilde to keep it up. She told her that both the Y and the city Parks & Recreation Department had sports camps in the summer. "We love our sports in Lupine," she told Tilde.

Jamila's father was a distance runner—he was Alison's student teacher in elementary school, but also an assistant track coach at the high school—and he suggested the girls focus on the long run. He said he thought it would suit them. "Just go out and run for the fun of it," he said. "Think stamina over speed for now." He met with them now and again to give them a pep talk and advice. Cross-country was a fall sport, but now was the time to start training. Next year, as eighth graders, they wouldn't have any opportunities locally for formal competition, but that didn't mean they couldn't train, and something might come up elsewhere in the state. He said, "Run for the fun of it, and if fun is enough, it's something you can do all your life. If running really bites you, though, you are old enough to start training and see what you can do. We could get serious in the summer." He told them about Maureen Wilton, a Canadian girl who at thirteen broke the women's marathon world record in 1967.

Tilde had been in school a week when her math teacher sent her for an evaluation after Tilde, with some apprehension, had said that she already knew everything in their workbook. A few days later, the teacher told Tilde she was quite advanced and she could work in the math lab at her own speed, if that was all right with her. Tilde had been impressed by the computer stations, books, and general

SANDRA SCOFIELD

atmosphere of the lab. The lab's students called it the Crib. She was
thrilled with the move.

Math became a revelation and a joy, and the Crib became home
base for a new kind of family. She joined five students there every day:
four boys and another girl. There was Jamila, daughter of Alison's
student teacher. Jamila wore her hair in cornrows. Tyler was quiet,
compact, fiercely proud, and laser-focused on school; he wanted to
go to Harvard, like his mother, an economist at the college, had done.
He never had much to say unless you asked him a direct question.
His father was a doctor. Emilion, whose family had immigrated from
Guatemala when he was a baby, was jolly and told dumb jokes, but
he could solve problems in his head without writing anything down.
His parents owned the Azteca Restaurant across the street from the
college. Zay, who lived with a married sister and never mentioned
parents, wore his sandy-blond hair long and uncombed and had a
funny habit of bouncing in his seat when he solved something difficult.
Otto, who wanted to be a physicist, was into athletics and came to all
the track days. His family ran a mobile home park. Mr. Willard said
the group was his own little U.N. —Unusual Nerds, ha ha. The group
sat together at lunch and more than once she had heard someone call
them "Willard's elves," but she ignored it, and besides, she didn't think
it was an insult. She was happy at school, and she wished Juni was, too.

Mr. Willard kept them very busy. They worked on computer
programs and in notebooks; there was a chalkboard that covered half
of one wall. Sometimes they played chess. Mr. Willard mixed them
up into teams to play challenging games he said were taken from past
state math competitions.

After a couple of weeks, Mr. Willard sat down with Tilde and
asked her to tell him how she had learned so much on her own. She

explained about the eighth grade book from the state, and also that she had had a computer up until a few months before they moved. She had found math games and lessons online. She mentioned that she had kept a math journal. The next day she gave it to him to read, and the day after that, he told her that he had given it to Mrs. Kenton to look at. She had a PhD in Mathematics Education and she would enjoy seeing how Tilde had studied.

Tilde wished that she could help Juni find something she enjoyed half as much as she enjoyed math. When she asked Juni if she needed help with math, Juni told her to mind her own business. When she asked Juni to think about coming out a day or two for track, Juni said no. She liked to go to Alison's and watch movies or play video games. And when Tilde suggested they go together to Alison's sometime, Juni said, "I like it when I'm there alone. I like not talking to anybody."

Juni endured school and walked away from it at 3:10. She definitely didn't want to put on shorts and run around after school for people to see her butt bouncing. Her body was changing so fast it felt foreign to her. She had to ask Eleanor to take her to get new bras, because it would be worse to ask her father and she didn't want to use her time with Helve shopping for underwear. She wore athletic bras with wide straps on the shoulders and under the breasts, which were like heavy round bowls jutting out from her body. Eleanor tried to give Juni a "talk." How she was a beautiful girl and now she was becoming a beautiful woman. How sometimes she would feel things and not understand what was happening, and she should know she could talk to Eleanor any time.

As if.

Juni never would say so, but Math had turned out to be her favorite class. She knew she was actually learning something there

every day. She had a chart to prove it. What had seemed impossible
had become likely. Ms. James was calm, soft-spoken, patient, and very
organized. Juni imagined her as the mother of little girls. She had told
Juni that she would catch up if she just did the exercises, day after day.
"The good thing about math," she said, "is that you can take it in little
steps, knowing you will get there." The class was broken into small
groups, and Mrs. James shuffled them like decks of cards the first four
days of the week. On Fridays, the whole class played games.

Juni had expected to love PE, but she didn't. There was a strange
vibe among the girls, too subtle, evidently, for Ms. Leyden to notice,
but often, someone was tripped, or chosen last, or taunted, sotte voce.
It was strange to Juni that PE brought the worst out in some girls.

They had recently been working on dribbling, passing, and
shooting from the foul line and from anywhere on court. They practiced using both dominant and nondominant hands. They dribbled
slow and fast. They dribbled sometimes in pairs, and on a whistled sig-
nal, switched balls. They dribbled backwards. Sometimes they would
dribble all over the court until a whistle blew, and from wherever they
stood, would shoot for the basket. It should have been a lot of fun,
because it was fast and demanding with lots of variety, and nothing
was at stake. There were balls into the basket, but mostly misses. There
were calls and whispers and hisses, not for many girls, but for some, like
Juni and Safi and two fat girls and the girl who wore thick glasses with
safety bands. There were "accidental" bumps and trips. The teacher
never seemed to notice.

One day, they had worked up a sweat doing layup drills, and
the teacher said to line up. Every girl would get two shots at the basket
from the free-throw line. "Do your best," she said. "Tomorrow we'll
focus on passing."

Nobody made a basket, but there was time for another round. It went much like the first time, until it came to Safi, who was in front of Juni. Safi missed her first throw—barely, bouncing off the rim—and sunk the second one. Juni cheered; a few other girls shouted or clapped; the teacher said, "Good shot." Juni went up next, and and slid the ball in both times. There were a few gasps at the second successful shot. Then a girl said, "Whoop-ee-do," quietly enough that the teacher didn't hear her, and girls snickered.

Ms. Leydon had them sit in a big circle. "Okay, one by one," she said. "I want you to tell me why you didn't hit the basket."

Nobody said anything. Juni almost spoke, but she didn't want the attention. She had thrown the ball too hard the first round.

Ms. Leydon said, "How you practice determines how you play in a real game."

There were groans. Ms. Leydon gave up. When she stood, the girls scrambled to leave the floor. A couple of them smirked at Safi as they passed her.

Safi and Juni were the last to go. They put the balls away. On the empty gym floor, they looked around and then at one another, and Safi raised her hand for a high-five. Juni slapped it and they went to change. In the locker room, nobody spoke to them, but a few looked at them brazenly, narrowing their eyes.

In the hall, Safi said to Juni, "I am so used to that shit." They slapped palms again an separated to go to their classes.

That evening after supper, Juni shot baskets until it started to get dark and Walter came out to see how she was doing.

24

At least once a week, and sometimes twice, the students in Juni's language arts class read library books at their desks. She liked those days. The teacher sat at her desk, and she read, too. So far, Juni had read and liked the novels *The Absolutely True Diary of a Part-Time Indian* and *Star Girl.* She didn't especially like writing about them, but she did, and Ms. Rondel told her she had good insight.

One day, Ms. Rondel said the whole class would now read a wonderful book that had won many awards. There was a copy for every student. They would read it in class over the next several days and they would talk about it and write about it. "It's short," she said, "and it is written in free verse, a form of poetry that doesn't rhyme, but has a beautiful sound to it." It was called *Out of the Dust*, by Karen Hesse, and it was set in the time of the Dust Bowl in Oklahoma. Ms. Rondel went on and on, talking about the weather and the lost crops. She said, "The author tells the story of a thirteen-year-old girl whose life is upended by a tragic accident, and of a family restoring itself after enduring great grief. Keep in mind that the book is fiction—made-up— though you are feeling what the character goes through—which we call empathy." She wrote *empathy* on the board. "In the end, you will see that the girl prevails, which means she goes on after her loss, and you are left with hope for her future. I tell you that so that you will know there is light at the end of the tunnel, because it is a sad novel. This story takes place in the 1930's. In high school, you will study the Great Depression in your American History class, and the *empathy* you have developed for this young protagonist will be important background for understanding that history."

Juni knew right away she wasn't going to like the novel. She didn't like the funny way it was written. And who needed a story about how poor this girl's family was and how bad the times were? She decided she would skim it as fast as she could.

On the following day, the class began reading immediately. The dust and the wind. A father who drinks. A pregnant mother and her daughter who both love to play the piano. Juni read faster and faster down the middle of the pages; it was like going down a slide toward fire and death. She shoved the book off her desk onto the floor. She began to tremble. She shook so hard her desk tottered. Someone cried, "Whoa, horsie!" and someone else, "Ms. Rondel, Juni's sick!" Juni moaned. Ms. Rondel rushed to her and knelt beside her desk and clutched her forearms. Juni's teeth were chattering. Ms. Rondel knelt beside her. She felt her forehead. "Are you sick?" she asked. "Do you hurt?"

Juni turned and buried her face in her teacher's shoulder; her sobs subsided to a whimpering. Someone giggled. Then it was quiet.

Suddenly, as if she just awoke, Juni looked around and jumped up and left the room. Outside the classroom door, she leaned against the wall, taking gulping breaths. Ms. Rondel went to the intercom on the wall to call the office. Two girls ran out to Juni and stuffed Kleenex tissues into her hands. "Blow!" one of them said; she obviously thought it was funny for Juni to fall apart over a book. The teacher came out and sternly sent the girls back to the classroom. She took Juni's hands in her own.

"Breathe slowly," she said. " Are you going to throw up?"

The sobs subsided. Juni was wracked with embarrassment and exhaustion. "I'm not sick," she whimpered. "I'm okay." She looked at the teacher's twisted, worried face, and she said, knowing she was going to be the mad girl now, "The book is too sad." The teacher was peering at her. Juni could see her thinking, yup, this girl is crazy.

Ms. Gregory arrived and stretched out her hand, saying, "Come with me," but Juni stepped away from her. Ms. Rondel went back to the classroom, saying to the kids, sit down, settle down, it's all over.

Juni said to Ms. Gregory, "I'm okay."

"I'm sure you didn't mean to."

Juni looked at her. "Didn't mean to what?"

Ms. Gregory said, "I don't know, Juni. I just got here. Come with me and you can tell me what happened. Do we need to call home?"

"I don't want to talk. Please don't make it any worse. Could I go to the library, just for the little bit that's left of class?"

"You can sit in my office until you feel better."

They walked together, Juni stiff and silent, Ms. Gregory murmuring.

In the counseling office, Juni sat in a comfortable chair with round soft arms and a cushioned back; she leaned into it and closed her eyes. If she cared what anyone thought of her, she would die right now, she thought, but truly, she didn't care. Ms. Gregory gave her a bottle of tepid water and sat on a stool she pulled close to the chair. "What happened, Juni?" More than anything, Ms. Gregory sounded curious, and Juni thought that was honest. She was calm now.

"We were reading a book about a mother and her baby dying."

"Oh dear, and you still so sad—"

Juni glared at Ms. Gregory. "You don't know."

"I can only guess."

Juni felt better, suddenly she was outraged. "It's a stupid book. We are just kids! There must be a million books and we read that one."

"I'm sure you don't have to read any more of it."

"Can I wait here for class to be over? I'll go to the next one. I'm all right." She swiped her eyes with the back of her hand. Her neck and breasts were so hot, she wished she could tear off her blouse.

"Yes, of course. The bell will ring soon. Don't worry. I'll talk to your teacher. You and I can talk later."

Juni gave Ms. Gregory a wan smile. She couldn't believe how stupid people were, to think that talking helped anything. She was sick of people asking if she was okay. She was sick of questions. The bell rang. She went on to her next class, and of course there were girls who came up to her; they wanted to put their arms around her, they wanted to know what happened. She shook them off.

She got a bathroom pass and went to her locker for her phone. She took it into the bathroom and called Helve.

"Please, can you pick me up?" It was Wednesday. She told Helve the dismissal time when she realized her grandmother was not going to drop everything and get her right immediately. "Please, please, please."

"What is it, Juni?"

"I feel sick. I miss you. I hate school."

"Has something happened?"

"My mom died!"

"Juni, Juni."

"Please, Mormie." She told Helve to park on the side street a block away. "It will be easier to get away from there." Helve would need to leave soon.

Helve came, bringing ice water in a thermos. She stood by the car to wait for Juni and when she appeared, hugged her and gave her the water.

Juni tried to tell Helve what happened, matter-of-factly, though her voice was quaky. "Everyone thinks I'm crazy now."

"No, darling, no one can think you are crazy for grieving for your mother, but hardly anybody knows what to say or how to act, either. What bad luck, a book like that just now. Come, let's get in the car."

"Can we just sit here for a few minutes?"

"Of course."

In those few minutes, Juni fell asleep. Helve waited for a little while and then drove to a grocery store and bought two oranges. She brought them back to the car and peeled them, standing outside the car, then got in the car and woke Juni. Slowly, in the parking lot, they ate the oranges.

Juni said, "I know I'm supposed to go to school, but I don't belong here. Maybe I don't belong anywhere."

"You have to be somewhere, dear," Helve said.

"I would rather be at your house."

"They won't let that happen. Not just your father and Eleanor. I mean—*they*—the authorities. You belong to your father, you see."

"Like a horse."

"I remember when my mother died. I cried until I thought I would die too. But then there was a day when I wasn't crying anymore. It will get better, love. It just does."

"You didn't kill your mother's baby."

"Oh dear, oh dear. Peter's death was an accident, my love. A terrible accident. Nobody blames you."

"Mom did."

"If she did, it was when she was sick with grief, and later she knew better. And anyway, Juni, it doesn't matter; your mother has no thoughts anymore. Death frees you from everything that once hurt. A dead mother has no memory. And you have no blame."

She suggested they walk a little while, and Juni stopped crying. They didn't talk. They walked back to the car. Juni asked Helve to drive by the school. There were kids on the field, shouting and laughing. Helve parked at the curb alongside the first of the nearby houses, and they got out of the car and walked along the alley beside the fenced field. Juni pointed out another house across the alley—it had a blue metal corrugated roof—and she rattled the chainlink fence on the school side.

"This is where I come and eat my lunch at eleven-twenty," she said. "In case you ever want to find me."

Helve put her arms around Juni and held her for a while. Then she kissed her forehead and said, "Sweet girl. We better get you home."

She drove to the Becker house and parked on the street. Nick got up from the couch as they came inside. He was in jeans and a crumpled black T-shirt. He was reading something that looked like a comic book.

"Juni!" he said. "They called me from school, but I only listened to the message a minute ago. What happened?" Juni and Helve stood in the doorway; Nick was by the couch. He looked at Helve suspiciously. "Did they call you?"

Juni clutched her grandmother's hand. "I called her. I needed her."

"We took a walk," Helve said. "Walking always helps." They stepped inside.

Eleanor had come up the driveway just then. She came in the house like a storm. "What is going on? You drove all the way from Frost Valley again?" She was talking loudly.

"Juni, go wash your face, dear," Helve said. Then she spoke politely to Eleanor and Nick. "She called me because she knew I could come. The hour she spent with me, she would have been alone, upset."

"About what?" Eleanor asked.

"We didn't actually talk about it. A book she was reading in class. A mother dies in the story, and evidently Juni fell apart right there in front of her classmates. I wonder if she might have cried more over that story than she has let herself cry about Karin all along. I'm sure it was terribly embarrassing, but it may have been a good thing."

Eleanor sighed. "I'll make coffee. Let's sit down. I'm sorry, I didn't know."

Nick and Helve sat at the kitchen table. Nick examined his knuckles. Helve had the air of a Buddha: calm, wise, immutable. Walter entered the house. He looked in the kitchen, held up his hand in greeting, and quickly went right back outside and down to the bungalow.

"She should see a therapist," Eleanor said. She poured coffee for them and sat down. "We've been fools to think she would just get better."

"I don't know about that," Helve said. "I'm not sure she wants to talk. I think she needs more time. You don't snap out of losing your mother. Maybe her health would improve if she weren't in school. I could be with her all the time."

"No," Eleanor said sharply. "She sees you every weekend."

"All right. Let's say I pick her up at school on Fridays, and one of you can collect her on Sunday afternoons. Really, two nights—not so much, but better than one."

"This Friday, all right." Nick said. "We'll see how it goes." The three of them sat quietly for a few moments. Then Eleanor sighed and said, "Poor Juni."

Helve thanked Eleanor for the coffee. She went into Juni's room. Tilde went in, too.

Ten minutes later, Helve went into the kitchen where Eleanor was preparing to cook. There was no sign of Nick. Helve said, "Eleanor, I am glad I could come when Juni called. I have no schedule, no commitments. I am available. You are good to her, and this is her home now, but she is fragile. Please consider if she should be with one of us all the time. I think school is too much for her so soon. Couldn't we talk about it—you and I and Nick?"

An image flashed in Eleanor's mind: little girl Eleanor on the old neighbor's couch, crying into her mother's sweater. Two days later, she was back in school and living in a stranger's house.

She said, "I expect it comes down to you and me." She suddenly felt humbled—not by Helve, but by the responsibility they shared.

"We aren't in competition, Eleanor," Helve said.

"It's not that, Helve. It's that as long as you are on call like you are, as long as you are her fail-safe, she doesn't bother to adjust to the rest of us. She doesn't give us a chance, or at least, not me. I think it harks back to her mother's attitude toward us. Juni is so resistant! If she stayed with you instead of going to school, wouldn't it reinforce her distance from her father, her sister? Do you think you could help her understand we'll do right by her? That we all love her?"

"I can try."

"And I'll make sure she knows she won't lose you. We don't want to keep her away from you. I think we can work out some kind of routine, don't you? Something she can depend on."

"Would Friday be all right, then?" Helve said.

"All right."

As Helve turned to go, Eleanor reached out and touched her arm. "Helve, why were we shut out? Do you know what Karin was afraid of?"

"Another time, Eleanor." Helve left quickly.

As soon as she was gone, Nick showed up again and said to Eleanor, "She won't stop until she takes them."

"Nonsense," Eleanor said. "You are their parent. She has no rights."

Nick pointed up. Eleanor didn't know if it was to the sky, or God, or maybe Karin.

After supper, she caught him as he was headed to the door.

"You should talk to the principal and make sure you understand what happened and how the teacher is resolving the issue. Should Juni read a different book? Do we need to help her find one? "

"You could talk to her," Nick said.

"No, you will. Really, it's time to step up."

"Fine!" He walked away. Eleanor saw Walter, standing by the bungalow, wave to Nick to come.

The next morning, Nick drove the girls to school. He let them out up the street from the school and parked, but he changed his mind about seeing the principal. It seemed as if everything had settled. He returned home, turned off his phone, and went back to bed.

At lunch, Juni went out to her usual spot by the fence and there was Helve, waiting for her on the other side. They clasped fingers through the links. Helve told Juni about the squirrel who had been coming to the corner of her porch. Juni put her forehead against the fence wire, and Helve kissed it.

The lunch lady spotted them and scurried off to tell Mrs. Gregory. Mrs. Gregory said to leave them alone for now, but a little later, she went to tell Mrs. Kenton. Mrs. Kenton called Nick, and when he didn't answer, she called him again fifteen minutes later, and once more time when he did answer. She described the situation. As in, "Here is the situation." She wanted him to talk to Ms. Sundersson.

Nick scoffed. He had been sound asleep. "You call that a situation? An old lady drives twenty-five miles and walks up an alley to console her granddaughter for a few minutes. She isn't on school property; the alley is public. Juni is safely secured inside the fence. Just what is the damned problem?"

Mrs. Kenton, who heard all kinds of disrespect in her job, always found it to be surprising when it came from an adult, though it was not unusual. She said, "We should have a conference and discuss how we can help Juni. When can you come in?"

The next morning, after the girls had gone by bus, and giving them enough time for classes to begin so he wouldn't embarrass them,

Nick went to the school. He walked straight into the principal's office, speaking as he arrived. Mrs. Kenton stood behind her desk.

He was saying, "Wouldn't the easiest thing here be to let Juni read a different book? Wouldn't the best attitude be, if Juni's grandmother can help her get by, she's welcome to try?" He had had to get past his own prejudices to come to that conclusion, and if he could, so could Mrs. Kenton.

Mrs. Kenton said they didn't want to set some kind of precedent.

Nick parried. "I'll tell Mrs. Sundersson she should call the school on a day she plans to see Juni. To inform you, not to ask permission. She won't just show up."

Mrs. Kenton said weakly, "It is irregular."

Nick said, "It isn't nearly as irregular as having your mother die suddenly right in front of you when you are thirteen years old."

In the following silence, both of them recognized their powerlessness. What was he going to do, take his daughter out of school? What was she going to do, call the cops?

"I'm very sorry, Nick," she said.

After that, Helve came to the school once a week on Wednesday, rain or shine. She brought a folding stool, which she set up opposite Juni, who sometimes stood and sometimes sat on the grass. Helve brought lunch for Juni. She always gave her a dollar.

Juni ate while Helve talked about her family in Sweden, beginning with a description of her grandparents' gravesite. The headstones had been carved by one of Helve's aunts, an artist who had a sculpture in the Moderna Museet in Stockholm. Helve told Juni who lived where now, and what kind of work they did, and many names. Sometimes she and Juni counted to ten in Swedish or named the days of the week. On Fridays she parked a block from the school and waited for Juni. There were no more outbursts at school.

25

Nick's chest hurt. He had awful reflux; often he gasped for breath. If he ate too little or too much, there was a fierce wretched pain that hit him in the solar plexus; and sometimes, higher, in his chest, came a worse pain. He was losing weight, but he washed and ironed his clothes and tried to look like he was somebody his mother didn't need to worry about. He got up almost every morning as the household awoke, dressed, and had a cup of coffee and a few bites of toast while Eleanor had her breakfast, and he sat with the girls while they had theirs.

After the girls had left the house in the morning, he shed his clothes, smoked, and returned to bed in his boxers and a T-shirt. He dozed and woke and smoked. He listened to the radio. The college had a good jazz and blues station. There was usually a nice enough hour somewhere in there when he relaxed and didn't think about whether life was worth living anymore. He took paperback novels from the living room bookcase and thumbed them and read pages randomly. When he discovered his father's collection of the old Swedish Martin Beck mysteries stored in the hall closet, he decided to read them all. He didn't have to make any decisions, he could just go to the next one in the series. He liked the way they progressed in steps, the voice stolid and impassionate, however violent the crime. Sometimes he read a page or two aloud softly, to keep his attention from straying.

In the late morning he showered and dressed and made fresh coffee. He ate a few bites of whatever was in the refrigerator. He was there when the girls came home. Nobody expected anything of him, though his mother reminded him now and then that he should see a doctor. He ate dinner with the family, often watched the PBS News Hour with his parents, then shot a few baskets with his daughters. He read at night or watched one of the late night talk shows on the TV in his room. Sometimes, when there was a clear sky, he walked down the hill and back. For much of the days—and sometimes the nights—he lay flat on his back staring at the ceiling. This was his life now.

The days were long. He helped his father clear out the bungalow, but he wasn't good for much. Mostly he moved things around and out the door, and his father carried debris to the dumpster. After an hour or two, his father sent him in to get a beer for them, and then they sat on the step and drank in companionable silence. Once in a while his father remarked on local news, or recalled a bit of fun the two of them had had in Nick's boyhood, but for the most part, both preferred not to talk when there was nothing to say.

Soon the bungalow had been emptied, construction began, and Nick went back to his solitary routine.

Neither parent pushed him about what he was going to do, except the one time his father suggested he look for part-time work for a pharmacy in a big box store. ("Soon," Nick said. "I already made some calls." Two lies.) He was in limbo. When his daughters came home from school, they said hi and went to their rooms or outside to play ball or hang out in the travel trailer, which they thought of as their club room. On the weekend, Juni went to Frost, and Tilde either went with her or spent Saturday with her friend Jamila.

He expected to hear more about Juni's problems at school, though he didn't know what he was supposed to do. He didn't know what to say to her. He didn't want to talk to anyone else about her;

it bothered him when his mother got on a riff about what he ought to do at school. He thought he was respecting Juni's autonomy. She didn't do the kinds of things for which kids should be punished. She wasn't weird or disruptive. She was just sad. He thought people—kids included—had to outlast their pain. You couldn't demand someone get over it. Weed helped, but the girls were too young.

Most days now, he turned off his phone.

He called an old high school friend, Andrew Dayton, who was a lawyer in town. He was embarrassed by the croak in his voice and he rushed to say he was having problems he needed to solve. Andrew said he would see him the next day. His office was a block away from the hardware store building.

Andrew had been a friendly, handsome nerd in high school; everybody liked him. He had gone out of state to college, then back to Lewis and Clark law school in Portland, then home to Lupine to set up his practice. He and his family lived up the block from his parents.

Andrew greeted Nick with a two-hand clasp and then pulled him closer, his hands on Nick's shoulders. "Man, long time," he said.

"Nice office," Nick said. It was. "I thought you'd be a doctor, though. White coat and all that."

Andrew laughed. "Organic chemistry—I just couldn't hack it. I liked law school. I liked coming home, too, you know? Where's it better? How can I help you?"

Andrew was dressed in casual but expensive clothes, and he had a good haircut. Nick knew he, on the other hand, looked like a loser, not that it mattered. He had worn his denim blazer—his nod to the seriousness of his visit—over a wrinkled shirt. He told Andrew about Karin's death and his living situation. He was hoarse, and glad when Andrew offered him a glass of water.

Andrew was aghast at the news about Karin, whom he had never met, and he was surprised at Nick's reason for seeing him.

Nick wanted to give his mother guardianship of his children.

"I don't know, man," Andrew said. "You mean, like give your parental authority to her?"

"Yes, that's what I mean. I'm not well. I don't want there to be any question about who they would live with, if, well, you know. I'm there; I mean, we all live together in my parents' house for the time being, but there's so much you have to take care of, with kids. There's the future. You have kids?"

Andrew nodded. "Boys." He stayed on topic. "Is your mother good with this? It's a big responsibility. She's in good health?"

"Yes to everything. She is already taking care of everyone. I want to make it official."

"So, we'll do a will. It's simple, I can turn it around this week, unless you have complicated finances."

"I have life insurance. A hundred grand. I think the premiums are paid for the rest of the year, from the job I just had. The girls are the beneficiaries. I'll keep it up."

He took the credit card bills out of his pocket and laid them on the table. "Take a look at these. Thirty grand in debts my wife piled up when I wasn't looking. There's no way I can pay them, I'll need to file for bankruptcy. I don't have much in checking and no property except a car that's six years old. I haven't got a job at the moment, though I'm looking." He looked Andrew straight in the eye. "Not a lot to show for a man my age."

SANDRA SCOFIELD

"We'll talk about the debt later. Let's address the issue of guardianship. A will, that's sound planning," Andrew said. "That's how you make your mother the guardian of your children upon your death."

"But I want her to be their guardian now. You know, deal with the school, the doctors, all of it. The decisions. They are girls, they need a mother—I can't do it, but my mother can."

Andrew scratched his head with both hands.

Nick said, "I can't take care of them, not properly."

"All right, I hear you. There are hoops. Steps in the process."

"Tell me what to sign, what to do. The custody, the will. I want something for my mother now, though, to say she's the boss—like, yesterday. I want to tell the school to call her and not me."

"We'll start with temporary guardianship. Come by day after tomorrow. Look Nick, this is pretty unusual. Are you going to take off or something? Are you in some kind of trouble? Whatever you tell me is absolutely confidential; maybe I can help. If you see something coming, we can get ahead of it. Or do you need to, you know—talk to somebody?"

"My wife's mother has her big wings over my girls and I don't want her to have them."

"Family stuff. I get it."

"You'll do the will right away, too? I'm sick, Andrew. I don't know if I will get better."

"Jesus, Nick. Have you got a good doctor?"

When Nick got the guardianship papers from the lawyer, he gave them to his mother. He caught her in the kitchen after all the supper dishes were done and put away. She was reading a magazine at the table. He was especially tired that day, but he wanted to get the matter taken care of.

"Something interesting?" he asked Eleanor. He wanted to sound casual; he wanted to slide into the subject. He didn't want to alarm her.

"Oh, it's a travel magazine, aren't I silly? A boat trip down the Seine." She closed the magazine and slid it away from her. "What's up?"

He explained what the papers were about. He thought she was going to faint.

"What did the doctor say?"

"Huh?"

"You saw him? Oh! Is that what this is about?"

"No, I haven't got in yet. I saw a lawyer. Andy Dayton, you remember him. Mom, I want you to do the things a mother would do for Juni and Tilde. The girl stuff. It's awkward for me. They need you to steer their lives. Doctors. School. Once I go to work, it'll just be work and sleep. Juni can visit Helve, but I want it to be clear that you're in charge—"

"But I'm not! You're in charge, Nick. You can't do this."

"I did do it."

"I didn't agree. I don't agree."

He was angry; he had expected her to say all right. "Then I'll have to ask Helve," he said sullenly.

She reached for his hand and caught it before he could pull away. "You need to take care of yourself. And you have to have something to do. Put your name in at Walmart and Walgreens, the hospitals. Start with part-time. Maybe just fill-in. You'll feel better once you're working again. You can't stop being your daughters' father. You can't do that to them. Didn't you stand up for Juni at school? Was that so hard?"

"Yes, it was. I don't have the strength for principals and teachers. I can't take care of anyone." He bent his head low. "Please do this. I'm thinking of Juni and Tilde, surely you can see that. It can just be between us, and when you need to show you have the authority. You can tell Helve if you want. Andrew drew up a summary of the formal papers, it's notarized. Half a page. Look, he laminated a copy, you can carry it in your purse. The girls don't have to know anything about it. I'm going to look for work. But I can't get through the days if I think my girls need any more from me than just being here. I love them, but I'm useless. In the best of times, I wouldn't know how to take care of them. You have to let me be. You have to look out for my girls, or Helve will end up with them."

"I think you are over-dramatising, you've worked up some sort of worst-case scenario, I see that now." She tidied the document, tapping its edges all the way around on the table. "I'll put these in our safe and we won't talk about them. Someone will need to go to end of year conferences. I'll call Abigail—Mrs. Kenton. The girls need to see a dentist. I can take care of those things. You know I am devoted to the girls. But you have to be present in their lives, Son. Little things would help. Take them to a movie. Ask them about their days. You have to make an effort. And Nicky, if I do this, you have to do something for me. See the doctor."

He laughed weakly at her rant, and reached for her, and she clasped his hands. He said, "Be sure to tell that principal not to call me." When he walked away, Eleanor noticed that he brought his hands up to his chest. He was halfway across the living room. She stood to go to him, but he moved on to the bedroom. She put the card in her purse.

When she told Walter about Nick that night in bed, she wanted him to say he would do something, that Nick couldn't evade his responsibility forever, but Walter just nodded and sighed. "It's probably for the best, Ellie," he said. "In some weird way, I think he's doing the responsible thing. He's a damned limp rag right now. Maybe it's too soon for him to look for work. He's a pharmacist, he needs a clear head."

She was too tired to push the conversation any further, but she did ask Walter to stay after Nick until he saw a doctor.

Walter scooted toward her and slid his arm around her and held her close for a moment, then released her, but lay near her. Neither of them pulled away. As they grew sleepy, they oozed apart like something dissolving.

26

The next day at work, Eleanor called Abigail Kenton. They had known one another since middle school, and though they hadn't been close friends, Eleanor was comfortable with Abigail. She explained that her son was not well and the school should contact her instead of him. "I have guardianship," she said.

Abigail didn't ask questions. Instead she said, "You've got two very different students here, Eleanor. Both are bright, nice girls. Juni is getting by. I think she tries to keep a low profile and does what she can. Her teachers are sympathetic, and they don't intrude. Tilde, on the other hand, is well-integrated. And Eleanor, she is a math prodigy. In fact, we have a singular group of kids in math. Their teacher and I have submitted a grant proposal in the hope that we can offer a summer program for them and similar students from schools throughout the valley. I'll let you know as things move along."

"Tilde hasn't said anything about her classes."

"She doesn't know how remarkable she is."

Nor do I, Eleanor thought. Tilde seemed comfortable in the Becker home. She often sat in a chair in the living room to read, unlike Juni, who almost never left her room. She went to the Y or shot baskets on the driveway with Walter. But Tilde and Eleanor had never discussed anything more significant than what to buy for lunches. Eleanor didn't want to pry. How do you say, do you miss your mother?

That evening, she went into the bedroom and called Helve. "I talked to the principal this morning," she said.

"Is something wrong?"

"Not at all. I just wanted to ask how you think the girls are getting on. Mrs. Kenton told me that Juni is doing all right, is that your impression? Do you feel she's doing better?"

"She doesn't talk about school," Helve said. "I don't ask her."

"Tilde, I'm told, excels in math, did you know that?"

"She is very enthusiastic."

"We don't really talk."

"She's fine, Eleanor. She likes living with you and Walter."

"She said that?"

"Yes. You don't need to worry about her."

"Do you still see Juni at school during the week?"

"Yes. On Wednesdays."

"I'm sorry."

"You needn't be. It helps me as much as it helps Juni."

"Thank you, Helve." They hung up.

Eleanor went into the living room. Nobody was there. She looked outside and nobody was there, either. She knocked on the door of the trailer.

"Hi, Mom," Nick said. Walter was with him.

"What's going on out here?" She hoped she sounded lighthearted.

"Poker."

"What are the stakes?"

"Pennies. Nickels."

"I'll leave you to it."

Walter said, "I'll be in shortly."

Back inside, she stood at Tilde's door. She could hear the television. Juni's door was slightly ajar.

She went to the bookcase and sat on the floor and looked at the history books. She chose *1491*. She vaguely remembered Walter raving about it, saying that the ancient history of the Americas should be taught in schools.

She opened the book and started reading, sitting there on the floor. The text was dense, and she had to concentrate. She could see immediately that the book would be both exhilarating and disturbing, the way so many things are when you pull the curtain back. She was ignorant, but she was hungry to know something larger than her own life. She opened pages at random and read passages. Any paragraph she chose was mesmerizing. She felt like laughing. She imagined her brain cells sleeping, waiting for something to come along worth their waking. And who did she think would make that happen if not her? She clasped the book so tight her hands hurt. She had put her education behind her when she married, like leaving one country for another. She hadn't grown intellectually since her sophomore year in college. Suddenly she remembered a document called *Colony at Roanoke*. It made her laugh, that she remembered. What did it matter now?

When Walter came in, she was still on the floor with the book. He offered a hand and pulled her to standing. He saw the book and smiled and nodded. She thought for an instant he would launch some kind of lecture, or worse, patronize her with praise at her choice of the book, but he didn't. She laid the book across others on the top shelf.

She took a long time in her bath. She thought about the British novel. It struck her that the story was ultimately about the corroding effect of suspicion on a marriage. The husband and wife forgave one another, but damage had been done. She liked that they knew their marriage would have to be tended. Maybe all marriages did.

How did you go about that?

She laid her wet washrag over her face and leaned back.

In the bedroom, the bed lamps were off. A slice of light from the bulb by the back door shone through the window at the edge of the shade. Walter was sitting up, his hands folded across his belly. He was wearing faded boxer shorts. He was waiting for her to come to bed. She stood by the bed for a moment, studying him. The moment felt familiar, and it comforted her.

He asked her what was on her mind.

She got into bed and said, "I was worrying about the girls at school, so I called Abigail Kenton today. And then I called Helve. Both of them reassured me."

"You called Helve? That's new."

"She told me that Tilde is happy here with us."

"That's nice to hear."

"I felt—talking to her—we are on the same side."

"Of course you are."

"I hope she'll help Juni understand she needs to be with her sister and her father."

"Maybe there's a compromise. If Helve has the girls for most of the summer, you would have a good break. We could do something, you and me."

"Like what?"

"I don't know, right off. Maybe go over to Sunriver? Or up to Cannon Beach? Water, sun, restaurants—"

"Oh that sounds fantastic, Walt. I'd love to."

She laid her head on his chest. He tugged her a bit higher and kissed her neck, her chin, her mouth. She wasn't excited, exactly, though she knew he was; she didn't mind. She felt tender. He was her husband. She loved him. She pulled her pajama bottoms off.

Walter caressed her, taking his time. Over the years, he had sometimes said, what would you think of a quickie? and she had grown to appreciate the expedient dispatch of his arousal. Yet she also remembered when she was excited just to think of being in bed with him, when she wanted lovemaking to go on and on. Now she thought she thought too much.

She touched him in a crude way she knew he liked, exciting him.

They lay on their backs after they made love, and he started saying something about a book he thought she would like, but she was so tired, she couldn't stay awake to hear what it was.

Nick told Eleanor that the doctor said he had been suffering from Broken Heart Syndrome. He had given Nick a prescription and a referral to a cardiologist.

"He said it is probably abating. You don't have it forever. He said to avoid stress. It's a big help to me not to deal with the girls' school, stuff like that. You're helping, Mom."

Eleanor looked up the syndrome online. Nick was downplaying potential damage to his heart. When she said how worried she was, he told her he would do what the doctor said to do—take his medicine, see a specialist. It would be a few weeks before he could get in. It wasn't an emergency.

27

Helve called Karl and asked him to meet with her at her house. She made coffee. He didn't seem concerned or curious, just his stolid self, waiting to hear what she had to say. He remarked on the fine weather and sat down at the kitchen table.

"I want to talk about the business," she said, to begin. "About my part in it."

"You have received two annual checks since Henry passed."

It was true that she received payments, but in the second year after Henry died, it dropped to a quarter of what it was the year before. There was no accounting to accompany it She knew the business hadn't declined. The farm supplied berries to a jam manufacturer in Wellen, and summer weekends, the farm was thronged with daytrippers.

Karl's skimpy payment didn't make sense, because what had been Henry's was hers. And it had been her money that paid for the farm. She should have had this conversation right after Henry died, but she had been depressed, and she didn't think of it for a while, and she let it slide.

"The payment was short. I should see an accounting every year. It's not enough to say, oh, we're family."

"I have a lot more responsibility and labor since Henry died, Helve. I pay myself a salary. And I paid Collin an hourly wage last summer as well. And I bought more acreage."

"Are you saying there was no profit?"

"No. I'm saying it was a smaller amount, compared to other years, because of the outlay."

"Am I not entitled to Henry's share of it, grand or not? Last year, and next year, and every year? As an owner of the farm?"

Karl shifted in his chair and scowled. Helve knew he was uncomfortable, but she didn't care.

"Well, no. You aren't entitled to Henry's share. You aren't really entitled to any income at all, Helve. You didn't work the stands last summer. You don't tend the bushes or do the accounts. I suppose we should have talked about this a while ago. I have been confident that you are secure. You have Henry's Social Security payments. You have your house. And up to this minute, you could still expect a payment out of the profits of the farm once a year, because I choose to give it to you. Half of Henry's share—a gesture of affection and respect; what Henry asked me to do."

She was stunned. "The business belongs—belonged to Henry, and me, and you." Ivy, who was Swedish-American, had married Karl almost ten years after the three emigrants had arrived in Frost Valley. Helve had a fleeting thought that Ivy was probably in for a surprise some day, too.

Karl said, "I'm sorry, Helve. There is a big misunderstanding here. You and Henry owned your house, and now you do. Ivy and I own ours. Henry and I owned the farm, and now I do."

She felt cold and dizzy. This was Henry's fault for not writing a will, and her fault for not insisting he do so. He had told her years ago that it wasn't necessary, because—she tried to remember—he said, "With the house deed, we don't need to pay some fancy lawyer to draw up a will." She felt herself coiling inside. The house deed. It was in a metal box on a shelf of a cabinet in the living room. But the deed for the land—she didn't think she had ever seen it.

It was her fault, of course, because she handed over the money all those years ago and signed something, but perhaps not the deed; and she didn't know, because she didn't ask questions.

She had been nineteen years old when she married Henry, she had been an ignorant country girl setting out on an adventure.

"Perhaps we should have this conversation before a judge," she said calmly.

"Now, now, Helve, don't get your skirt in a twist."

"I will take a copy of the deed to a lawyer. If you get right down to it, you should have a reasonable salary, and the profit ought to be mine. I bought the land, after all."

Karl smiled, and the smile made Helve shiver.

"You are not on the land deed, Helve. You have never owned this property. Henry and I bought it as joint owners. When Henry died, the property became mine. Come to the house so I can get the deed out of my safe. I will show you. I will make you a copy. I don't have to give you anything at all. I have done so because you are my brother's widow."

"It was my money."

"I wouldn't know about that. Henry had the money and he said both of us should be on the deed, that we were going to farm and prosper together."

"But inheritance law says that a husband's property passes to the wife."

"It was our joint property. His and mine; and now it is mine, Helve. Go to a lawyer if you like, and he will explain it to you."

She saw stars. She forgot to breathe for a minute. And then she just felt old.

She didn't know if Karl was right—she was going to find out—but she knew now that Henry had intended for Karl to own the land if he died first. He thought to protect Karl against the possibility that Helve might sell the land. He did not protect her. He had loved his brother more than his young wife.

Henry and Karl had stolen her inheritance, and she had let them.

When she had a chance, Helve told Ivy about the deed. At first Ivy didn't believe her. There had to be a mistake. Helve shook her head and didn't argue. Then Ivy said there had to be a reason, and Helve got up to go. Ivy grasped Helve's forearm.

"You can go to the minister. He can help you sort this out. We're family."

"I need a lawyer," Helve said, though she knew she was unlikely to find a way to set things right. Ivy insisted, though. She argued with Karl about it, until he agreed to sit down with Pastor Malberg.

"I'm not promising anything," Karl said. "I'm looking for the Pastor to help you understand you don't have a leg to stand on. Business and kinship aren't the same thing."

Their visit to the pastor lasted fifteen minutes before he told them to go home, pray, and come back in a week. He said, documents are of the world, but the bonds of love are spiritual. Helve thought he leaned toward her favor but didn't want to get in the middle. He said the deed was legal, but Karl could change it to give Helve Henry's share. The second time, Karl opened the discussion, saying he allowed that it would be a great relief to have Helve and her quarrel out of his hair, and he was prepared to raise the annual amount he paid to her, though he didn't say how much he had in mind. Helve shook as she pointed out that *her* land would eventually belong to *his* son instead of *her* daughter. It wasn't fair. She had understood that Karl was part of the deal when she married Henry, she wasn't quarreling that he had a right to a salary plus a share of the profits, but she wanted two-thirds of the profits—the shares for her and Henry. She wanted Elin to be an heir, along with Karl's sons. Karl turned bright red and then had a coughing fit before he stomped out.

Helve went to see a lawyer with a xerox copy of the deed Karl had given her. The lawyer had been recommended to her by the handyman, Otto Hagen. The lawyer shook his head and rubbed his hands together. "I never saw a situation quite like this," he said, "though I can tell you families cheat each other coming and going. That said, it might have been ignorance or bad advice, you all being immigrants and such. Perhaps your husband thought his share would pass to you, that would have been Tenancy in Common. But this deed is Joint Tenancy, and your brother-in-law does solely own the land, as the survivor. I don't know how this compares to ownership and inheritance in your own country, but I think what we have here is probably a misunderstanding." Dumb Swedes, Helve thought he implied. Her own country!

She thought, *and I am going to have to pay him for this.*

She finally decided to ask Karl to pay her what she had put into the land originally. When the attorney heard the amount, he pointed out that she would be much better off taking the shares Karl had offered. To be fair, at the very least, he said, they would need an appraisal of the farm, a consideration of the decades of Henry's labor; and starting from those figures, they would have to arrive at a fair payout for her to surrender her claim, such as it was.

Her head was spinning. She finally told Karl she wanted to settle the matter now, between them; she didn't want the quarrel to go on and on. She wanted him to give her her initial investment, which was a laughable sum now, fifty years on, plus $25,000—a little over five hundred dollars a year for the years since the purchase. She thought he should borrow to pay her if he had to. Karl laughed at her.

After a few days of anguish, she asked him what he was willing to do. She said he had to give her some consideration, and he agreed to repay her initial investment. At least she had her pitiful stake back.

Some time after, she went to speak with Ivy. She said she didn't want to go through all the tiresome details of what Karl had done to her—she did say "had done to her"—but she wanted to give Ivy important advice.

"You must demand that Karl write a will, if he hasn't already, Ivy. You must know what your status in the marriage is."

Ivy shook her head. "I trust Karl and my boys to take care of me." Helve wanted to shake her.

After that, Ivy came over a few times, but though both of them tried, they couldn't get around Karl and their dispute. Helve saw how painful it was for Ivy to think that Helve had been cheated— or, at least used—by the men they loved. She learned nothing from Helve's experience.

When the girls asked to see the chickens, Helve told them they were sick and couldn't be around anyone but Ivy for a while.

She was ashamed to lie to them, but she didn't want them to know her heart was hard.

28

A Saturday. Eleanor and Walter were invited to dinner at Steve and Alison's. Alison told Eleanor that she wanted to celebrate her marriage, her home; being settled. Eleanor offered to help, but Alison was firm that she could take care of everything. It would be a nice group: Steve, Alison, her parents, and Nick; Steve's cousin Jonas—also an electrician—and his girlfriend, Kizzie; her student teacher, John Kenyanjui, and his wife, Amy; and of course, Alison's best friend and fellow teacher, Charlotte, mother of Fiona's best friend, Daphne. Alison had called Helve to ask, somewhat timidly, if she thought Tilde and Juni might come. Only if they want to, she said. It would mean their giving up time with Helve. She didn't want to insist. Helve had been gracious, congratulating Alison and wishing her well; and she had spoken with Juni. It was only one weekend. When Eleanor mentioned the occasion to Tilde, Tilde was quick to say, "We heard about it. We're coming," and Eleanor didn't feel she had to pursue the question of how it got worked out.

Eleanor, in her own kitchen making deviled eggs, was wondering what she should wear. The guests mostly knew each other, but it was an occasion, and she almost never had a reason to dress up. Steve's house on a hill was modern and quite nice. The upper floor had two bedrooms and a bath off a long hall (the garage on the other side) as you came into the house, and then it opened to a large space with lovely large windows. At one end was the kitchen and a long table with stools; further on, there was a sofa, a club chair, and several stylish translucent plastic folding chairs. Along one side was a wall of cabinets; on the other, sliding glass doors opened onto a deck. Stairs led downstairs to a daylight basement with two small bedrooms, a bathroom and a kitchenette. Steve's house made the Becker house seem old-fashioned, which of course it was. When she had first met Steve, Eleanor wouldn't have thought of him having a contemporary sense of style, but obviously he did.

"Will you change anything?" Eleanor had asked Alison the first time she went to the house, and Alison said, why would I? No other woman had lived there. The two of them had sat at the long glossy table drinking coffee, and Alison talked about how well Steve was doing, how smart he had been to buy this lot at an estate auction. Many had passed on it because it was difficult to bring in utilities, and hook-ups would be expensive. It had turned out that the utility hookup fees had been paid decades earlier; the lot was a bargain. Eleanor thought that Alison, with her bit of bragging, was grasping, but for what exactly, she didn't know. Eleanor's approval of the house? Of Steve?

Eleanor had put her hands on Alison's and said, "Just be happy, Alison."

She laid wax paper across her stuffed eggs and taped the edges to the platter. Juni came in the kitchen still in her pajamas, though it was past noon. She took out a bowl and poured Cheerios—she ate them dry—and stood at the end of the table, looking out the window.

"When Tilde gets back, I'll take the two of you over to Alison's," Eleanor said. Tilde and Walter had gone to swim at the Y. "You can play games or watch TV."

Eleanor waited for a moment, looking at Juni's back. Finally she said, "Juni, could you please look at me when I'm speaking to you?"

Juni turned around slowly and set her bowl on the table.

"After you eat, take a shower and get dressed. Wear something nice."

"I don't really want to go to Alison's house. I don't feel so great today. I'll be okay by myself."

"We are all going, Juni. It is a family occasion. You can rest or play downstairs until guests come. Then you and Tilde can say hello to people, have a bite, and go back downstairs."

Juni got up and left the room.

Tilde came home, showered, and huddled with Juni to dress. Eleanor was delighted to see them in pretty outfits, their shiny hair pulled back into long loose braids. Tilde was in black leggings and a bright flower-print blouse, and Juni wore a crisp yellow cotton flared skirt with a scoop-neck white pullover. Both had pulled their long hair back in a single braid.

Eleanor said, "How pretty you look!" Tilde smiled; Juni turned away.

It was three o'clock by the time Eleanor and the girls got to Alison's. At the last minute she was afraid Alison would bark at her about bringing food, but in fact, Alison seemed pleased; she ate half an egg right on the spot.

There was some conversation between Alison and the girls about school—mostly Alison's questions and their yes's or no's, and then the girls went downstairs. Alison made white wine spritzers for her and Eleanor. It was a warm spring day. They went out onto the small deck and sat on the steps. There was an expansive view of the town from there.

Alison said, "Lupine was a great place to grow up in. I felt like I knew everybody. I felt safe."

"Why, yes," Eleanor said, surprised. She remembered how sour Alison had been in adolescence, full of complaints about school and her hair and her chores and her father's teasing. She had resented her brother's popularity, had complained about his friends in the house. She hadn't been outrageously rude, only sullen. One "cheer up," and she would leave a room. She had been so difficult to please, so quick to take offense. And then Ben had made her lose her sense of power over her own life, first as a wife, and then as an ex.

"We were a nice family," Alison said.

Eleanor thought she might cry. She squeezed her daughter's knee.

Alison went on. "I want you to know that I wish as good a childhood for Fiona. She's been very lucky to live with you and Dad. Now I'm trying to make a good home for her."

"Fiona is a happy child, darling. She is much loved."

"I was a nervous wreck, introducing Steve to Ben, but they were cordial. Ben said congratulations, shook hands with Steve, and actually smiled at me. He hasn't brought up custody again."

"Maybe he won't."

"Maybe. I told him that sometimes we could bring Fiona over after work on Friday—Steve and I could go out to dinner or to a movie in Wellen. He would have two nights. He didn't say a word."

Eleanor didn't want to say the wrong thing. How pathetic that sounded: two nights. Not that she was on Ben's side! But divorce, child custody arrangements—all of it was innately cruel to someone, if not everyone. And as the custodial parent, Alison lived with a constant sense of jeopardy.

Eleanor stood. "Are you okay with the girls here? I want to get home and wash my hair. When should we arrive?"

Alison slid the doors open and led the way back into the house. "I said six. Early and uncosmopolitan, but I thought good with the little girls—Daphne is going to spend the night. Jonas and his girlfriend can still go out after the rest of us call it a night."

"Sounds like a plan." Eleanor stood at the top of the stairs and called to the girls. "I'm going now, see you in a while!" There was no answer, only the low sound of a TV.

Walter was in the yard when Eleanor got home. They talked over plans for a moment and she went in. She decided to wear a pair of dark brown slub silk pants. She laid them on the bed and opened a drawer and found a cream-colored blouse. She thought Walter and Nick might need a snack— they would be drinking at Alison's—so she went in the kitchen to lay out cheese and pickles and crackers.

Nick appeared, wearing long ratty pajama bottoms and a white T-shirt. She asked him if he was hungry.

He said he wanted juice, if there was some. She handed him a large bottle of orange juice and he drank from it. She said, "Alison is expecting us at six."

He sighed. "Me too?"

"Of course you too. There'll be Steve, his cousin, and Alison has invited her student teacher, John, and his wife, Amy. Their daughter is Jamila, Tilde's friend. Haven't you met them?"

"No. Can you call me in an hour?" He took a piece of cheese and left the room. He passed Walter, who said hello and took some food and sat at the table.

All of a sudden Eleanor wanted to lie down. That little bit of wine had hit her. She hadn't had much to eat. Walter looked at her and asked her if she was okay. She said she was going to take a short nap. She would set an alarm.

Walter grinned. "I could stretch out, myself."

Eleanor put her hand on his shoulder for a moment, then went into the bedroom and shut the door with a firm click. She truly did want to sleep.

It was almost five when Walter woke her. He had picked up her ringing phone from the kitchen table, and Alison wanted to talk to her, *right now*.

At Alison's, Juni had come upstairs and asked Alison for a couple of Tylenol. A little later, she came up again and said she wanted to take a walk. Tilde had fallen asleep on the couch downstairs. Alison, busy reviewing her food preparation, did little more than nod. She said, "Don't be too long, sweetie," not turning around. Juni made a face, tugged her shirt, which felt too tight, and headed out.

She picked her way down the hill, ignoring the path. When she came to the street, she turned right and walked past two houses, until she came to a narrow, roughly-paved perpendicular street, almost an alley. If she went straight, she would approach a cul-de-sac; if she turned, she would practically walk into back yards. She needed to go the other direction. She stood stock-still, feeling her heart pounding. She was feeling strange, not quite in pain, but definitely not right. She felt too big, too tall. Her breasts, only recently full but very round, with nipples straight out like big buttons, had become heavy, like ill-risen dough.

She turned around to see a girl approaching her, waving wildly, smiling like an idiot. She was short, with curly hair and a chubby face. She was wearing jeans, stylishly ragged at the hem, and a blouse with a peplum and a monkey pattern. She had a small dog on a pink leash.

"Amanda," the girl said.

Juni said, "Got ya, Amanda."

"And this is Josie."

Juni looked at the dog. "Hi, Josie."

"So, you live around here?" Amanda said.

Juni pointed to Steve's house. "I'm at my aunt's for dinner."

"It must be pretty cool all the way up there. Can you see downtown?"

Juni shrugged. "Don't really know. Like I said, it's my aunt's house."

The chihuahua started yapping and hopping. Amanda laughed. "Want to come to my house?" The dog rubbed Juni's ankle. It was noisy, but cute in an ugly sort of way. Juni bent down and scratched the dog's head. She felt a stab of pain in her abdomen.

Amanda's house was close by. They passed the front door and entered the house along the side. A small porch with an overhang opened into Amanda's bedroom. She bent to let the dog off leash and the dog ran to a cushion in the corner. Around and around it turned, then burrowed into its bed.

Juni sat on a chair with a ruffled cover. Amanda sat on the bed.

"What do you think about Lupine Middle?" Amanda said. "Some of the teachers are pretty lame, right? But mostly it's cool. My fave is art, and sometimes English, if we read a good book. I love the days when they just let us read, don't you?"

Juni winced but managed to say, "School's okay."

"Who do you have for home room?" Home room was a fifteen minute time-waste first thing in the mornings.

"I don't remember her name. Gray ponytail."

Amanda giggled. "That must be Mrs.—Mizz—Tracey. Did you know she used to write romance novels? Like, years and years ago."

Juni turned to look out the glass door. Amanda said, "So. Where did you come from?"

Juni sighed. "I need to get back pretty soon." She noticed a shelf on the wall, on the other side of the bed. There were odd little dolls arranged like a parade. Amanda saw her looking, and jumped up.

"Oh, you have to see my collection. We went to Japan last summer for two weeks. Tokyo, Kyoto, Hiroshima, all over. I would have starved, but they had McDonalds everywhere."

Juni got up and joined Amanda at the display. The strange dolls were roly-poly, like eggs with no arms or legs. They were painted with pink or green or white kimonos and black hair with bangs, and there was some kind of red screw sticking out on top. Juni thought, one maybe, but—eight, nine, ten?

"They're called kokeshi dolls," Amanda said. She chattered on about them for several minutes, but Juni wasn't listening. She was thinking the dolls were like obese babies in bundles. Creepy.

"And I have these little toys, too." Amanda scooped up some tiny objects from a bowl on her dresser. She showed them in her open palms. They looked like fat pendants, with little creatures trapped in the middle behind plastic windows. "You're supposed to take care of them. Feed them and stuff like that, but I sort of forgot."

"I better go," Juni said. She had a sour taste in her mouth and she felt a little nauseated.

"Can't you hang a little longer? Let's get a drink." Amanda led Juni down a hall into a spacious white kitchen with a large island. Josie followed, pitter patter. Through a skylight sunshine flooded the island. The room looked like a surgery, except there was a red tile backsplash at the stove. Along the island were stools with white cushions trimmed in red. The white and red made Juni think of an ad for Coke.

The dog settled down in the hallway.

Juni looked around for an exit. The large kitchen windows looked out onto the side of another house that was set a little lower than Amanda's. The house had those panels that make electricity. Juni wondered how hot they got.

Amanda set a glass of Coke down in front of Juni. "It's cool that you know where I live. We can hang out again."

Juni felt a sudden cramp. She gulped her drink and sat down on a stool, breathing shallowly. The soda had burned her throat going down, and she felt a knifing pain in her abdomen. She shifted on the cushion. It was made of thick, soft foam. She took a sip of her drink. Then she yelped, "Ow!" and doubled over. "I think I'm sick."

"Like, are you going to barf?"

"No." Juni stood. "I just have to go." Her head was pounding. She felt sticky at the top of her legs. She felt faint. She bent over at the waist and laid her cheek against the cold island top. Just for a minute, she thought. She closed her eyes.

"Gross!" Amanda cried. "Ew. My mom is going to have a fucking fit."

The back of Juni's pretty new yellow cotton skirt was splotched with bright red blood. So was the cushion where she had sat.

Eleanor was in the bedroom; she was just about to get in the shower. She took the phone from Walter. Alison was practically screeching.

"Mom, I need you. First of all, you've got to pick up some sanitary pads for Juni. I have tampons, and Juni had a fit when she saw them. She's in the shower right now. She can wear some of my clothes. Just bring the pads, and then you have to take her to Frost. She's crying that Mormor shit. You have to let Helve handle this. I have guests coming soon!"

Eleanor appeared twenty minutes later, wearing jeans and a T-shirt. She had packed a small bag with a few things for Juni, including a package of pads. She took Juni aside and gave her one. While Juni went to the bathroom, Eleanor told Alison not to worry about when she would get back, not to save food for her. "I can't come looking like this, I'll have to change," she said. "If there's still time."

"It's okay, Mom, you'll get back in time to get mellow with me." Both of them tried to laugh.

Eleanor asked Tilde if she wanted to go, and Tilde asked Juni if she needed her. Juni narrowed her eyes, and Tilde went away.

Alison gave Juni a pink pill and some water.

Eleanor pulled Alison aside. "What was that?" she asked. She would wring her daughter's neck if she had given Juni a prescription drug.

Alison shrugged and said, "It's just a Benadryl. It will make her a little drowsy, don't you think that will help?" Eleanor frowned.

Juni lay down on the back seat, her seatbelt on but loose, and spoke not a word on the way to Frost Valley. Eleanor had asked Alison to warn Helve to expect them. When they pulled up, Helve came quickly to the car and helped Juni out. Juni immediately began sobbing.

Eleanor got out and stood by the side of the car. Helve said, "Please don't go yet, Eleanor. Come in." Eleanor followed them inside and sat on a kitchen chair while Helve ushered Juni into the bedroom. She could hear Helve's voice but not the words, and then Juni's whine, and Helve again. Eleanor got up and found a glass for a drink of water. She finally had time to think about what was happening: the histrionic child getting her way, Helve the heroine, Eleanor the chauffeur. She felt foolish and manipulated. This was not an emergency; she should have put Juni to bed and told her she would feel better in the morning. They had made way too much of something healthy and natural. Perhaps the surprise—the embarrassment—had set Juni off, if she had never had a heavy period, but Alison had already done what needed doing. Eleanor could have taken Juni home—to save Alison's party   and given her some sweet chamomile tea and a warm bath. Instead, here Eleanor was, cooling her heels in Helve's house.

If they let Juni make an emergency of it—well, they already had, hadn't they?

Her meandering thoughts were interrupted by Helve and Juni. "Are you doing better?" she asked Juni, who walked away.

"I'll make coffee," Helve said.

Eleanor stood. "I won't stay," she said.

"We need to talk."

"It's just menstrual cramps and she's tired and I see she is lonely for you."

"Wait until she settles down. She'll go to sleep, you can see she is exhausted. I'd like to talk to you."

"Thirteen, it's all still a surprise. "

"Yes. Please, Eleanor, sit."

Helve went into the bedroom again with Juni. Eleanor heard her quiet voice. Eleanor looked around the room. There were no magazines or newspapers.

When Helve appeared again, she said, "Now, coffee."

"You needn't."

Helve smiled. "I do need. We need. Eleanor, we are in this together, you and I."

Eleanor sat silently as Helve prepared coffee in an elaborate pour-over fashion.

Helve put a plate of Danish butter cookies on the table with milk, sugar, and mugs and spoons.

When the coffee was poured and they had had a few sips, Helve said, " Juni has been calling me every day, before school and after school and late at night."

"But—I've never seen her use the phone."

"I gave her a cell phone. I thought it would help if she knew she could call, but I didn't expect her to call so much. Yesterday she called midday, whispering; she said she was in a bathroom stall and hoped nobody would find out, they would take the phone away."

"Look, Helve, she has been fine. She is playing games with you."

"I always say to her, have you spoken to your father, and she says, he is in his room."

"He is grieving. I will coax him."

Helve rearranged the sugar and cream containers.

Eleanor added cream and stirred her coffee, which was too strong. "I do understand that Juni wants your comfort, Helve. I do know that you and she are close. But you must understand, she lives with her father in our home for now, and he and Juni have to be allowed their relationship. The hole in Juni is her mother's absence. Nobody can fill it for her. Or you. Perhaps you should grieve for Karin without trying to replace her with Juni."

Helve blanched; Eleanor thought she had hit home, but she didn't feel good about it.

Helve spoke, her chin high, her voice brittle. "Juni is special to me in a way that Tilde is not. I want to explain to you some history of our connection, and then perhaps you will—you will be more sympathetic."

Eleanor got up. It was time to go.

"You have had these children as your own all their lives. Of course they aren't close to me, to Walt, they hardly know us. You have to back off and let them learn that we love them, too, because we are Nick's parents and they are going to be with him. The girls need all of us, but they also need stability. They need to know where their home is. All this back and forth—"

"Please, Eleanor, sit. I ask you humbly, please stay. Juni is a wounded child, you will see. There are things you should know. I will tell you."

29

Henry's and Helve's first daughter, Elin, had been born in Oregon, but had nevertheless been a Swedish child. Henry and his brother Karl spoke Swedish to their firstborn children until they went to school. Elin never stopped speaking Swedish to her father. She was a confident, vivacious girl who excelled in school and sports, and she went off to Scandinavia at nineteen and didn't come back.

Karin was different. Though Henry tried to speak Swedish to her, he was defeated by school, TV, and ultimately by Helve, who said it was time to admit they weren't Swedish anymore. Karin was an ordinary child. She behaved, though she hit a patch of sneakiness around the time she was in fourth grade, and in some way, it became part of her character. Her grades were at or just above average. She read a lot. She enjoyed building things, from play dough when she was little to birdhouses with her father when she was older. Helve's memory was that she and Karin were close as she grew up, that they liked to be in the same room, even if they were occupied with different things. They hiked in the hills and along the river. They helped out at church events like used clothing drives and spaghetti dinners.

In Junior High, on the school bus into Wellen, Karin met Jennifer, whose family had moved to Frost Valley recently from Southern California. They became fast friends all through high school and after. Jenny married at nineteen, Karin at twenty, after working two years at the grocery store in Frost. Henry and Helve were happy to see Karin settle with a husband who had a good profession, and they were glad that the couple stayed close by. Nick Becker was a solemn sort, polite and shy, but it was obvious that he adored Karin. Her parents missed her, but they were stalwart folks, with a farm to run and family next door. They looked forward to being grandparents. They invited the couple to attend church with them, but only Karin would go, and after a while she didn't. They invited them to dinner, suggesting that Jenny and her husband would be included, but plans never materialized. Karin made it clear that they didn't like for Helve to drop in. Their sense of privacy smacked of rudeness; it was hurtful. The time between visits grew longer.

Henry and Helve owned a bungalow in a quiet old part of Wellen that they rented out with year-long leases. It was small and cozy with a fenced back yard. It had a washer and dryer in the garage. Karin was seven months pregnant when the house became available. Without a second thought, Henry offered the house to their daughter and son-in-law for a below-market rent—enough to cover the insurance and taxes. Nick and Karin moved in with a bed, a dresser, an old-fashioned aluminum-legged table, and two chairs from Goodwill. Helve bought a crib and took Karin shopping for a layette. Karin showed no interest.

That night, Helve told Henry she hoped the baby would come soon. Karin would be herself again. Henry, waspish, said there was no Karin anymore, only the dyad, Nick-and-Karin. How true that was would be proven soon enough.

Helve had asked if she could be present at the birth, and Karin said she would think about it, but when Helve heard from her, the baby had been born—eight pounds and healthy. Karin had named her Juni, from a list of Swedish names she found in a book. Two nights later, Nick called Helve at two in the morning and begged her to come.

Karin would not stop crying. When Helve arrived, Karin was sitting on the side of the bed, clutching the sheet. Her hair was wet with sweat, her clothes soaked, too. She looked at her mother with hateful eyes and said, "Go home." Helve approached her, speaking in soothing phrases, and Karin fell back on the bed and put her face down in a pillow. The baby was crying.

Helve changed the baby and walked her. Nick sat at the table looking like a man who had just lost a job or a wife. He didn't offer Helve tea or coffee, or a glass of water.

"What is going on here?" she asked.

"Karin doesn't sleep more than an hour or two at a time. She cries and snarls at me, and then she lies there staring at the ceiling. Last night she got up while I was asleep, and when I looked for her, I found her out in the yard, walking around in circles."

"Is she nursing the baby?"

"No. I've been giving the baby bottles. I have to work."

The house smelled musty, smoky. It was too warm, a July night. Helve told Nick to scrub the kitchen sink, then fill it shallowly with lukewarm water. "Get me a washcloth. Then go to bed."

She bathed the baby and put her in her crib and went to her daughter. Karin was weeping. Helve sat gingerly on the edge of the bed. "Dear one, could you take a bath? I'll make you something to eat."

Karin rolled over to face her. "I don't want her, Mama," she said. "I can't do it."

"It's early days," Helve said. Karin hissed at her!

Nick brought in a bottle and a kitchen chair. Helve fed Juni. She changed her and walked with her and put her back in her crib.

Karin went to sleep.

Helve said she would be back before Nick went to work. She was there every day. Henry ate supper with Karl and Ivy. Helve lost weight.

Karin seemed to be getting better. She walked around the little house. She bathed and ate and sat with the baby on her lap. They ate takeout, canned chili, and cereal. Nick came home from work and slept until nightfall, so that he could get up if the baby cried. Helve came and went. It worked for two weeks, and then one morning Helve arrived to find the baby naked on the floor on her back. She was gurgling and wiggling, and Helve gasped with relief that she was all right. Karin was in bed, red-eyed and angry. She said the baby had been screaming foul names at her.

Alarmed, and without asking Karin or Nick, Helve packed everything up and took Juni home. Every day she took her into Wellen to be in the house with her mother. Some days Karin held her and gave her a bottle. Most days she wasn't interested. Some days Karin cried; some days she slept. Some days she lay in bed, staring at the ceiling, and wouldn't speak. She never dressed. She smelled bad. Eleanor bought her four pairs of cotton pajamas, underwear, two more sets of sheets, and a portable fan. She told Nick his job was to keep his wife—and their bed—clean. He was thin as a nail, but calm, and he wasn't missing work. He told her he was grateful for her help.

Helve noted the smell in the house again and asked Nick what it was. He acted baffled. "What smell?"

She glared at him, and he said, "I'll smoke outside."

That was when she realized she was smelling marijuana. She had never known anyone who smoked it. She didn't know what it looked like. She didn't know what effect it had on a baby. She was as ignorant as a child. She didn't know what she could do, so she did nothing. It was illegal then, but she had a hunch that if she questioned them, Nick and Karin would stand shoulder to shoulder and throw her out. She told Karin that she wasn't going to bring the baby into town every day anymore. Karin never wanted to hold Juni anyway. The back and forth was hard on Helve and Juni.

"I stopped going to their house at all after a month. Karin had been to a doctor at last, and was better, but she remained indifferent to her child. Juni lived with me until she was nine months old. I knew we were fugitives, but that time was joyous. She was truly a little person, so cheerful and curious. I knew her body, her cry, her gurgle. She liked to sit on Henry's lap while he sang to her. Sometimes he clicked spoons for her and she screamed with delight. She was happy with us. She slept and ate well. I knew it could not go on forever, but I lived day to day. Then one day Karin showed up looking fat and sloppy, and took Juni away. I felt as if my guts were ripped out of me. Juni screamed and kicked in her mother's arms. Karin was hateful. She said I had had 'quite enough time' with her baby. There was no thank you. She hadn't actually looked Juni in the face. It was as if she had come to scoop up some laundry she had forgotten about. I stood in the door of my house and listened to Juni's screams until they drove away.

"After that, I went to their house every day. I went in quiet as a thief. I was very polite, very solicitous. On a good day, I could take Juni out for a while. We would sit in the park four blocks away. If the weather wasn't nice, I took her to the mall, where there was a little indoor play yard. I fed her. She screamed when I left. I was afraid that Karin would accuse me of displacing her—which of course I had done—but she didn't. She just took Juni out of my arms and held her, dangling, and shut the door."

Eleanor hadn't said a word. At moments, she had wanted to get up and run out. Sometimes she had wanted to cry or to take Helve's hands in her own. But she had sat and listened, shaken. Now it seemed Helve needed a break. She was sopping with her story, looking at the table, wringing her hands. Eleanor took a deep breath.

"I went by many times but Karin never let me in," she said. "I called Nick and he said there wasn't anything he could do about it. He sounded sad; Walt said he was spineless." She remembered Juni peeping out from behind her mother's legs.

She looked at her lap, suddenly stony with fury. "You could have called me. I could have helped."

Helve shook her head. "She didn't want to be observed."

Eleanor said, "Now and then I came home from work to find him stretched out on his old bed sound asleep. I would wake him, feed him, and tell him I would do whatever he wanted me to do, and he would say, it will get better, Mom. Then he would leave."

Helve sighed. "Was I wrong? I put the baby first. Karin was suffering. I told Nick that he had to get her to a doctor again. She did seem to be taking some kind of drugs, but now I think probably she and Nick were smoking every day. They began showing up at our house every few weeks and leaving Juni. Karin wouldn't get out of the car while Nick brought Juni in to me. Sometimes it was for the afternoon, sometimes for the night. Once they didn't come back for a week. Henry said we should go to court and get custody. But I knew that if we lost, I would never see Juni again. I told Nick I thought Karin needed psychiatric help, and he told me to go away and leave them alone.

"And then one day Karin came to see me with Juni, and I realized that she was pregnant—well along. She had cut her hair so short it was spiky. Her belly poked out and her legs were thin. I said she needed to talk to her doctor about the way she had been after Juni was born. She looked at me, smiling, and said, 'I'm much stronger now.' I felt such dread, I fell onto the couch and lay there until Henry came into the house. 'Foolishness, another baby,' he said. That was a lot for Henry to say.

"I had Juni once more for an extended time, after Tilde was born. Two months. Then Karin and Nick came to get her and said that they were moving to Salem. He had a better job there. She acted very sweet. When we went to the Wellen house after they cleared out, to clean and do minor repairs, we discovered filth and disorder. They had flooded the bathroom and the water had run into the other rooms. The floor was buckled and we had to pull up linoleum and carpet. My daughter! Taught to say please and thank you; to carry her dish to the sink; to scrub the tub; to rake leaves—"

Eleanor got up and pulled her chair beside Helve, sat down, and put her arm around her. "Breathe," she said. "Just take some breaths."

Helve went on, talking, talking. "Nick called me when Karin went into labor. He said if I could stand to sleep on the pullout couch, I could stay with them and help with the new baby and they would really appreciate it. Of course, I was happy to be invited. I stayed almost a month. Karin was distant, dreamy; sometimes I wondered if she knew I was there. And every day, all day, Juni followed me around like a puppy. If I sat down, she crawled on my lap. I bought books for her and she carried them around the house. She slept with me on the couch. When I left for home, she screamed. She called me 'Mormie.' It broke my heart. Once I had been this attached to Karin, but she didn't matter to me anymore, not like Juni.

"God is good, though, I thought; Karin didn't have that terrible depression after Tilde's birth, and besides, Tilde was an angel from the start. I thought both girls would be okay. And in a while, sisters, they would be there for each other. I hoped Karin could be their mother.

"I felt exhausted and defeated by sorrow, though I am a sturdy person. I was desperate to get my own life back. I went to see them at increasingly longer intervals. I thought they were getting on, in their own way. The girls seemed healthy; they were growing. The family seemed stable. They visited us at Christmas and in the summer. I always felt as if we were standing on a wobbly floor, but I was grateful for signs of ordinary life.

"Then Peter."

Neither Helve nor Eleanor spoke for a while. Eleanor walked into the living room and back again; she repeated the circuit; she moved her seat to the other side of the table. "The baby's death broke Nick's heart," she said. "All our hearts."

Peter was six weeks old and Juni was five when she rolled over on him in her bed and suffocated him. (No one ever explained to Eleanor why the baby wasn't in his crib.) When Karin saw the baby, she slapped Juni and pulled her hair. Nick was working a night shift at the hospital. When he arrived home, it was to the girls screaming, Karin wailing, the baby lying on the mattress like a discarded blue-faced doll. He called an ambulance and then he called Eleanor. It would take her hours to make the drive; he took the girls with him to wait in a hospital waiting room. A nurse put them in a spare admitting room and they slept under a white blanket, their heads at opposite ends of the examining table, until Eleanor arrived.

Karin was transferred and committed to Salem Psychiatric Center for twenty-one days. A psychotic break, the psychiatrist said, when he had seen Karin's records. Postpartum depression. There was a brief formal investigation, mostly consisting of Nick's account of what happened, and there were no charges against anyone. No one spoke to Juni about it. She will forget it, Nick said. She will have had a brother who died, but she won't remember the details.

"Peter," Eleanor whispered. She had never seen the infant. She remembered Nick's awful call. The baby's crib had been in the girls' room. Juni had picked the baby up and taken him to bed with her, apparently to stop his crying. Asleep, she had thrown her shoulder across the baby's face, or rolled over on him. It was a tragic accident. Nick asked Eleanor to take off work and care for the girls while Karin was hospitalized, so that Helve could be with Karin every day at visiting hours, and he could work.

They made me do it, Nick told Karin, of her commitment to the hospital. He blamed Helve and the doctor for the decision. She might have been jailed if she had not gone to the hospital. Karin told Helve she would never forgive her, though Helve thought she forgot, in time. Eleanor called a rental place and had folding beds delivered to Nick's house. She and Helve shared the house and the children for a week. Then Eleanor went home; she had to work.

The baby was cremated and stored in the trunk of Helve's car until she eventually buried the urn in the family plot, attended by her husband, his brother and sister-in-law, and their minister. Neither Nick nor Karin ever went to the grave—until, of course, the burial of Karin herself.

Helve said, "Karin and Nick lived like desperados. They existed in a vapor of intoxication and— can it be called love? The thing that kept me sane was that she left the girls with me in summers. I would see them playing in the field, stuffing their mouths with berries, or curled on the couch with books, and I would thank God they had survived.

I gave them vitamins and caramels. I trimmed their hair and nails. They were happy in those times.

"For a while each summer, Nick and Karin could live the life they really wanted—together, secretive, with their drugs. Nick took vacation and they camped on the coast—or slept in their car, I don't know. A few times they drove all the way to southern California."

"You might have invited me to see the girls," Eleanor said.

"I should have. I am sorry. But I felt crazed to protect them. We never left our property. I felt I was saving them."

"Excuse me," Eleanor said. She went to the bathroom, washed her face and hands, and sat down on the toilet lid. She felt battered by Helve's long monologue. She wondered if everything Helve had told her was an invention—if Helve was so malicious as to vilify her own daughter in order to claim the girls. But so much fell into place. Nick's long absences between his drop-by solo visits. His go-to-voice-mail phone. His refusal to engage in any discussion of the welfare of his family, his peevish reaction when they offered help of any kind. Eleanor and Walter knew he was an addict, but they told themselves and each other that it was only marijuana. It was deemed medicinal in Oregon then; now it was legal.

Nick had always held a job, hadn't he? The girls grew big and strong, that was what mattered. The rigid wall between the Beckers and the Sunderssons—that was Karin's doing; and how could Nick fight his wife for his parents?

Eleanor knew that Helve was waiting for her to say something, but surely not what she did say: "I'm starving, Helve. I'm dizzy with hunger. I was supposed to go to dinner at my daughter's house. Do you have some cheese, maybe? Crackers?"

Together they made sandwiches with wheat bread and cheese and mustard, and sat on the couch and ate in silence. Eleanor's appetite surprised her. She finished her sandwich, while Helve ate little of hers.

Juni wandered into the living room where the women were sitting. She sat squeezed between Helve and the arm of the couch. She took a big bite out of Helve's sandwich.

"All better?" Eleanor asked.

"Sort of," Juni said. "I was wondering, could I take a bath?"

Helve jumped up. "Of course." She got towels, some kind of salts, and a bathrobe. She came back to join Eleanor, and they both sat in silence for a little while, listening to the sounds of water running.

"I guess the emergency has passed," Eleanor said, careful to speak kindly.

"If she sleeps well tonight, she should be fine tomorrow."

"Nick can come for her in the afternoon."

"Perhaps she could miss school on Monday. We could play cards, cook something. She could rest."

"You want to coddle her."

"I want to reassure her. These things come to a woman. Maybe she has questions."

Eleanor thought for a moment, then said, "All right. By four on Monday, Nick will come for her." She stood and spoke slowly. "It must have been difficult to tell me these things. I am truly sorry for your suffering. And I respect that suffering as your own, Helve, so different from mine, which was from ignorance and embargo. We have both lost a child to this marriage. But the girls? They are my son's children. They should be with him." She was shaky, but she thought her voice was firm.

Helve spoke her turn. "Karin was always Nick's priority, even when his children needed him. He knew Karin was never there for Juni, he knew she sometimes reminded Juni of Peter's death, but he forgave her easily. I wonder if he ever thought of her as a mother. They were lovers, and that came first."

Eleanor laughed hoarsely. "But of course! Karin couldn't help herself! It's Nicky's fault. I should have seen that coming."

"No more than my daughter's," Helve said.

Eleanor was at the door. "What were they thinking, the two of them?" She was suddenly dizzy. Helve moved quickly to put her arm around Eleanor's waist and urged her to sit in the nearest chair, then pulled another chair close and sat facing her.

She said, "If I blame Nick, and you blame Karin, we won't have helped Juni and Tilde. Nick was there when Karin was lonely and tired of her parents' life; he offered her an opportunity to leave home without going through the scary part of being on her own."

Eleanor said, "Nick had had too much achievement and enthusiasm. He was smoking because it made the world a quiet place."

"Hook and eye," Helve said.

Eleanor was embarrassed. She sat up straight and ran her hand through her hair. "I didn't know Karin, I can't judge her, and I know nothing about their compact, but I can tell you, I blame my son for his behavior, then and now. I don't think I know him." She looked at Helve as if to plead. "He was the sweetest boy. A brilliant student."

"The other day—you said, it's down to us. You and me."

"Yes."

"I don't want to take the girls away from their father, or from you, either. I have my own life and plans. But right now Juni isn't doing well. She isn't as strong as Tilde. She doesn't have math or running or friends to keep her going. If she could stay with me for a while, it would relieve the pressure on her. We would fill our days calmly. What would she miss, a few weeks of school? My house, my ways, they are familiar to Juni. She can fall into my routine. She can be a little girl with her grandmother for a while. Could she stay with me, Eleanor? Just for a while?"

It would be so much easier, their life without Juni; there was no denying it. But how then would she ever come back to the Beckers? Whatever Helve's promise of temporariness, she was asking to take Juni away. How could Eleanor agree to that?

She got up and went to the door again. "You will have to ask Nick," she finally said, and Helve sighed.

Driving home, Eleanor caught herself holding her breath, her chest rigid. She pulled into a rest stop and walked around for a few minutes. She got back in the car, turned the ignition, then turned it off again. She closed her eyes and counted breaths to ten. If there were villains in this story, they were Karin and Nick. Not Helve.

She resented Helve's role in the life of her son's family—the rescuer, the standby, *the mother*, but it was lucky Helve had been there. It was not Helve's fault that Nick shut his parents out. And there was such strangeness to the history of Nick and Karin. Why would anyone want to shut the world out, not just for themselves, but for their children? What did they fear so much?

She told herself it was time to go home. She texted Alison: *Juni ok. Sorry to miss the party.*

30

Eleanor stopped at the grocery store to buy some fruit for breakfast—
bananas, oranges, apples and grapes—and orange juice and milk.
It was too late to dress and go to Alison's, and right now she wasn't
much interested in company. She had a lot to think about. She had
known all along that Nick and Karin were living strange lives, cutting
themselves off from family and the world at large, but Nick always had
a job. He had some sense of responsibility. At least she thought he did.
She had worried about the girls being out of school, but she had tried
to be broad-minded, to see the family as contemporary in some way
she didn't understand. Lots of parents homeschooled. She had gone
through emotional ups and downs about how Nick had cut himself
off from her and Walter, but she had never seen anything she could
do about it, even if it were her business, which it was not.

She had seen Helve as an abettor whose intimacy with her
daughter had infringed on Nick's ability to reach out to his own parents. She had resented Karin, to whom she felt she had lost her son.
But she had not let herself blame Nick. And she had thought Helve
selfish in her relationship with the girls. Hearing that Helve had borne
her own suffering had been a shock and a rebuke to Eleanor. Most of
all, though, Eleanor was appalled to have Nick revealed to her not just
as a besotted husband, but as a negligent father. Eleanor had always
blamed his absence on Karin, but now she saw that his addiction was

at the heart of his isolationism. He simply couldn't be bothered to communicate. She felt as if there were a hot stone on her breastbone. She gagged.

She washed and cut up the fruit. She put it in a bowl and covered it with Saran Wrap. She sat down at the kitchen table and stared through the window at the darkening sky. She had to confront her son. Her heart was pounding so hard she thought it might burst. Then Walter and Nick arrived.

Walter came through the door saying how great the evening had gone, how good the company was, how disappointed he was that Eleanor missed it.

She stood in the middle of the living room. Nick went right past her to his room and shut the door.

Walter said, "He hit it off with John, who is a golfer, too."

"Walt."

"Is something wrong?"

"I just spent two hours with Helve. She had a hell of a story to tell."

"What? Here, sit down. I'll get you a drink."

"I don't want a drink. I don't want to sit down. I want you to listen to me. Helve has a strong argument for her hold on the girls."

Walter waved his hand. "Let her think what she wants."

"She was ruthless about Nick. His passivity. I couldn't defend him. And if anything, she was harder on Karin."

"Come in the kitchen, please, I'll pour us a little wine."

In the moments it took to get settled she calmed down. "A glass of water for me, please."

"So tell me," Walter said.

"There is a whole narrative we knew nothing about. Karin chronically sick. Filthy houses. Kids left to their own keeping. They needed help, yet Nick never talked to us. He didn't trust us. It hurts, Walt." Suddenly she was too tired for details. She shrugged. "He chose Karin over everyone," she said. That was the sum of it.

"He was loyal to his wife, hon. That was only right."

"You aren't hearing me. They should never have had children."

Walter said, "It's irrelevant. Here they are, two beautiful girls." He yawned. "Let's go to bed."

She reached for Walter's glass and drank the little bit of wine left in it, and got up and put the glasses by the sink. She leaned against the counter and said, "We are strangers to our grandchildren, and our son is a stranger to us."

Walter put his arms around her. He brushed her hair off her face. "So we let the girls know we care about them, just like we have been doing. They're children, they are resilient. You know that."

"I feel so sorry for everyone—the girls, us, Helve, too." She wiped her eyes and moved away. "I'm so angry with Nicky. And with myself for ignoring his stupid addiction. The pernicious, utter self-ishness of it."

"Pernicious? Jeez, Eleanor, he hasn't got much to be happy about. I think it's better than being a drunk. He's making an effort."

"Go on to bed, Walt."

"Aren't you coming?"

"I just want to sit here a little while. I'll be in." She touched his cheek. "You think I'm overwrought, and I am. You think Nick is a good person, and somewhere deep inside he is. But we are sanctioning his drug use by ignoring it. And he is using us—"

"Wait. That's harsh. You went up there and brought them to our house. He is our son! I don't remember any doubt about where they belonged. You wouldn't want him to pack up and take Tilde and Juni away."

"No, that would be terrible. But I shouldn't have let Nick hand me the responsibility for them. I know what he is doing. He's prepping us for his vanishing. His demise." She began sobbing hard, gulping and gasping. Walter held her, rubbing her back. She pulled away and said, "I think he is sick and doesn't care. I think he wants to die. He talks about Karin like she's calling to him." Her heart was pounding. She was scared for her son.

"Hang on, El. It's not that bad. It's late. Let's go to bed."

So they did. Eleanor curled into a ball, facing away from Walter. Her stomach was hurting. Beside her, Walter fell quickly to sleep.

She heard Nick.

She got up. He was in the kitchen, gulping water, his head under the faucet. She reached over him and turned the water on full force.

"What the fuck!" he cried. He turned off the water and grabbed a towel to wipe his face. His T-shirt was soaked around his neck and shoulders. He tried to step past her.

"You wait," she said. "I have something to say to you."

He looked around the room. "You are having a bad dream."

"No, I'm wide awake. You listen to me."

"You're scaring me."

"I saw Helve today. She entertained me with the chronicle of your marriage. What did you think you were doing all those years, Nicky?"

Nick leaned against the cabinet and looked at the ceiling. "It is the middle of the night."

"Karin was dysfunctional. I get that your life might have been too much for you. You could have asked us for help, but you shut us out. You let Helve in when you needed her, but never took any real responsibility for your children yourself. Couldn't you have kept them in school, where people would look after them five days a week? Was it too much trouble to get them there? You let Karin abuse your children because she mattered more to you than they did."

"Whoa. Way off base, Mom. Karin never—"

"Never hit them?"

"She didn't."

"And you think that's the only way to hurt them? Day after day, both of you stoned. And now you shut yourself up in your room and lie there dreaming about her, don't you? Instead of looking after your daughters." She was gasping for air.

" I couldn't get past you if I did want to get to them."

"I can't throw you out, because Juni and Tilde need us and they need you. But you have to get yourself together. Start by getting off drugs."

"You are so out to lunch. It's *marijuana*, Mom."

That did it.

"Get it out of this house right now, tonight! Put your—your— *stash* in your car or the trailer!" She was screaming. "Do it now!"

Nick held his hands up like someone facing arrest. He looked over his mother's shoulder and gasped in relief.

Walter had appeared. He held Eleanor's shoulders gently, exhaling into her hair. "It's okay, El. I've got this. Go to bed. Go on."

Curled in a ball of anguish on her bed, she thought she might die of frustration, but exhaustion swept through her, and she fell asleep.

31

In the morning, the first thing she saw was Nick's bedding in a mound on the floor in the hallway. The door to the bedroom was open, as were the two windows in the bedroom. Eleanor rushed to the front door. Nick's car was still there.

Eleanor texted Amy. *Not coming to church. Will be there to pick T. up.* Amy texted back: *We'll drop her off.*

She went out of the house when she heard the car later. She invited the family in, but they were on their way somewhere.

Inside, she offered to make Tilde something to eat.

"Thanks, I had breakfast."

"Juni is at Helve's. She's going to spend tomorrow with her and then she'll come home."

"Okay."

Walter was raking the yard of the front house. Velma was sitting in her doorway. She was in her same old house robe. Eleanor went to her, waving at Walter on the way. She opened the sliding doors and pulled up a chair.

"How are you doing?" she asked Velma, and it worried her when Velma only nodded and said nothing. "Was Andrew here? Did I miss him?"

Velma's lips trembled. "I'm hungry," she said.

Oh my God, Eleanor thought. She hadn't been in Velma's house in at least a week. "I'll fix you something," she said. There was damned little to fix. She toasted some bread and buttered it, and cut the dry edges off a small bit of cheddar cheese. She set it on the table with a glass of water, and Velma hobbled over to sit.

"Are you not feeling well?" Eleanor asked.

Velma said, "Fine." She wolfed down the bread and cheese.

"I'll bring you some supper later, love," Eleanor said.

Velma smiled. "I'll watch TV."

Eleanor turned on the television and found a station with an old black and white movie. She didn't recognize the actress, who had platinum hair and thin arched eyebrows. The movie was a démodé comedy.

Eleanor held Velma's arm and got her settled in her lounge chair. She bent to kiss her cheek, her hand resting lightly on her shoulder, and she got a whiff of sour body odor. "I'll come back this evening," she said. "I'll help you take a shower, okay?"

Velma patted Eleanor's hand.

At the house, Eleanor searched through a kitchen drawer and found Andrew's number. She dialed and it went to voicemail.

"Your mother isn't doing well, Andrew. She's made a turn of sorts. This is Eleanor Becker. You need to get over here. Tomorrow, latest."

Meanwhile, Walter had come along the drive. He met her as she left the front of the house again.

"I have neglected her," Eleanor said.

"She isn't your responsibility," Walter said. "Her son should move her to Klamath Falls."

"Where is Nick? Did you talk to him?"

"Yes. He'll sleep in the trailer."

"And?"

"And he said fine. What did you think he would say?" He was a little testy.

"I'll make some coffee," she said. They went in the house. "Are you hungry?"

"Not at all. I think I'll lie down a while. Want to join me?"

She shook her head. "I'm going to clean out the refrigerator."

She had everything out to make spaghetti. Tilde appeared and offered to help, which pleased Eleanor. They shaped meatballs, and chatted for a little while about school. She said that Jamila's father, John, was going to coach her and Jamila. He was part of the staff for the high school cross-country team, he knew what he was doing.

"He said the three of us could get together on Sunday afternoons, and then Jam and I could run during the week on our own. And we'll have lots of time in the summer. "

"Tilde, love, that is terrific! What great luck to have made such a good friend."

Eleanor explained to Tilde that she was going to visit Velma briefly. "You can put dinner together, I really appreciate it. Cook the meatballs in the skillet, they'll brown, and you just sort of stir them on all sides; then put them in the saucepan and add the can of tomatoes. A pinch of each of these seasonings. Then wash and dry the lettuce and tear it up in a bowl."

Tilde didn't look happy.

"You don't want to, honey?"

"I don't know how to do lettuce."

"Then it's time!" Eleanor explained washing and draining and tearing up by hand. She demonstrated with a leaf.

"I'll probably be forty-five minutes, okay? Then when I get back, we'll do the pasta and set the table. I sure appreciate the help."

Tilde's smile was enough to wipe away a lot of angst.

Eleanor took a can of chicken noodle soup to Velma's and heated it. While Velma ate, Eleanor found a thermos and filled it with not-too-hot sweet tea, and set it by the couch. Then they went down the hall.

"Now, don't you be shy with me, Velma, haven't I known you thirty years?"

Velma nodded. They were standing in the bathroom beside the shower. Eleanor slowly unzipped Velma's robe, held her arm while she stepped out of it, and guided her to step aside a few feet. She ran the shower, tested and adjusted the water, and helped Velma step in. She got a washrag wet and gave it to Velma to wash her face and front, then rinsed it and got it soapy and wiped Velma's back and buttocks. How old and small and frail Velma had become—it seemed it was all of a sudden, which was a ridiculous notion, of course. Eleanor just hadn't paid attention.

"Now I'll do your hair with a dab of shampoo." Eleanor felt Velma go rigid. She whispered soothing assurances, and helped Velma turn around so she could put her head slightly under the stream of water. She was glad Velma's hair was very short. Her daughter-in-law, Roberta, had cut it recently.

She patted Velma with the towel and rubbed her hair dry. She had found a cotton gown, and she slid it over the old woman's head, pulled it down and adjusted it. She kept Velma steady while she stepped into panties (one pair inside another), and then she helped her put on a sweater.

"I'm going to move the TV a little, so that you can sit on the couch to watch, and when you get tired, you just lie back, is that okay with you? I'll put the remote right here beside you."

Eleanor had padded the couch with folded towels, and over them a sheet. When Velma was settled with a pillow and blanket, Eleanor sat down on the edge of the couch.

"I talked to Andrew a little while ago. He and Roberta will be here later to spend the night with you. If they aren't here when I'm ready to go to bed, I'll come back to help you. And here's your phone, you can call me."

Velma lay back and closed her eyes. Eleanor rearranged the television to face her, and turned the volume on low. A cowboy movie was playing. What was the name of the star? Eleanor stood watching until it came to her: Alan Ladd.

She felt sad for her neighbor, her friend, though she felt sure that Velma would say she had had a good life. She felt sad for herself, too, that she had not been able to do these things for her mother.

Supper was a quiet affair, with thanks for Tilde's cooking. She looked pleased. Eleanor told Nick about picking Juni up Monday afternoon, and he nodded and left the table. Tilde excused herself. "I'm going to call Juni," she said. She hesitated, and then she said, "I have a phone, from Helve."

"I know," Eleanor said. "That's fine."

In a minute, Walter said, "We're all going to be okay, you'll see."

Eleanor went to check on Velma and found her sound asleep. She left the TV on low, tucked the blanket, and patted Velma's hand. There was a light on above the stove, and another outside the sliding doors. Velma's son should arrive soon.

When she got back to the house, Walter was watching a mystery on TV—something Scandinavian, she knew, because there was snow. "Where's Nick?"

He looked up and paused his show. "In the trailer, just like you told him. He's going to sleep out there so he can smoke, Eleanor, you know he is. It's how he gets through the nights. He's doing the best he can. If he doesn't come in the house, it's not our business. Let him be."

"I think I should tell you all that Helve told me."

Walter turned off the television.

She sat down beside him. She talked for a long time, staring at her lap. He listened. When she had told him the things Helve had told her; when she had cried, thinking about Juni and the baby boy; when she had been angry all over again that Helve blamed Nick, although she was furious with him herself—then she looked at Walter and grasped his hands. "I always thought they were happy, the two of them. Selfish, rude—but happy. Now it seems as if they were children who never grew up, who didn't know how to face a problem or ask for help. They didn't want help. They wanted to live like they did."

"He must be sick," Walter said, his voice raspy, his words halting. "He needs help."

"He has to want it."

"He will get better," Walter said, "because he will have to."

32

Nick brought Juni home Monday at five. She went into her room and shut the door until Eleanor sent Tilde to call her to supper. After the meal, Eleanor asked Juni to help clean up. She had her empty the dishwasher and she showed her where the various dishes should go. She was self-conscious, trying to keep her voice mild and cheerful. Juni moved slowly, eyes cast down, but she complied. Eleanor noticed that she was wearing a necklace of sterling silver beads that she hadn't seen before.

When they were finished with the dishes, Juni started to leave, but Eleanor asked her to wait. "Sit down for a minute with me, please." She took a Coke out of the refrigerator and divided it between two glasses.

Juni didn't meet Eleanor's eyes.

"I'm sorry you have had a hard time at school," Eleanor said. She took a drink and waited. Juni still had a little more than a month of school left, and Eleanor hoped she could make it through without any more disruptions.

Juni sighed. "You sit all day and none of it matters."

"It does matter. It's the foundation for the next step, and the next one after that, for your future. The year is almost over. If you could try your best, you might be surprised to find you've learned something, and maybe it will all go faster for you. Next year will be better. In high school, you aren't a kid anymore."

"Uh, it will be the same people, the same everything."

"No, it will be a new environment, with teachers new to you, who will get to know you just like they do everyone else, from day one, with no history. I'm sure classes will be more interesting, too."

Juni took a gulp of her drink. "I'd rather go to school in Frost."

"There is no secondary school in Frost, honey. It's in Wellen. You would have to spend two hours a day just coming and going on a bus. And you would have the same problems there that you have here, you would have to get past being a new student—"

"I can ride a bus. I'm not a baby. I want to live with my real grandmother. Why do you care?"

Eleanor thought, the gulf is too wide. The "real grandmother" remark was more spiteful than she had expected of Juni. She couldn't let Juni hurt her, though. She wouldn't empower that.

She said, "You can talk to your dad about it, but I am sure he wants you with him and Tilde."

"My mother didn't like you." Juni pushed her glass away and slouched in her chair.

"Karin didn't know me, Juni," Eleanor said quietly. "And neither do you. Not yet. You can make things better for yourself. If you are busy, you won't mope." She wished she hadn't said, 'mope.' "You could ask a friend over."

Juni gave Eleanor a look of contempt. "Would that be the queen bitch from social studies or the fat boy with pimples from math?" She started crying.

Eleanor got up and knelt beside her chair. She took Juni's limp hands in hers. "It is the saddest thing ever to lose your mother, Juni. I know." She touched a bead of the silver necklace on Juni's throat.

Juni bumped Eleanor, getting up abruptly, and went to her room. Shortly after, she went outside and Eleanor heard the thumping of a basketball against the garage. Eleanor sat at the kitchen table and lightly pounded on it with her fists.

A little later, Eleanor walked past Juni and knocked on the trailer door. Nick opened it and stepped outside; she could smell marijuana. For just a quick moment she wished she could be high herself, which— good girl that she always was—she never had been.

He seemed relaxed, as if he didn't remember the things she had said to him. It would do no good to be angry again. She asked him to take a walk with her. Juni had gone in the house.

"Give me a minute." He slid a window open.

When Nick came out, Eleanor put her arm through his and they walked without speaking. Near the bottom of the hill was a house with a second-story addition under construction; they stopped to appraise the work. Next door, a woman was kneeling in her flower bed, turning the soil with a spade. Trees had leafed and grass was turning green.

The gardener glanced up and smiled and said hello. Eleanor knew her name, but couldn't think of it; she said hello and walked past with Nick. At the end of the block she stopped and faced him.

"Are you okay in the trailer?"

"Yup."

"You are alone so much."

"I get up every morning, Mom. I see the girls off to school. I do things."

"What is it you do?"

"What do you want me to say?"

"You're stoned all the time, aren't you?"

He spoke quietly. "I'm not your little boy anymore. You have to let me look after myself. I'm not going to argue with you. If you don't want me here, I'll move."

"No, please, that's not what I want."

"The girls have to be with you and Dad, though. Otherwise, they have to be with Helve. I can't be responsible by myself. I love them, Mom. That's why we are here with you."

A little boy on a scooter was coming their way, shepherded by a young woman. Nick and Eleanor stepped off the walk onto the grass. The boy waved and grinned. Once they had passed, Nick touched his mother lightly on her arm.

"You have to understand, Mom. It hasn't been very long since Karin died. I want to keep being sad about it for a while. Smoking helps me bear it. It helps me be with her."

Eleanor, startled, stumbled and reached out for Nick's arm to steady herself. Her neck and chest were hot, her legs were weak. She couldn't look at Nick, she was afraid she would hit him, or screech. His excuse for staying weak was a paean to weakness itself, a hoop of self-pity: being stoned made him feel better. He had no sense of his role in his daughters' lives. It wouldn't help to accuse him or chastise him, she had to find some other way to reach him.

They started walking up the hill again.

She spoke hesitantly. "Would it help to see someone? To talk about your grief?"

"Talk isn't going to bring Karin back."

"We're all struggling, Nick."

"Look after the girls, Mom, please. They need you. I'm sleeping a little better; I'm going to look for a job soon. I miss working." He laughed feebly. "Handling meds, it's a blast."

When they were at the mouth of the driveway, Nick said, "I appreciate all you do. I trust you. I know it isn't easy for you, but I've felt better since—well, you know—since I got those papers for you. Just knowing the girls have you."

"They need you."

"You worry too much about Juni. She's always been a little sullen."

Juni and Tilde were shooting baskets. Nick grabbed the ball when it bounced, and dribbled in a little dance that made the girls laugh. Eleanor watched them for a few minutes and then went inside.

Andrew and Roberta closed up Velma's house and took her clothes and possessions away. Soon after, a truck from a Wellen charity came and loaded furniture and drove it away, too. Another van came from a professional cleaning company. There was a dumpster. Painters pressure-washed the outside and repainted all the trim on the house and the garage. Yardmen came to rake and water, trim the edges, and set out new flowers. Old appliances went out, new ones in. New windows in the main area, including the sliding doors. There was so much going on in Velma's house, Eleanor stopped noticing. All good, she thought. No one minded an upgraded house next door.

A FOR SALE sign went up. Eleanor and Walter looked up the listing and almost fainted when they saw the price. They went in at the first Sunday open house and walked through. Everything was light and bright. The kitchen was snazzy, with new lower cabinets and the old ones off the walls, replaced with paint and shelves. The carpets had been pulled up and stone-patterned laminate laid all through the house. The doorways of the master bedroom and the bath across the hall had been widened and the shower was new, with no lip to step over. The toilets were dual flush, sleek and easy to clean. Eleanor said it was too bad all that hadn't been done for Velma, but on second thought, she didn't think Velma would have liked seeing her home changed. The house, well-built to start with, now felt new and modern.

Roberta called to say that Velma was doing just fine; she was happily ensconced in a foster home with two other old ladies. One of them was from Oklahoma, one town over from where Velma grew up. "Oh, please tell her we are thinking of her!" Eleanor said. "Tell her we miss her." Roberta laughed. Why, Eleanor couldn't guess.

Eleanor and Walter were inspired by the rejuvenation of Velma's house. They laughed when both of them admitted they wanted the sleek new toilets, defensible because the new ones used less water. They decided to upgrade the living room. Walter painted their kitchen and the living room a warm white, with some help from Tilde on the trim. They went to a discount furniture store in Wellen and bought a love-seat, and rearranged the front room into a cozier configuration, with the old couch against the wall and the new one in the old spot, farther forward. Across from the old couch were the club chairs with a table in between and the bookcase behind. It was almost like making the room into two rooms. Behind the seating, there was now ample space to walk back and forth from the bedroom wing to the kitchen, and to access the closet. There was a clear path to the French doors onto the back yard for the first time in years. They bought a new folding table, good for puzzles and games. They kept it against the wall next to the bookcase, easy to get to. Eleanor moved a long, high, narrow table to the back of the loveseat, where they could throw their keys and books and mail. She and Walter loved the new layout. They settled themselves there in the evenings to read or watch television. The girls preferred their rooms, and Nick seldom came indoors except to use the bathroom.

One evening when they were alone in the house, Walter stood near the front door facing into the room, and made a sweeping gesture.

"Good enough," he declared.

"Good enough," Eleanor said, too. For that sweet moment, it was just the two of them in the whole world.

MAY

33

Nick came out of the trailer and found a job in a day. He had talked to a pharmacist in town who said he had heard the hospital was looking for someone, and they were. He applied; they called Portland; two days later, they hired him. The schedule had been off-putting to other applicants, but it was perfect for Nick. They needed someone to work all night on the weekends: Friday, Saturday, and Sunday. It was a full-time job. He would start at seven in the evening and end at seven in the morning. His main duty would be the prep for night meds and the first ones of morning. He would be available for calls throughout the shift. He might have other administrative duties, checking stock, that sort of thing, although most of that was done by staff during the regular work week.

"All night?" Eleanor said when he told her. She was dubious.

"There is a nice cot. They said I would almost surely have time for a nap. I saw a blanket and a pillow. I don't mind being up at night, remember. I'm used to it, and I'll be by myself most of the time. It's perfect." He sounded positive for the first time since Karin died. Once she got used to the idea, Eleanor saw the logic of it. Nick would be able to sleep in the day; he could avoid the family entirely four days of the week. But he seemed genuinely pleased about the job, and she had worried about him trying to interact with people all day in a pharmacy, anyway.

"I'll start giving you money with the first check," he told her.

"Will you have insurance?"

"Sure. For me and the girls. It'll pick up on the tail of my old policy."

"It sounds just right for you."

She went in her bathroom, sat down on the toilet lid, and sobbed with relief.

One day when Juni was sitting in the back of the bus on her way home, she saw that Amanda, in the front of the bus, was trying to get her attention. It made Juni want to scream. She got off at the corner before their usual stop and took off in a new direction, avoiding Amanda, but when she got to Alison's, there she was, sitting on the deck! Juni couldn't think of anything to say, she was so surprised at Amanda's nerve.

Amanda jumped up. "This is your aunt's house, right? The one on the top of the hill. I guessed right, didn't I?"

Juni nodded.

"It's as pretty as it looks from afar. Can I see inside? Is it really modern?"

"My aunt would get pissed if you came inside. I had to promise that nobody would be in the house with me when I am here alone." Juni half-smiled, hoping this would be enough to get Amanda off her back. "Sorry."

"So, you could come to my house. Mom didn't know who was there, that other time." She gave Juni a hopeful look. "You'd never know it happened."

"I'm not feeling so good."

"Okay, just forget it."

Juni stepped past Amanda and keyed in the code to open the door. "I have a headache. I'm going to lie down. Sorry, really." She didn't have another moment's thought about Amanda. She was happy to be alone. Inside, she got a drink and went downstairs to watch an episode of *Sex Education* on Netflix.

The next day, she decided to go straight home and do her laundry so that when Eleanor said, "It's time to do your laundry, Juni," she could smile at her like a movie star and say, "I already did it."

A lot of kids got off downtown. She scooted away fast and started up Cherry Street. Halfway, she had a funny feeling and looked around to see if she was being followed. There was a group of girls—she recognized them, vaguely—but they were in a huddle in front of a house, showing something around among themselves, giggling. One of them raised her hand about waist-high and gave a little wave, just her fingers.

Juni walked on.

She had just gone into her room at home when the doorbell rang. She had never heard it ring in all the time she had been living there. It startled her so, her shoulders twitched as if she had been goosed. She went to the door, opened it, and there stood four girls, all of them grinning and looking foolish.

"Amanda, what a surprise," she said, heavy on the sarcasm. "Lisa." Lisa was one of the girls who sat at the table with the embezzler's daughter Melanie. She was in PE, too. Juni narrowed her eyes at the other two. "Do I *know* you?"

All the girls giggled. One of the nameless ones said, "You're like, the secret student, Juni. We wondered where you live."

"It's kinda dark," someone else said. The blinds were drawn in front during the day when no one was there.

Juni wondered if her dad was in the trailer. She couldn't remember what time he went to work. What day was it?

The girls took a few steps. "Is this an old house?" one of them said. "Like, wood floors!"

"What do you want?" Juni asked. It was scary to be so easily invaded.

Amanda said, "You always wear such pretty jewelry. We wanted to be able to look at it, you know—away from school." She looked around at the other girls.

"Could I try something on?" a girl asked.

"I'm thirsty," said someone else. "Do you have any soda?"

Lisa said, "How come you have so many fancy necklaces? Are you rich?"

"Is this your room?" somebody called from Juni's bedroom. They all traipsed in. Juni had boxes of jewelry on the chest right by the door. She moved toward the chest, to shove the boxes into the top drawer, but the girls were ahead of her.

"Look, boxes and boxes of necklaces!"

"Oh wow. Cool."

"Gosh, is this an emerald or what?"

"It's a topaz," Juni said, thinking, *duh*.

Someone held up a necklace with a single pearl. Another necklace had a cluster of CZ stones.

The girls were trying the jewelry on, holding it up to their necks, fastening each other's clasps, laughing, oohing. "You're so lucky!" one of them said, smiling wide so that her braces gleamed.

Juni, fighting tears, said, "I want you all to put my stuff down. Right there where you found it."

The girls were laughing.

"Now, fucking now!"

"Oh!" They did stop, and they looked at her as if they just noticed she was there. "Are you mad?" one of them said. "Don't be mad."

"Where did it all come from?" somebody said.

Juni glared at her. "My mother."

It was suddenly quiet. The girls looked at one another, not sure what to say.

"Can I have a drink of water?" That was from a girl Juni was sure wasn't in any of her classes. None of them had any business in her house. What would Eleanor say? Would she say, oh how nice, your friends came over? Would she say, you should have asked first?

Juni lost it. She slapped at the girls' hands, she shoved, she yelled, "Go home!" One of the girls started crying. Amanda yelled at the girls to leave, too. She tried to tell Juni she was sorry, but Juni slammed the bedroom door as soon as the last girl left the room. In two minutes it was over and the girls were gone. Juni frantically checked every box. One was missing its necklace, and her heart raced, but she saw it on the floor.

She sat on her bed and sobbed. She was reeking with perspiration.

She called Helve and gave her a short version of what happened.

Helve said, "I didn't realize you were there alone after school. Where is Tilde?"

"She's at track."

"When will someone be home? Where is your father?"

Juni had calmed down. "I think he's asleep. Eleanor will be home soon."

"Juni, lock the front door, put your jewelry inside your bottom drawer, get yourself a glass of water, and sit down. Breathe slowly and sip the water. Go on."

Hours later, after supper, Helve called Eleanor, and afterwards, Eleanor asked Juni into the kitchen to talk. Juni couldn't believe Helve had called Eleanor. She felt like throwing up.

"Helve said there were girls you didn't know in the house this afternoon. She didn't think they should be here when you are alone. I agree. We don't know their families. Who were they?"

"There were four girls from school, that's all," Juni said. "I didn't know they were coming. They followed me from the bus."

"What did they want?"

"I don't know. They were pushy, looking at my things."

"What do you mean?"

"None of your business!" Juni ran to her room.

Eleanor asked Tilde if she knew anything about it, and Tilde went to talk to Juni. She was upset when Juni told her about the girls and the necklaces. "You have to put that stuff away," she said.

"It's my room."

"Juni, kids see you wearing Mom's necklaces. You're asking for it."

Juni touched her neck. She was wearing the silver beads.

Tilde shook her head. "They're just necklaces, don't be dumb."

Juni pushed Tilde out of her room and shut the door. She pounded the door and cursed.

That night, Tilde told Eleanor that girls were talking about the jewelry, and she was afraid they were going to mock Juni or maybe try to grab something off her neck. It was embarrassing and worrisome *and it wasn't Tilde's problem.*

Eleanor waited until the following Monday to talk to Nick after supper. She told him what had been going on. She wanted him to talk to Juni.

"Why are you telling me?" he asked, and yawned. "Do what you need to do, Mom."

"Go in there and speak to Juni as kindly as you can, then gather up all the jewelry and put it in the safe. Tell her she can have it when she's older. Tell her she can keep the beads for now."

"Jesus, Mom, I don't want to do that. I'm not going to. That's why I made you their guardian. You tell her."

The next day, Eleanor came home at lunch, took all the boxes of jewelry she could find in Juni's room, and stored them in the safe in her bedroom. She left work early so that she could be home when Juni arrived. She sat Juni down on the new loveseat, sat at the other end of it, and explained what she had done and why. She told Juni, "It won't do any good to cry about it or go to Nick or call Helve. Eventually you'll understand that I'm protecting you."

She was tired of the damned jewelry. She was tired of Juni's petulance. She was sick of Nick's lassitude. She was carrying the load all by herself.

Basically, Juni never spoke to Eleanor again. Nor, for that matter, did she speak much to Tilde or Nick. She was a silent boarder. She came home after school and shot baskets, alone or with Walter if he was around, then went to her room at the sound of the front door opening. She did laundry and ate leftovers in the middle of the night. Sometimes she slept on the couch under a throw, curled up like a baby. When she came home from Frost on Sundays, she was always clean and her hair was washed, but the rest of the week she didn't bathe. Eleanor pulled her aside and said, as gently as she could manage, that the bottom line was, during the week, she had to wash her face, her teeth, her pits, and her jay-jay every day. "If I think you aren't doing that, I'll stand there until you do." Juni's eyes were wide, and she said, "I hate you!" and ran off, but she complied, as far as Eleanor could tell.

Eleanor finally called Helve and confided that she and Juni were quite out of sorts and it was worrisome, and Helve—kindly, Eleanor thought—told her that Juni was suffering grief and projecting her suffering onto the Beckers, and it couldn't be fixed. It was like a long-lasting flu, and it would have to fade in its own good time. And Helve was sorry. She didn't say what Juni was like with her.

Eleanor did consider packing Juni up and taking her to Frost, but she thought that it would be the worst possible lesson for Juni if her inappropriate behavior got her what she wanted. She thought if Juni lived with Helve it would be the end of her for the rest of her family.

And then, for a moment, she wondered if that would be such a bad thing for any of them.

34

Eleanor asked Amy Kenyanjui for a counseling reference, and she rec-
ommended a woman in her early thirties who specialized in treating
adolescents, Meghan Lewis. The woman had an annoyingly high-
pitched voice, but Eleanor thought perhaps Juni would be comfortable
with her because she was young.

Walter picked Juni up at school and took her to see Meghan
twice, and then Meghan called Eleanor and said that if Juni didn't
want counseling, it was basically futile and maybe cruel to make her
go. She said she had established that Juni could say anything at all to
her confidentially—to Meghan—and that there was no right or wrong
about feelings, but Juni had not said anything. Not a single word.
Meghan said that Eleanor should tell Juni she could ask to go back to
counseling any time she wanted, but then they should leave her alone
about it. Just be there, she said to Eleanor. And, she added, perhaps it
would help if you saw someone, yourself.

The therapist's remark felt to Eleanor like a clap of two hands
in front of her face. The therapist probably thought Eleanor was
overinvested in Juni's behavior, but what came to Eleanor's mind had
nothing to do with Juni. *All I do is monitor other people.* And the standard:
Is this all there is? At work she kept track of students who weren't where
they were supposed to be. She sometimes talked to them on the phone,
asking them why they weren't at school. She passed their names on
to the truant officer when the absences were too many. At home, she

was stuck in a role she had stepped into without looking and couldn't get out of: again, she was monitoring. Walter was out from under the store, and he already had promised to coach Little League and do who knows what else; Patricia Tennison was retiring and planning a summer in Florence studying painting; Barbara had her summer garden and little grandchildren. It wasn't that Eleanor resented working—she was younger than any of the others—but she suddenly recognized that she had too short a perspective on her own life. She was just getting through the days, working and then coming home to worry about supper and the laundry—and the emotional state of two orphaned girls, and their father as well. She felt drained to the dry bottom of her well. She had been worrying so much about other people, she hadn't asked herself what she needed for herself and what she had to do to get it. If Juni stopped scowling and professed to like school, as good as that might be, it wouldn't exactly fulfill Eleanor.

She had caught herself looking at teachers at the high school and thinking: I'm as smart as they are. There was a knot in her that was coming undone. She didn't just want to read Walter's library. He thought it was cute when she picked one of his favorite books to read, but she didn't want to be a dilettante. She wanted to take her mind out of the closet. She didn't want to paint or write a novel or travel through France. *She wanted to go to school.* There it was. God, it was so obvious. She wanted lectures and discussions and research papers. She wanted criticism and grades. She wanted to wrangle with *ideas.* She wanted dedicated time. She didn't care if she was old; if she would be a fish out of water. She wanted to finish her undergraduate degree, the one she abandoned when she got pregnant with Nicky. There it was; that was it. If she went to therapy, the only question she would have was, why did I go to work instead of back to college when Alison started high school? It hadn't even been a decision! Nobody stopped her. She simply had not thought of school as an option.

Why didn't matter, because it was about the past; the question was why didn't she do something about it now. And hadn't Walter said, as he stomped out of the house, *Do what you want?*

She made an appointment and went to see Amy Kenyanjui at the Admissions Office at the college one day after work. She asked her to review her transcripts. They talked about what it would take for Eleanor to complete her undergraduate degree, and Amy was very supportive and optimistic. She assured Eleanor that she would not find it difficult to fit in: "College is no longer just for the young!" Eleanor had the required basic courses done, plus two courses in history and two years of French. Earning a degree would take her two more years, whether she went full time at the college—which meant quitting her job—or did the coursework online while continuing to work—which meant an incredibly demanding schedule. Continuing her education was a formidable proposition, but it wasn't an impossible one. She wasn't too old to study. Patricia Tennison, who was almost ten years older than Eleanor, had just retired from teaching second grade, not because she couldn't work anymore, but because she wanted to start over as a painter.

Amy had made an interesting observation. "There have been a lot of changes in undergraduate education in the past forty years, Eleanor. You're going to be astonished at the depth and breadth of it." What was wonderful was that Amy didn't ask Eleanor what she wanted to do with her education.

After she left Amy, Eleanor sat in her car in the parking lot for a while. Her heart was pounding. All she could think was, what was

I waiting for, an invitation? She went home with brochures and a list of websites to check.

When Walter had described the money they had, he talked about it as if it was hidden away. But it wasn't irretrievable. When he asked what she would do if she didn't work, it hadn't been a question of money, it had been a question of her capacity to fill her time! As if she had no potential for a life away from the attendance desk at Lupine High School.

She would soon be sixty years old. She could take early state-employee retirement—seriously discounted, but still a substantial, dependable income—and she could continue to buy their excellent insurance through the state system, albeit without the subsidy she had while employed. Walter could start Social Security, or they could draw on their investments, whatever he thought was best. There would be the bungalow rent income. Walter's building hadn't sold, but he had leased it to an arts group for a year. He wouldn't clear any profit, but at least it wouldn't be a drain, and eventually he would get something for it.

She didn't care what pot they took the money out of; she cared about turning this page in her life. Blood gushed to her head; she leaned forward and put her head on her knees and breathed slowly. She and Walter would have to sit down again right away and do a further accounting, with her aspirations on the table. She thought he would be surprised to learn she had some.

35

A few nights later, she had just fallen asleep when Walter woke her, shaking her shoulder gently.

"Something is wrong with Nick."

She sat up. "Huh?"

"I heard him scrabbling in the bathroom cabinet. I asked him what he needed and he said he had a headache. I found some Tylenol and gave it to him. I went to bed, but I couldn't sleep. I checked on him again. He looked sick, all right. He's in bed out there now, sweating buckets, shivering. Then I realized, this is a night he works. I called the hospital and they said he had called in, he was all squared away."

She found a thermometer and went to take Nick's temperature. It was 103 degrees. She and Walter helped him into the house. Walter took off Nick's sweat-soaked pajamas and wiped his face and chest with a cool washcloth and ran a towel over his body; he got him into clean pj bottoms; he put him into the bed in the back bedroom. He found a fan in the closet and turned it on. Eleanor sat on the bed and tried to talk to him.

"When did this start, Nicky? How long have you been sick?"

But Nick had nothing to say. He raised one hand and limply waved her away.

She called the hospital hotline and spoke with a nurse. The nurse said to help Nick drink some water—slowly, in case he was nauseated. He wasn't short of breath or confused and he didn't have a stiff neck, so she said to just make him comfortable under a sheet. Give him 500 mg of Tylenol. Check him every two hours. She said, "If his fever hasn't gone down in four hours, or anything new develops—like a rash or incoherence—call your doctor's emergency line and ask if you should bring him in to the hospital. Or just take him. Set an alarm and try to get some sleep."

They went back to bed. In a little while, Eleanor said she was going to go lie down by Nick; she couldn't sleep, worrying that she wouldn't know if his fever got worse. Walter said he was going to go to sleep, because somebody would need to be awake tomorrow.

In the morning, Nick's fever was 99.5 degrees and he wasn't nauseated or confused or upset. He took some Tylenol. He had called work.

He slept most of Sunday, then got up in the evening and ate a scrambled egg.

Monday afternoon he went to work. He looked thin and tired, and Eleanor thought he sounded raspy, but his fever was gone. "No big deal," he said when Eleanor fussed over him. Though he continued to sleep in the back bedroom instead of the trailer, they hardly had a glimpse of him the rest of the week. On Saturday, Eleanor sent Walter out to clean the trailer; he came in with a laundry basket stuffed to overflowing with dirty clothes and bedding. Walter cleaned the trailer thoroughly, but Nick never went back to it.

Eleanor's birthday fell midweek, and when Walter brought up the idea of going out to dinner, she said it wasn't worth the trouble. Sure, she could prepare a meal ahead of time, and maybe Nick could manage to get the girls to the table, maybe he could load the dishwasher, but she would worry about it and want to get home early. She said it was enough to have the day remarked on. She was sixty.

It turned out to be a beautiful warm spring evening, and they went with Walter's alternative plan: Indian take-out that Nick picked up, and then Walter and Eleanor took chairs to the back deck and drank gin and tonics and watched it get dark.

"This is nice," she said. "I'm glad we stayed home."

"I have something for you," he said. He got up and went in the house and came back with a gift-wrapped package.

"Books," she said, because you could see that was what it was.

"Of course," he said, and they laughed about it.

One book was a new biography of Eleanor Roosevelt. Eleanor was delighted. The other book was *Agrippina: The Most Extraordinary Woman of the Roman World*.

"She was at the heart of the Julio-Claudians," Walter said. "Nero, Caligula—"

"How did you find it?" She was surprised and very pleased.

"Lauren, at the bookstore. I told her I was looking for a birthday present for you, and I wanted something historical about a woman. She practically leapt to get this book, she said you would love it, but to warn you that it is shocking. She said all that with a smile, of course."

She could hardly speak. "Shocking, huh. And *Eleanor*, not so shocking. A perfect pair of books, Walt, thank you."

"I got a cake, too. Let's go call everybody together and cut it."

"What kind did you get?"

"Devil's Food, of course," he said. They went in the house laughing.

36

In PE, the teacher often reminded the girls that the purpose of physical education is to develop strength and agility of the body; skills; and a lifelong love and habit of hearty activity. The girls knew better. Whatever they did, everyone wanted to win. The teacher tried to be on top of the competition in class, often reminding them to be good sports.

The girls who loved P.E. were the ones in the middle. They didn't make fools of themselves, but they also never made the best shot, and they never ultimately got the ball from the winners. They stayed clear of the Lisas and Karlys and Melanies, but they also stayed clear of Safi and Juni. They ran and bounced and got out of the way and had a good time.

Juni envied them.

She and Safi were always the last to leave the floor, because they picked up and stored whatever was left out. Ms. Leydon appreciated their help, but she didn't make much of it.

On that day, Juni and Safi were the last into the locker room. Most of the girls were gone. A few were chatting, tidying their things. Heading out.

Juni's and Safi's lockers were four doors apart. They got to them at the same time. The few girls left in the room froze in place for a moment, then scooted away.

On each locker someone had taped a blown-up photoshopped picture of a giraffe. On Juni's giraffe they had drawn a bra with huge bra cups, and a necklace of chain links. On Safi's giraffe, there was a cartoon version of an Afro, drawn with a black felt marker, and the lips of the giraffe had been enlarged.

Safi kicked her locker and looked over at Juni.

Juni slumped onto a bench and gagged.

They were alone in the room.

Safi came over to Juni, sat, and put her arm over her shoulder. She said, "They are so dumb. They don't like it that we're friends. Don't let them get to you, Juni."

Juni looked up. "It's because we're good athletes. Because we're serious. "

"It's because I'm Black, dodo."

Juni blushed.

"Come on, get dressed. We'll be late for class." There was one more thing to say. "Don't let those stupid girls see you upset."

Juni reached toward the paper on her locker, but Safi put her hand on her forearm. "Don't take them down."

While they were changing, Ms. Leydon looked in and when she saw what was holding the girls up, she said gruffly, "This cannot be tolerated." She moved closer to them. "Are you okay, dear girls?"

The girls shrugged, their shoulders tight.

Ms. Leydon told them to go to class. "I'll get these," she said. "I'm so sorry."

Safi said, loud and clear, "Lisa. Melanie. Karly," and then she tugged Juni's arm to get her out of there.

Juni wanted to cry, but there wasn't time and there wasn't a place. She got through her last class and hurried to her locker and out of the building to the buses. She sat in front and got off quickly and ran to Alison's house.

She planned to have a soda, take her shoes off, watch cartoons or listen to music. She wouldn't think about the stupid pictures in PE.

She entered the hallway, threw her shoes off, and walked into the kitchen. There was a guy at the table playing Solitaire. There was music playing, something she had never heard, a girl's voice, high and trembling. She liked the music immediately; she felt it.

She felt herself blush; her neck was hot.

The boy was older than her and very good-looking. She stopped four feet away from the table. She bent her head back, put her hands to her neck and slid them under her hair and lifted it, leaning back more so it would fall straight. She shook her head and looked at him.

The boy raised his eyebrows and bit his lip. In a moment, he said, "Hey!"

She couldn't think what to say.

He laughed and stood. "Brian. I'm Steve's son." He walked around the table, stuck his hand out, and they shook hands.

"I'm Alison's niece. Juni. What's that music?"

"Skott. She's Swedish."

"I like her. I'm Swedish, too!"

"Is it too rude to ask, where did you come from? Sweden?" He was grinning.

"I live nearby and I come here sometimes after school."

"Yeah?"

"I hang out downstairs before anybody's home. It was Alison's idea. She said it's so I can have some space."

"Where do you live?"

"About six blocks away."

They stared at one another, then laughed. Brian said, "You hungry? Want a snack?"

"Maybe a soda or something?"

They both moved to the refrigerator. There were six beers lined up in the door. They looked at one another and Brian raised his eyebrows. "Split one?"

"Okay."

He poured and gave her a glass. He set the bottle on the floor by the cupboard. The beer was very cold and it stung her throat, but she didn't cough, though for a moment she thought she would. They sat on stools across from one another.

"Are you visiting?" Juni asked.

He said he had always lived in Texas with his mother. "We had a big fight and she shipped me to my dad. I'm going to live here. "

"Are you good with that?"

"Oh yeah."

"Were you guys out of school already?"

He told her what they had worked out at Lupine High that morning. It was way too late in the year to get in line to graduate from LHS, but the school would cooperate with his Texas school so he could finish his credits and graduate long distance.

"Sounds complicated," Juni said.

"Nah. They didn't blink. "I've got a high GPA and never gave anyone any trouble. LHS put me in chemistry and calculus classes and then I'll spend some time with the alternative school kids for the rest."

Juni drank the beer. The taste wasn't so nice, but it was cold and fizzy.

"Did you know Alison before?" she asked.

"I met her last summer. She's cool. I'm glad my dad, you know, got married."

"I love this house. Sometimes I pour a soda in a wine glass and walk around and out on the deck like it was mine." Now Juni was embarrassed.

"Is it bad where you live? Am I being nosy?"

Juni shrugged. "I live with my dad's parents. They're okay. I have a sister and my dad."

"Your parents separated?"

"My mom died."

"Oh shit."

"I guess I'll go home."

"We could play cards. Or watch something?"

"Like what?"

"They have Netflix and HBO—"

Juni laughed. "I know. I've been watching *Sex Education.*"

"Ha!"

"I'd be embarrassed to watch with a guy. We could play Foosball."

"Oh, I'm good at that."

"Me, too."

They went to the basement.

By the time Alison and Fiona got home, Juni had curled up on the couch in the basement and gone to sleep. Brian was back at the kitchen table with his Solitaire game. The beer bottle was in the recycling bin.

"Brian!" Fiona called as she came in. She ran toward him, stopped short, and wiggled her foot, toe to the floor.

"Hey, kid," Brian said. Fiona giggled and ran to her room.

"How was school?" Alison asked.

"It's all okay. Filling time until the year ends. Well, except for calculus."

"Sounds good."

"Yeah. Hey, your niece is here. Juni."

"Where?"

"She's asleep on the couch downstairs."

"What?"

"We hung out, played Foosball a while, she seemed really worn out."

Alison walked past him quickly and down the stairs. Juni was awake, sitting up with her knees under her chin. She was rubbing her eyes. She said, "Hi."

Alison sat down on the couch. "Juni, sweetie, you can't come anymore after school—"

"Oh."

"You can't be here with Brian, just the two of you."

Juni frowned. "He's nice."

"It's not—not appropriate. I'm sorry, I hadn't had a chance to talk to you to say things have changed here. You can come on the weekend when I'm around. Come on, Fiona and I will take you home."

"Right now?"

"Yes. I need to go to the grocery store, I can drop you off first."

Juni went upstairs and retrieved her backpack. She managed to give Brian a look and a shrug: *what the hell?* Brian brushed past her and went downstairs.

"He's nice," Juni said in the car. "Very polite."

Alison didn't react. Fiona said, "He's my stepbrother!"

Everyone was home at the house except Nick. Tilde was on the couch, reading. Walter was in a chair with a New York Times crosswords book. Juni was in her room with the door closed. Eleanor rushed from her bedroom, where she had been folding clothes, and gave Fiona a hug, crying, "What a nice surprise!" Fiona jumped onto the couch next to Tilde, who laughed and put her book down under the edge of the couch.

Alison asked Eleanor to step into the bedroom with her.

"Mom, I have a big complication in my life right now. Steve's older son arrived from Austin day before yesterday without warning. He got in trouble and his mother put him on a plane with no notice."

"Oh my, what did he do?"

"He says nothing, but it all had to do with a picture a girl sent him on the phone. She's fourteen and he's almost eighteen. Both mothers went crazy. I would, too."

"What kind of picture?"

"*That* kind. Well, just her bare boobs. He said he didn't ask for it, and when he got it he deleted it, but she had sent it to another girl, and that girl sent it to someone else, you know how that goes. It was all over school. A cop came out and gave them a warning, and then on to Brian's parents."

Eleanor clasped Alison's hands. "Listen, love, this might be a good thing. Maybe this is where the boy needs to be."

"What do you think Ben said?

"About Brian? It's none of his business. You told him?"

"Yes, I called Ben, because I didn't want the news of Brian to come out of the mouth of babes. I said Steve's son had come to live with us, and right away Ben said, how old is he and what did he do, just like you did. I said Fiona would never be in the house with Brian alone, and would never ride with him driving a car. And Ben said, 'It might be better for her to be with us.'" Alison started to cry. "He is looking for a reason to take her away from me. I can't be scrupulous enough to satisfy him."

"You are magnifying this. Ben is a blowhard. I would think he of all people would respect Steve's relationship with his son. Stop worrying about Ben and think about how you can help Steve make his son welcome in your home. And Alison, Ben doesn't have any right to details about your life. Step back. You both need a lesson on boundaries. Maybe you should get some professional advice about dealing with him and with your need for his approval."

"A lawyer! Do you know what that puts in motion?"

"I was thinking a therapist."

Alison said crisply, "I thought you would understand."

They went into the living room and Alison said, "Come on, Fiona, we have to go."

"No!" Fiona cried. "Can't I stay, please?" She had pulled out the Checkers board and Walter was putting up the game table. He said he would bring Fiona home after supper if that was all right. Alison wearily agreed. "Seven, latest," she said. Fiona ran to grab Eleanor around her waist.

After supper, Walter and Eleanor went together to take Fiona home, so they could meet the boy. Steve and Alison both looked tired, and Eleanor hoped she wasn't misreading their body language, which seemed tense. The boy was downstairs, where he had a bedroom and bath, and Steve said he was already in bed.

In the car, Walter asked, "What will he do, coming at the end of the school year?"

Eleanor said, "Oh, they'll work something out with the alternative school, probably to let him graduate from the Texas one. I am guessing that will be the least of the problems."

Abigail Kenton called Eleanor just as they parked at the house. Eleanor stood in the porch alcove to talk.

Abigail said, "Did Juni talk to you about what happened in P.E.?"

"No. What did?" Walter looked in and she waved him off.

Abigail described the ugly posters in P.E. "I'd like for the girls to speak briefly with the counselor in the morning before they go to class. Do you think Nick would want to come, too?"

"No, he works nights; he'll be sleeping. And I'll be at work. Do I need to take off?"

"It's not necessary. We just want to assure Juni and Safi that what happened is unacceptable and we are very sorry. We won't go into details except to say that the three girls involved have been suspended."

"I confess I'm shocked this would happen in the school, I didn't think our kids were like that."

"My impression is that the three girls thought they were up to mischief—they definitely wanted to goad Juni and Safi—but I don't think they had any real notion of how disgusting their prank was. Part of what has to happen is some consciousness-raising. We will be meeting with their parents tomorrow, and I'll let you know what we work out. I want Juni and Safi to know we have their backs, and I want the other girls to get a wakeup call."

"That sounds like a tall order."

"Yes, well, big bucks, you know. How has Juni been doing? None of her teachers have said anything since the book incident."

"She seems okay. She doesn't talk about school, but even tonight, after what you say happened in P.E., she didn't seem upset."

"Millie Leydon, the P.E. teacher, says Juni is close to Safi. Maybe it helped that they were together. Listen, I'll call you tomorrow. Or if you have a break, feel free to call me in the afternoon. We're meeting at 1:30, so after that."

"Juni's in her room. I don't know whether to say something or not."

"Safi's mother is quite upset, she sees it as a racist incident. Millie says the other girls—the culprits—are jealous of Safi and Juni's athletic skill. Safi's mother says Safi doesn't want to talk about it and wishes nobody knew it happened, but on the other hand, Safi named the girls.

I think that both Juni and Safi are suppressing their feelings, but I'll leave it to Mrs. Gregory and the families to explore that."

Eleanor had to sit a while to take it all in. Her heart ached to think of Juni seeing the mocking picture on her locker. And she wondered why she had never heard of Safi. She knocked on Juni's door. Juni was stretched out on her bed with her phone on her belly and earplugs in, listening to music. She was fully dressed including her shoes. She hadn't turned a light on and the room was dim. Eleanor suppressed her urge to tell her to sit up.

"The principal just called and told me what happened in P.E. today. I'm so sorry, Juni. Do you want to talk about it?"

Juni stared at the ceiling. She made no move to turn off the music. Eleanor made a gesture—take out your earplugs—and Juni did so with a big sigh.

"When you get to school in the morning, Mrs. Kenton wants you and Safi to meet with Mrs. Gregory, the counselor, before homeroom. Juni? It's about the girls in P.E."

"If they make it a big deal, it will only be worse."

"Juni, those girls were mean. I came in here to tell you how sorry I am it happened."

"Okay. Can I have my jewelry back?"

Eleanor exhaled audibly.

"Can I have a lock on my door?"

"No. No. Did you tell Tilde?"

"No."

"She's your sister."

"So?"

"I've got some laundry in the dryer, I think your pjs are in there. I'll bring them to you. Why don't you take a bath and get comfy, and we'll look for something all of us can watch on TV."

Juni groaned and swung her legs around to sit on the side of the bed, and looked directly at Eleanor. In a weary voice she said, "Would you please please leave me the fuck alone?"

Eleanor didn't say anything. She took care to leave the room without rushing or looking back. In the hallway, though, she leaned against the wall for a few moments and collected herself.

Later, the girls were in their rooms and Eleanor and Walter were watching TV when there was a light knock at the front door. Eleanor went to open it. A girl stood there looking woebegone, clutching an envelope.

"Hi, I'm Amanda," she said. "I'm a friend of Juni's."

"Honey, Juni has gone to bed."

"Oh, that's okay, I just wanted to give her this." She handed Eleanor the envelope. "To say I'm sorry about what happened today."

Eleanor startled. "You—"

"No! It wasn't me. But I heard about it. I told my mom I couldn't go to sleep if I didn't tell Juni I'm sorry." She turned and pointed down the driveway. "She's waiting for me, I have to go."

Eleanor gave Juni the envelope in the morning, but never heard anything more about it.

Lisa, Melanie, and Karly were suspended for three days, with the caveat that in order to return, they had to meet with either the counselor at school or a therapist of their parents' choice, to talk about the implications of their prank. They were required to write letters of apology to Safi and Juni. The letters were mailed to the girls' homes.

When Eleanor gave Juni hers, Juni said she would rather eat them than read them, and Eleanor, who saw Juni's point, tossed them in the trash.

Safi told Juni that it had worked out for her. She had parlayed the blow-up into her mother's concession that Safi could spend the whole summer, not just two weeks, with her father in Chicago.

"Lupine isn't a good place for me to live," Safi said. "Just about everybody is perfectly nice and it's really pretty here, but it's like living on another planet after growing up in Chicago. I want to be in a big city again, and I want Black friends."

"Wouldn't you miss your mother?"

"Some. But not as much as I miss my dad now. My mother has been away from us for long periods of training, and it wasn't fair to make me follow her here when I've always been with my dad in Chicago."

Safi's mother was a wildlife biologist who had spent two years of work and study in African game parks, and she had got her dream job at Lupine's world-renowned wildlife forensics laboratory. Animal remains, bones, and so on, were sent from all over the world for the lab to determine how they had died—or in many cases, been killed. Her mother was happy in her work and with her fellow professionals and staff. Safi's little brother, who was in third grade—and in Walter's softball group—was happy, too. But Safi wanted more than friends; she wanted a community, and there weren't enough girls like her in Lupine to make one. She hoped she wouldn't have to come back from Chicago. When she told Juni all that, Juni started crying and so did Safi, but they didn't hug or say anything about feeling sad. Both of them had known loss, and they would make do.

37

Eleanor insisted that Alison's family come for a barbecue early the next week. She went all out, with steak and locally made frankfurters and pricey first of the season strawberries. She felt it was important that they welcome Brian, and she wanted to see how Alison and Steve were doing. Brian seemed like a nice boy. He was certainly good-looking, built like a tennis player. He had good table manners, a strong Texas accent, and he put ketchup on his steak.

Juni sat across from him at dinner and hardly looked up, but while the adults were having coffee, and Tilde and Fiona were playing Checkers, she and Brian went for a walk down Cherry, over and up the back way and across the field to the back door. They walked briskly, not talking, but looking at one another once in a while.

"I want to get your phone number and give you mine," he said. They were standing on the back deck.

"What for?"

He laughed. "In case we want to talk some time. Or maybe you'll need my help, and you'll know how to find me. My dad gave me a truck to drive." He grinned. "An '88 Toyota Tacoma. Red. Sometime we can take a drive."

"I'm thirteen. Eleanor would not go for that."

He laughed again. "Nor Alison. I'm the bogeyman. Listen, Juni, I'm living in a house with a nine-year-old and her mother, who thinks

I'm a bad boy. You have a look about you—like you're on the sidelines in your family, too, and I just want you to know I'll be your friend. Like a big brother. I mean, we are family, sort of."

"I guess."

When they got back to the house, Juni got her phone out of her bedroom and they sat on the back step and exchanged numbers. Juni thought Brian was okay, but she didn't care about boys.

She did ask Brian why his mother sent him to Oregon.

"I grew a foot in the last year, and I think I scared her. What could she do to me? In a few months I'll be eighteen anyway, and she knew I would come to Oregon then. This way it's her idea, it's spiteful, and she can feel she washed her hands of me."

"That's awful, I'm sorry."

"Don't be, it's all good. I just wish my little brother could have come with me. He's kind of fucked up." He reached for her hand and held it for a moment. She felt a tingle in her chest, and then her cheeks burned. She jumped up and went to her room.

Later, when the house was quiet and everyone else was asleep, Juni called Brian. He answered right away.

———————————————————————

Helve was busy with her house. She and Otto Hagen kept a running list of repairs and improvements to make, and she was relieved to be in his good hands, checking things off one by one. He said the house had been well-built and was in great condition overall. He put an awning over the back porch. He put an accordion gate across the top of the stairs so that someone would not stumble down the stairs in a nighttime misstep—how lucky they had been with the girls! He came many times. They had coffee together, and sometimes she made lunch for them. She enjoyed his tales of growing up in the valley. He had been married, but his wife died young of pneumonia, and he had no children. He had siblings and cousins and their kids; he said he had a busy business and family life.

She thought he liked her. She had her hair cut and bought a new blouse. When he wasn't there, she thought sometimes that it would be nice if he kissed her. It wasn't a good idea, though, because she was going to leave in the summer, and neither of them needed to be hurt. She did tell him her plans, and sensed his disappointment, but then he was more interested in the house than ever. He picked up a couple of realtors' pamphlets and brought them for her to see. She was shocked by the high prices, but of course her house was basically a one bedroom cabin. He had his ideas about the price range she might fit in, and he said she should have a realtor come to talk to her, unless she wanted to sell it herself, word of mouth.

An electrician came to put a panel in the garage. Otto laid new flooring in the bathrooms. She bought a new kitchen range. She hadn't yet cleared the closets and cabinets—she dreaded doing that—but otherwise the house was spotless.

She sat in the evening, studying the sales flyers. There were two century-old homes in town, but she didn't think her house compared to them. There was one cabin in the woods, with a wood stove; it wasn't like her house, either. She thought the closest houses she might compare hers to were the basic two bedroom one bath ranch houses—built, almost surely, with materials inferior to her house. And her house sat on seven-eighths of an acre. She decided she wanted what was being asked for the nicest of the small ranch houses. She would call a realtor right away.

Before she did, though, Collin came to see her. She was surprised, but soon realized that Karl hadn't said anything about his quarrel with her. Collin was completely at ease, happy to see her and to talk about his plans. Lily would be graduating at the end of the month and would come immediately, because both of them wanted to work the summer on the farm. They would stay in his parents' house, in his old bedroom. And oh yes, they were planning a small wedding soon.

"Mom told me you are going to go to Sweden, Aunt H. At first I thought, oh no! because we will miss you so much—Mom especially—but then I realized you will probably be selling your house. Is that right?"

"Yes. I've had everything fixed that needed it, and then some. The handyman says it is solid as any house can be."

"Well, Lily and I would love to buy it!"

She needed a few minutes to absorb that news, though it was perfectly obvious that they would live in her house if they could. For Lily, a city girl, it would be a kind of adventure; for Collin, who grew up across the fields from Helve, it would be an extension of his childhood, right into the house next door. He would work with his father, maybe work in town off season, live in Helve's house. From the farm, he would draw a salary—and later, a share, and later still—he would own the farm.

The skin on her arms prickled.

"Have you priced it yet?" he said. "I've been to the bank. Lily's parents are giving us money for a down payment as their wedding gift, and I have a job here at the farm. So I qualify for a modest mortgage. Wouldn't it be great if we could buy it and you would stay until you go to Sweden, of course, and you wouldn't have to pay a realtor?"

Helve thought of the price of the nicest of the small frame houses she had studied in the flyers, and then she thought of how Karl had cheated her, and she added twenty-five thousand to the model house's price, and blurted out the sum. She said, "That's if you buy from me directly, of course, where there's no payment to a real estate agency. If I sign up with them, I'll list it for more. I'm supposed to see an agent this next Wednesday." She hadn't called anyone yet, but her heart was racing, and a deadline would put pressure on Collin.

He looked stricken. He probably thought his aunt would give him a good deal on a cheap house. She wouldn't. And he wouldn't find anything as good for less.

"I don't think I can borrow that much, you know, make the payments. They spelled it out pretty well so I'd know my limit. Geez. I wasn't thinking, uh, houses cost so much here."

"Maybe Lily's parents could help you with a larger downpayment."

"They've already been generous, it would be hard to ask for more."

"Then you'll have to ask your father. I can't take less, Collin, this is what I'll live on for the rest of my life."

"Oh yeah, I understand, sure." He looked downhearted, and she was surprised that it didn't touch her. He, after all, was the heir to her farm.

She patted his hand. "I'd be so pleased to have you youngsters in this house. Keep it in the family, the house your father and uncle built."

She could see that he was shaken. He gave her a hug and went away.

She thought she would like to see Karl's face when Collin told him how much money he would need to buy Helve's house. She was sure Karl would say he couldn't help, though saying no would cost him in another way.

But he didn't say no.

He didn't argue with Helve, either; indeed, he never spoke to her again. He sent her a cashier's check, certified mail, for twenty-five thousand dollars, and everything was set in motion for the sale of Helve's home to Collin and Lily.

38

On Wednesday, three weeks before school let out, the Lupine public schools had an early dismissal day so that teachers could have inservice in the afternoon. They did this every year, although parents hated it. One of the eighth grade girls, Gabby Genari, had let a few girls know that they could come to her house to swim. Amanda, who always managed to be on the periphery of what was happening, considered herself included when Gabby told two girls at lunch while Amanda was sitting right beside them.

Amanda caught Juni between classes on Tuesday and told her that her brother would give them a ride to the Genaris' house. Juni could come home with Amanda and they would go from there. Juni demurred—she hadn't been invited—but Amanda was persistent. What else did Juni have to do? Actually, Juni had wondered if Brian would be at Steve's house, but then she thought he would probably hang out with guys from high school, and besides, she wasn't supposed to be at the house when Alison wasn't there. Brian was like a pen pal anyway, except that they talked on the phone instead of writing letters. She didn't think he would want to be seen with her in public.

So when Eleanor asked the girls how they would spend the free afternoon, Juni said she was going to Amanda's, with no mention of the pool party. Tilde was going to the Kenyanjuis', where Jamila would be responsible for her little brother, a third grader.

At Amanda's house, Juni tried on some swim suits that had belonged to Amanda's big sister, but they were a size or more too small. Amanda assured Juni that there would be suits at Gabby's house. They ate a lunch of chocolate bars and apples. Then Amanda's brother, Kyle, showed up and hurried them along, because he had somewhere else to be. When they got to the Genari house, though, he told them not to get out yet, because he had something that would help them have more fun. He lit a joint and passed it to Juni. She had never smoked anything, so she gagged and coughed, but Kyle showed her how to inhale, and coaxed her to keep trying. By the time they got out of the car, Juni and Amanda were giggling.

The Genari house was on a road with the feel of a country lane, a quarter mile from an intersecting road that led to the freeway in one direction and to a dairy farm in the other one. Below the house was the panorama of a horse farm.

The Genari parents were out of town, and the big sister, who was in charge, was in classes at the college. There were no adults on site. In the pool vestibule, Juni found a two-piece suit that fit her, except that the top squeezed her breasts into fat mounds and there was a fold of belly above the shorts.

The day was blindingly sunny and hot, perfect for being in the water. In the kitchen, Gabby had put out soft drinks, chips, and pickles. Amanda looked in the refrigerator and found two six packs of beer and half a bottle of Chablis. She and Juni split one of the beers.

The water was cold until you dunked yourself and got used to it. Juni wasn't so sure she liked it, but the marijuana and the beer had affected her, and the sunshine was soporific. She slid into the pool and stayed near the side, holding on lightly, gently bobbing, eyes half-shut. A couple of girls were in the pool in their underwear. There were eleven girls, counting Amanda and Juni, the last to arrive. Stripped as they were to near nudity, the girls were friendlier than at school. One of them even came over and adjusted Juni's suit bra to make it looser.

Then a group of boys driving around looking for fun spotted a couple of the girls sitting on the steps at the side of the house, below the pool. They shouted to the girls, who giggled and ran back to the pool. The boys followed, five of them.

Juni didn't like it when the boys showed up. They were a lot older than she was, probably had been drinking, and were whistling and calling out to the girls in the water, who were nervous and giddy. She was self-conscious about her exposed breasts. She was feeling chilly.

She went into the house and called Brian. She didn't know where he was or what he was doing, and she didn't care. When they talked late at night, he always ended by saying, I've got your back anytime. She asked him to please come and get her. At first he tried to put her off, but she was pleading, so he told her get the address and he would be there as soon as he could.

When he drove up, she was sitting on the steps off the back deck in her swim suit, with her T-shirt on and her jeans folded in her arms and her bra tucked inside. She was barefoot; she hadn't been able to find her shoes. He told her to get dressed and he would take her home, but she started crying and said she wanted to go right then.

Brian took her by her arm and led her to his truck. He opened the passenger side door. She climbed inside and he gave her shoulder a squeeze. He backed the truck up, banging into someone's car, slapped the steering wheel, then roared away. Juni put her hands on the open side window and looked out. Her wet hair was whipped in the air.

"Put on your seat belt," Brian yelled. She groped for it and got herself buckled in. She was shivering. "What were you doing there?" he asked her. "What were you thinking?"

Juni started crying. "It was supposed to be just girls. Nobody invited those boys." She lifted the hem of her T-shirt to wipe her nose.

A police car entered the road down at the intersection, where Brian was headed. Brian slowed down and gave the cop a wave as they passed one another. Then he floored it. Juni was curled up with her legs under her, her head against the edge of the window, the seatbelt loose.

"Bet some neighbor called the cops!" Brian shouted to Juni.

At the road, Brian could stop and turn left, then cross the freeway and get Juni home in no time; except, he didn't stop. He also didn't see the large woolly dog in the road until it was right in front of him when he made his left-hand turn. He had only an instant to avoid hitting it, and his instinct was to turn sharply away. He did everything wrong.

The dog loped across the road away from Brian's car, down into the brush. Brian was stomping on the brake as hard as he could, but there wasn't room to stop, because he had turned too sharply left as the dog ran right; the truck bounced into the ditch and fell hard into it on Brian's side of the truck. An approaching car skidded to a stop, and the driver took out his cellphone to call for help.

It was four o'clock in the Lupine Community Hospital Emergency Room, and it had been almost eerily quiet until Brian Nichols and Juni Becker were brought in. Brian's ID was a Texas driver's license. Juni had nothing to identify her, and she wasn't responsive to questions.

The police found Steve's name and address on the registration card in the truck's glove box, but there was no phone number. Someone thought to go back to the truck to look for Brian's cellphone and found it under the seat.

While the ER nurses and doctors began assessing Brian and Juni, the police called Steve. He gave them Juni's name and Nick's phone number. Nick's phone was turned off. When Steve arrived, he explained who Juni was, and said he could get hold of the family. He called Alison, who was at the babysitter's house collecting Fiona; Alison called her mother just as she walked into the door at home. Tilde was at home, and she was frantic when she heard about the wreck. She begged to go to the hospital, but Eleanor said she should stay at the house. Alison and Fiona would arrive right away.

Walter was in the yard and when Eleanor told him what was going on, he went to wake Nick in the trailer. Nick was incoherent, soaked with sweat, and shivering uncontrollably, his teeth chattering. Walter called an ambulance and waited for it while Eleanor drove to the hospital alone. Soon, both of them had reached the hospital in their separate cars. Nick was taken to the ER and straightaway to the ICU. Walter went up to that floor. Eleanor went to the ER.

Steve was in the ER with Brian. Brian had hit the inside of the door in the crash. His left ulna was fractured and his left knee was dislocated and swelling fast. His head had struck the side window. He was in shock. He was assessed for internal bleeding and a subdural. They splinted his arm. With oxygen and fluids, he calmed down and was coherent. Then he had a mild seizure, and the hospital admitted him for the night. Steve called Alison, and she said she and Fiona were staying at the Becker house until someone showed up to be with

Tilde. Steve said he was going to stay at the hospital until he could bring his son home.

Alison called Eleanor, who was in the ER with Juni. Eleanor tried to tell Alison that she couldn't talk, but Alison was upset and talking rapidly about how angry she was with Brian. Eleanor kept saying, "I've got to go," until Alison said, "It's so strange being at your house right now, where I don't live anymore." That was when Eleanor had to just hang up.

Juni, protected by her airbag and her distance from the impact, didn't appear to be significantly injured. At first she had been agitated—thrashing and resisting—but as fast as they could discuss what to do with her, she calmed down, though she was confused and mute. They did a neurological exam and labs, and she seemed okay, but she was remarkably pale. The bloodwork showed the presence of cannabis. When she was touched she recoiled. When asked if she was in pain, she didn't answer. She lay on her back with her eyes open, staring at the ceiling. She was given oxygen and fluids. A second doctor examined her and asked Eleanor if anything had been going on with her before the accident that might help to explain her remoteness. Eleanor explained that Juni's mother had died in late March, that she was moody and sad, and had problems at school. She said she was very surprised about the marijuana, she was certain it was an anomaly.

The doctor said Juni should have a psych exam, but she explained that there was no one at the hospital to do it. Juni would have to be transported to Wellen and admitted to their psych ward. Eleanor said she would have to think about it. She stepped into the hallway to call Helve. She assured her that Juni wasn't seriously injured, though she seemed traumatized; she didn't need to say that Juni needed Helve. She explained how Juni was behaving and what the doctor was suggesting.

Helve was adamant that Juni should not be taken to a psychiatric ward, or to a psychiatrist. She said, " If you take her to Wellen, I can tell you, you won't know when you will see her, or what they are doing to her. She will never forgive you. Juni has had bad things happening for weeks, and now this alarming afternoon—who wouldn't want to crawl inside herself and wait for everything to get better? She's not hurting herself or anyone else. We can let her find her own way at home, with everyone around her."

The "everyone around her" startled Eleanor—the assumption that they were all in it together, the implication that Helve would come to Lupine. Eleanor had expected Helve to immediately launch an argument to take Juni to Frost Valley.

"Will they release her yet today?" Helve asked.

Eleanor said, "I think they will pretty soon."

"I'll meet you at your house. Tell her I will be there. If I'm early I'll sit in the car."

"Alison is there with Tilde. Yes, Helve, meet us there."

"I will sit up with her tonight. She needs to feel safe."

Eleanor couldn't think what to say for a moment. Part of her felt overwhelmed by Helve's confidence, and part of her was grateful for it, because her fear for Nicky's condition was shaking her to her core.

"Helve, pack a bag. We have a bedroom free for now, plan to stay a day or two."

She called Alison and asked her to change the bed in the back room, to get it ready for Helve. "Please make it nice," she said. "Put out towels and a water glass."

Someone came to check Juni again. Shortly after, someone else brought her a cup of orange gelatin and a lemon soda. Juni pulled herself to a sitting position. Eleanor moved to help her—the hospital gown had slipped off her shoulder—and Juni recoiled and bent her head almost to her lap. Eleanor stepped back.

"We'll go home soon," she said softly. "Your grandmother will be there waiting for you."

Juni lifted her head and looked right past Eleanor. She, took a drink of her soda, set it on the side table, and slowly ate a spoonful of gelatin. She looked composed but distant.

Eleanor sat on the chair by the bed and dabbed her eyes with a tissue. She had no idea how long it was before someone came and said the doctor would be there shortly. Juni could dress. They could go home.

39

While Eleanor threw a late supper together—mac and cheese from a box, peas from the freezer, and chopped lettuce—Helve ran a bath for Juni, helped her dress in pajama bottoms and a clean T-shirt, and got her into bed in the back room. She had pushed the bed against the wall with the window. She brought a kitchen chair and put it beside the bed and sat down. She had with her the little book by Astrid Lindgren, _The Children of Noisy Village_, and she began reading the chapter, "How Olaf Got His Dog." Juni stared at the wall for a while, then closed her eyes. Helve read the chapter, "The Big Snowstorm," and then she read the dog chapter again. By then, Juni was asleep. Helve left the door slightly ajar and went to join the family in the kitchen.

"If she wakes up in the night, she will have to crawl over me to get out of bed," she said. She had locked the window.

Eleanor apologized for the food, but everyone was quick to say it was fine, and all of it was eaten. As they were clearing the dishes, Helve went to sit with Juni until she fell asleep again.

Alison and Eleanor stood by the stove while Alison said that she had talked with Steve and he said they might send Brian home, but probably not until the next day. "He will be in a cast and will need physical therapy. I told Steve Fiona and I were going to spend the night here to keep you company. I hope that's all right."

"But what if Steve and Brian do go home tonight? And where will you sleep?"

"If Steve is alone, he'll go straight to bed. If Brian is there, Steve will be downstairs with him and won't care if I'm in the house or not. That's how it has been ever since Brian arrived. They play video games. They watch sports. They play foosball. They come up to eat when I call them, and turn right around and go back downstairs. Then there's Davis, who is eleven. They call him every night. Brian says he has a bad time at home and school both. The only reason the mother didn't send him, too, is she doesn't want to lose the child support. Steve is sure it's true, and he wants to go get him now— though he would be here in July anyway! When Brian told him their mother put Davis on medication for his behavior, Steve went crazy. He says he'll pay his ex off if he has to. So now I can look forward to two messed up boys in the house with Fiona. I didn't sign up for this when I married Steve, Mom."

"You knew he had kids. Alison, I'm disturbed to hear you talk like this. Imagine if Steve said he doesn't like having Fiona in the house because dealing with Ben is a bother. You married a man with children, where is your generosity?"

"I'm exhausted, Mom. I'll sleep in Juni's bed, and Fiona will sleep with Tilde, they've already worked it out. I called in sick for tomorrow, so I can help Helve with Juni. I can make some food. Steve will understand."

Eleanor said, "Maybe a good night's sleep will help you see things better tomorrow. But call Steve now, please. Give him some support." She put her arms around Alison. "It takes time to feel like a family." She rubbed Alison along the wings of her back, like Alison had loved as a child.

Late, Walter called to update Eleanor about Nick. He had septic pneumonia. He was on big-gun IV antibiotics, fluids, and oxygen. The doctor said that as bad as it was, it could improve quickly. He was lucky he got in when he did.

Eleanor left work at noon on Thursday to spend the rest of that day at the hospital with Nick, who was still in the ICU, but improving. Back at home, she could not have been more surprised at how comfortable Helve's presence was. Helve sat and read in the bedroom while Juni dozed and lay half-awake; she read to her, walked up and down the driveway with her, fed her snacks. Thursday night they were up much of the night, wearing a path around the living room.

Friday night, after Juni was asleep, Eleanor and Helve sat up and talked. It just happened. At first, they talked about Juni, of course—Helve was reassuring—and then Eleanor confessed her worries about Alison, who didn't seem to have settled into her marriage very well. She explained a bit of Alison's history with Ben, and expressed worry about their ongoing friction and the effect it was having on Alison.

"Maybe women should put off childbearing for a year or two, until they are sure they've landed in the right marriage," Helve said with a chuckle.

"Good idea, but a lot of marriages are like mine; I was nineteen, a college student, and then I was pregnant. Walt and I had talked about marriage, it was okay to move it up a little, but when I look back—I was very young. My mother died when I was eleven. I spent my adolescence in foster care."

"I had no idea. You're a strong person."

"Oh, hardly! I'm a one-foot-in-front-of-the-other person."

Helve patted Eleanor's hand. "Women have to be."

Eleanor said, "The girls will want to spend the summer with you. We might all go to the coast for a week, but beyond that—"

"Actually, I'd like to take them to Sweden for the summer."

"Oh!"

"It's late to plan, there were things I had to settle. They will need passports."

"I saw their birth certificates in Nick's things when we packed up in Portland," Eleanor said. "We will need to get photographs. I'll send the application by overnight mail, with the expedited fee."

"I'm relieved. I didn't know what you would think. I'll get tickets when we have the passports. Of course, I'll pay for everything."

"And how long will you be gone?"

Helve smiled. "I'm not coming back."

Eleanor gasped. "Oh no! Are you sure?"

"I have nobody left here except the girls. My daughter Elin has two children, a boy and a girl. I have a sister. Cousins. I want to be with them, and then, some day, to be buried by my mother and father. I will show Sweden to Tilde and Juni and introduce them to their family; I hope they will come again and often. At summer's end, I will put them on a plane home to you. Or, you are welcome to come for them and spend some time."

"But Juni—"

"Juni will be all right, you'll see. She won't be miserable forever."

"How old were you when you emigrated?"

"Nineteen. I was very innocent. My mother had died when I was thirteen, and my sister, who was still little, was raised by our aunt and uncle, who lived in Malmo. I stayed with my father—he had a prosperous farm—more or less stepping into my mother's shoes in the kitchen and laundry. Then Father had a heart attack. There I was with a farm! Imagine. I was friends with Henry, from school. He lived on a less successful farm not far away. He was a second son, and he had a younger brother. The oldest son would have the farm. All Henry talked about was going to America. He had relatives in Minnesota.

"Of course I had to sell the farm. I couldn't wait to do so. My uncle saw to it. My aunt said I would go to university, but I had done poorly in school after my mother died, and I didn't have the confidence for more education. Henry said if we married we could have this adventure, you understand? Then he said his brother would come, too. The proceeds of the property were divided with my sister, but I had a substantial stake. I didn't know what I would do if I didn't marry Henry, so I did, and we left Sweden soon after. In Minnesota, my money wasn't enough, but someone told us about the Frost Valley in Oregon."

"Oh my," Eleanor said. "It's like a movie. My whole life has been right here in Lupine."

Helve said, "There is a lot of good in that kind of life." Then she said she would go to bed. Eleanor wanted to ask her—something—but she wasn't quick enough to think what it was.

Eleanor lay awake a long time that night. When Walter came home, she wanted to tell him about Helve, but he crawled into bed and fell asleep. She kept thinking of what Helve had told her, and she realized that Helve's story didn't sound at all romantic. She had been orphaned, with no education. The way she talked about Henry didn't have a shred of sentimentality to it; it sounded like settlers sharing a covered wagon, heading West. Of course it was all just a summary, but there hadn't been warmth in Helve's telling.

Helve, Eleanor, Tilde, and Juni went into Wellen to Walgreen's the next afternoon and had the girls' passport photos taken. Eleanor had hers done too. Juni stayed close to Helve. At one point, Eleanor saw her holding onto Helve's blouse in the back.

Afterwards, they went to a bookstore and bought a travel guide to Sweden for the girls. Shortly after they arrived home, Walter called from the hospital to say that Nick was out of the ICU. He would probably come home Monday. A little later, Helve asked if they could order Chinese food, something she seldom had a chance to eat. Eleanor said of course. Walter picked it up on the way home from the hospital. The girls were pleased with the food.

After dinner, Helve said she would go home in the morning, and what did Eleanor think of her taking Juni for the rest of the school year? It was only a couple weeks. Helve had a lot to do to get ready to leave her house, and Juni could help.

Eleanor agreed. She tried to imagine Juni traveling, and wondered how she would cope, but then she imagined her left behind, and wondered how she would survive.

Walter went to bed early, and the girls to their rooms. Eleanor and Helve drank a bottle of Pinot Grigio, sitting side by side on the new couch. Eleanor poured the last drops into Helve's glass and said she was anxious to have Nick home. She was worried about his job.

"But he's ill, and he works for the hospital, right?" Helve said. "They will understand. They will want him to return when he is well."

"Yes, but my worry isn't that they won't hold his job, it's that he won't be able to do it."

"Because of his drug use?"

"Mostly, I guess. I think he restrains himself on the days he works, but I don't see how he can go on and on like he is, barely present in his own life, let alone in Tilde's and Juni's. And he's not well, in general."

"There's probably nothing you can do, Eleanor. He's got to want to take care of himself. And he did get a job, that's a start."

They sat in silence for a while, and then Eleanor spoke. "Have you sold your house and your share of the farm?"

"Yes."

"Where will you live in Sweden?"

"My daughter and her husband have a small house on their property that they usually let in summers. I'll move there in the fall."

"She has children?"

"A boy, fifteen, and a girl, only eight. They don't know me, but they will."

Eleanor set her glass down and folded her hands. "I am taking a big step, too, though nothing so radical as moving to another country. I am going back to school in the fall to finish my degree in history. At my age."

Helve nodded. "Good for you," she said. After a short while, she said. "When you get right down to it, going home to Sweden is the first decision I've ever made on my own."

"I feel that way, too. Don't get me wrong. Walter is a good person. What I want to do has nothing to do with him or our marriage."

"Henry mapped out my life."

Eleanor laughed lightly. "I guess I would say Nick mapped out mine. You know, getting pregnant. I was lucky, because Walt and I were in love. But I was young."

"At least you had some education. I learned English easily, and I've read a lot," Helve said, "but I'm ignorant as a rock."

"I doubt that," Eleanor said. "And I'm starting to think you are wise."

Helve looked surprised. "Wise enough to know that you are doing something good. You're still young. Who knows what lies ahead?"

"I don't have any big goals. I don't want to be a teacher, say, or write books. I just want to know more than I do. I think learning—knowing—it's worthy in its own right."

"We must toast that," Helve said, but their glasses were empty, the bottle was empty.

So instead, Helve opened her arms and the women embraced.

40

Monday, Eleanor went from work to the middle school to catch Abigail Kenton and bring her up to date on Juni's condition, and to explain that Juni had gone to Frost Valley with her other grandmother.

Abigail said, "I'll talk to her teachers, I think we can give her grades from what she has done. We just want to know that she has the basic skills she'll need to start high school, and I think she does. Right now, the most important thing is her health."

"The summer will be restorative."

"Yes." Abigail smiled. "And I have some good news for you. Our grant went through—the summer math camp for gifted kids. We will host it here in the middle school. It starts the week after school stops, and goes on through the third week of July. We have a great team. Ryan Willard will head it up. He's Ernie Willard's son, a post-doc scholar at U of O in mathematics. He was a boy genius, went to the Duke summer program as a kid, finished his BA at seventeen. Ryan and another doctoral student, Ken Scotland, along with Ernie, will teach. There will be visitors from the college and the community; we have a retired Harvard physicist in town who wants to be involved. And I'll make sure they have snacks and a great lunch! We have an extraordinary crop of kids who will learn and bond, and they will have each other in high school."

The camp would run Monday through Thursday, and would comprise mathematics, along with some time for sports and recreation. The kids, twenty of them, were seventh or eighth graders from Lupine and Wellen, Grants Pass, and Eugene, and a freshman transfer student from Portland. There were six who lived at a distance, and they would need to be housed in Wellen Sunday through Wednesday nights.

"I'm sure I can find families for them, and I can offer a stipend," Abigail said. "I'm excited about this. When you see what Tilde accomplished on her own, and then how fast she progressed just since she arrived here, you know she is very special. The LMS students and the transfer student will join a select sophomore group at the high school in the fall for math."

"But Tilde is only a seventh grader."

"I've recommended that the seventh graders in Ernie's group go on to high school, if parents approve. Research shows that math prodigies do well academically, socially, and psychologically, if they are allowed to progress at their own speed. They tend to be more mature for their age. All their teachers approved the acceleration."

"So you need hosts? We can take two girls. Sure, let's do it."

"Don't you have your hands full, Ellie?"

"No. Juni will be with her grandmother for the summer. We have spare beds."

A little later at home, Eleanor talked to Tilde about the school. She told her she didn't have to go, if she would rather go to Sweden when her sister did. Tilde knew about the program, and was eager to attend it with her friends, as Eleanor had expected. When Eleanor told her that two of the girls in the group would stay at the Beckers', Tilde clapped. So Eleanor called Juni to join them, and explained about the school and its timeline. Tilde would still be able to go to

Sweden for the month of August, and Eleanor would come with her to accompany their return trip.

Tilde ran to call Jamila. Jamila gave the phone to John, Tilde gave hers to Eleanor. John said, "The family is going out for pizza, and we'd love to have you join us."

"Would it be be all right if we waited for another time soon? With all that has been going on, Walt and I haven't had any time to talk, just us." The two couples agreed to go out for Indian food the following weekend, while the girls babysat Jamila's brother.

Walter was very happy with the evening plans, and immediately started suggesting where he and Eleanor could go to dinner, but Eleanor pointed out that there wasn't time for a restaurant meal. So they strolled down to Main, picked up sandwiches and a couple beers at the deli, and walked to the park. They found a bench at the duck pond.

"What a fine day," Walter said.

"It makes me think of when we were first dating," Eleanor said. "We came down here all the time."

"I was a cheapskate," Walter said. They both laughed.

"It's a beautiful park." Eleanor took a big bite of her reuben sandwich.

In a while, when they began walking on a path, Walter asked her if she was up to a "semi-serious future-prospects kind of discussion."

"What in the world does that mean?" Eleanor stepped off the path into a patch of sunshine, and Walter followed. The prospect was about the property they owned at the end of Cherry Street.

"I had a call from a developer interested in buying it. Kracken. He did that golf course project south of town. We would get a wad. They don't make more land like ours, right in Lupine."

"And you think we should sell? Why?" She needed a moment to orient herself, but her first reaction was anxiety. She had never thought about what it would mean to sell the parcel, but for sure it would mean the end of the open space, the quiet; it would mean a change in their environment. The whole neighborhood would be affected.

"I'm just telling you I got a call. That it's a possibility, if we're interested. If we don't sell now, we can sell later; or we can hold it and the kids can sell it down the line."

"Are the taxes so high? Why sell it now?"

"The taxes are a bite, but they've been in our budget all along, they aren't a reason to sell. The cash would be a backup if we drag out our lives and need long-term care. Of course, if we were in that situation, we could sell it then, couldn't we?"

"I don't understand what the sale would mean."

"Kracken would build high class houses, meaning spacious and expensive. Gardens, lawns, gazebos. He would improve the two streets and add offstreet parking. It would upgrade our neighborhood. His houses would be set apart from our smaller, old ones. A row of trees, maybe. Or a fence."

"That doesn't appeal to me."

"Or we could do something good with that land if we developed it ourselves. It's been on my mind. The city is short of housing in general and desperate for affordable units. Steve and I have been talking for a while about building skinny townhouses and apartments, with units set aside for low-income families—some to rent, some to sell. A small playground; xeriscaping. It would be nice to have more children on the block, wouldn't it?"

"Where would that kind of development money come from?"

"I think we could get some public funds. And—you borrow."

She didn't like the way he said that, it was condescending. She stared at him. What drove him? Why didn't he just take care of what they already had?

"Not our money, Walt. When I just found out we have it."

He took out his handkerchief and blew his nose, and then said, "Maybe we could turn it into a great big community garden."

She couldn't tell if he meant to be funny—to appease her—but it wasn't working. He didn't know when to stop. She had an engine inside her that turned things over and over in her mind, and right now there was a lot to worry about. Walter didn't do that. He thought about things neatly, with a start and a stop. He had to be in motion. He had to have a project all the time.

"Couldn't you just coach another team? I can't take in something this big right now." She felt a wave of resentment that he was so blithe, when they had a full house and she had plans of her own.

He said, looking away from her, "There's no hurry." He scuffed the ground with the toe of his shoe. She could see he was disappointed in her reaction, probably miffed. His sulk reminded her of the early days of their quarrel about Celeste. She almost remarked on his childishness.

But then she thought—of course! She blushed head to toe. Of course. Celeste had been a damned project, too. She had needed help, and he was good at help. It really had been all about her house, her stuff, her preparations to depart, and not about her—not in any way that Eleanor should have minded. Why oh why hadn't she seen that then? What would have happened if she had said, oh, you're so nice to help her? We must have her come to dinner. Walter had been exasperated because he couldn't believe that after forty years, Eleanor still didn't know him. And she had been exasperated for the very same reason.

He expected her to be excited when—and because—he was excited; maybe that was a good thing. He had posed this building idea as a way to do something good for the people of the city. She loved Lupine. She had never lived anywhere else. It was her home, though it had been gussied up by California retirees and tech titans—and he was right, she loved her neighborhood. She didn't want an enclave of wealth next door. She would rather have young families, singles, people who worked and came home and sat out on the lawn and watched their kids play.

The city offered little to its cooks and clerks and cleaners and sanitation drivers; to teachers and nurses and cops. What Walter was proposing, if she understood him, would be a small rock of good in a pond of urban change, but it would be worthy.

She took his arm and smiled. "You guys are something else. I look at that property and I wonder when the mowing guy comes next. You look, and see a whole community. Let's come back to it, Walt. Soon. Let me get the girls settled for summer. You'll have to explain a lot of things to me. But I'm not opposed. I don't want to sell to Kracken, either."

He lit up. His happy spirits were contagious. She felt her bad mood slide away. He linked arms with her and they started along the path out of the park.

It would be nice to go home and make love, but she thought then what they really needed to do was sit down and evaluate the changes in their lives. There was a lot they needed to talk about. First were all kinds of practicalities. She wanted money issues to be openly, jointly resolved. She wanted to know how they would be engaged with one another's endeavors, if only to promise to keep each other informed, and how they would make time to nurture their marriage. She wanted to know if they should hire a housekeeper.

For the first time since she was nineteen years old, she had her own dream, and if he had his, well, that made it easier to enter hers. She wanted Walter's companionship; she wanted to be his lover—a better lover, in fact. She wanted to mother the girls, but with a light touch.

And she wanted her own separate life, in which she took care of no one else, answered to no one else—not all the time, of course not, but some of the time. The fabled room-of-her-own was hers to have; she only had to step into it.

41

On Friday evening, Alison showed up, this time alone after dropping Fiona off at the Corry house in Wellen for the weekend. She had come to talk to her parents about her exasperation with her home situation. Steve was going to fly to Texas on Sunday, and he had told Alison he didn't know how long it would take him to consult with an attorney, maybe go to court, but he was going to stay until he could bring Davis back to Lupine. Brian hadn't been able to return to school; his fractures were complicated, and he was depressed. He was on medication for the time being, and he just had to wait until his leg healed enough that he could begin physical therapy. For now, he was basically confined to the basement, where he had everything he needed, as long as Alison shopped for groceries. He had two appointments coming up, and Steve had arranged for his cousin Jonas to get Brian to them.

Walter, Eleanor, and Alison were at the kitchen table, the site of so many shifting paradigms of family that spring. Eleanor opened a bottle of sparkling water and set out a dish of salted peanuts, like it was a cocktail party.

"I told him that I can't take care of his son by myself," Alison said, "and he just about exploded. He said all he's asking me to do is get groceries. That's absurd. Brian can't be in some kind of solitary confinement down there, and I'm not going to go watch Hulu with him. I said either Jonas has to move in—in the basement—or Brian has to stay at Jonas's place. So Brian is going to Jonas's apartment. I am sure Jonas isn't happy, but he did step up."

Which was what Alison did not do, Eleanor thought.

Walter said, "He'll be alone there all day while Jonas works. It would be better if he stayed here."

"Oh no," Eleanor said. "I'm not up for that. Tilde sharing a bathroom with her father *and* a boy she doesn't know? I won't do it."

Walter said, "Brian is an injured boy, and I am with Alison on this. He needs his father's full attention. He barely knows Alison. Steve can go get Davis after school is out. Brian needs him now. What is the hurry? What is he thinking?"

"Oh, Dad," Alison said, and burst into sobs. "Oh thank you for understanding."

Eleanor stood. "We don't need to get involved."

Walter put his hand on Eleanor's arm, urging her to sit again. "Of course we are involved. Steve and Brian are family now. Alison is out on a limb. Why don't I go over there now and talk to Steve? The two of us can talk to Jonas tonight. I'll propose that Brian sleep at Jonas's apartment, and I will pick him up each morning to spend the day with me. Jonas has to work. I can get Brian to his appointments. He can ride around with me while I run errands. He can hang out here. And Steve can let up on the gas. Three days is enough time to find an attorney and spend some time with the boy. He can get back here by Friday. This is not an immediate crisis. Davis can come up for the summer while the wheels grind with lawyers. Steve can try to work things out with his ex-wife without fireworks. He needs to think of Alison, too. Most of all, he needs to think about Brian."

He looked at Alison. "I am so sorry about all this, and I understand your feelings, and I'm not going to spend too much time thinking about what is going on between you and Steve, and how upset I am with both of you. The needy person is Brian. He can't be abandoned. And honestly, Alison? I am surprised Steve would ask you to take care of him. Did anybody ask Brian what he thinks? What Steve is asking is too much physical responsibility for you; and your reaction isn't to say you can't do it, it's to say you don't want to."

At that, Walter left.

Alison, stunned, sat quietly while Eleanor began to prepare supper. Tilde, who had kept herself tucked away in her room, appeared and offered to help. Eleanor gave her vegetables to wash and peel, and Alison slunk away to change Juni's bed for herself.

The days that Steve was gone were good ones for Brian. Walter brought him to the house, set him up with food and the TV, took him on drives around the city to point out the sights, and showed him what they'd been doing with the bungalow, which wowed him. When Walter mentioned that he needed to do something with the long yard between the two houses, though it was late in the season for landscaping, Brian surprised him with a long description of what grew in the part of Texas where he had grown up, including not just plants and trees, but snakes, birds, and small mammals. Brian was a whopping big bright kid, starved for talk, and as he and Walter got to know one another over the week, he not only seemed happier, he got along better on his cast and crutches.

His mother, Brian said, didn't like boys. It was the heartbreak of her life that she hadn't had a little girl with her second husband, but instead had yet another boy. He thought she ought to adopt.

"Maybe she didn't get enough mothering, herself," Brian said solemnly. "Maybe she doesn't know how to do it."

Walter was moved and amazed at Brian's insight and generosity. He took him in the house and split a beer with him. Brian was shocked, until Walter explained that it was legal because they were a boy and his step-grandfather, at home.

Eleanor was tidying the kitchen when Nick entered into the room. He had lost weight, was pale and a little stooped, but he had gone back to work. He kept to himself. Walter said he saw to it that Nick ate something during the day. He coaxed him into running errands with him, or going to the bungalow to see the renovation as it was completed.

She offered to make an omelet or warm some soup, but Nick ate a banana and drank a glass of water. She had hardly spoken to him since the night she made him leave the house; it seemed like a year ago. Since he came home from the hospital, he slept in the back bedroom, but he almost never ate a meal with them.

He told her that he had some things he needed to tell her. She sat at the table beside him, their chairs turned so that they were close and face to face, but his eyes were cast down.

"Is this about your heart?"

"No, and don't worry. I'm on medication, and I walk a little every day. I'm fine at work, I like the job. It takes a lot of attention to manage a pharmacy in a hospital, and when I'm doing it, I'm not thinking about other things. I'm okay, Mom. Even if a broken heart is forever, the syndrome isn't."

"What cures it?"

"Time."

"You have to want to be well."

"It's not psychological, Mom. And anyway, I do want to be well." He smiled. He had beautiful straight teeth that had cost them a fortune. "There was a moment in the hospital when I thought I would just let go, but I couldn't do it."

"Oh, Son."

"I want to ask something of you. I want to live in the bungalow. I was just out there yesterday and they were cleaning up. They said they were finished."

"Yes, they're done. But I have to rent it, Nicky, I'm sorry, a lot of money went into the renovation. I wrote out an ad a while ago for the paper."

"Of course I'll pay you rent. Just hear me out. I'll be a great tenant—no parties, no pets. I'll only smoke in the yard or on the porch, I promise. I'll be close by. I can have dinner with you and Dad and the girls on nights I don't work. I want to be there for them, but I have to live by myself."

She was silent for a few minutes. He had one hand on the table, his middle finger tapping, tapping.

"So, can I?"

"You're still putting it all on me, Nicky. You just want to wave as the bus goes by. You're never going to be their father again, are you?"

"I'm going to try, in the best way I can, so they know I love them. And part of that is admitting I'm in no shape to be their parent."

"When was the last time—ever—you had a real conversation with Juni or Tilde?"

"I pick Juni up on Sundays from Frost. We talk on the way home."

"Tilde tells me about Jamila's father. 'John has these great running shoes. John took us to the high school track for some timed runs.' Don't you think she would like to do things with you?"

"I have provided for my family for fourteen years, Mom."

"All right, all right. You can live in the bungalow."

"Thank you. Tell me how much and I'll give you a check right now."

"There's a coffee pot out there, basic things, already. I'll get you some bedding." She remembered his filthy apartment. She would have someone in to clean. He wouldn't like it, but it would be part of the deal. "I have to think about the rent."

He leaned over and kissed her cheek. "Now, please make us some coffee, because I have a story to tell you, Mom. I thought I was going to die in the hospital and all I could think was, I can't take this story to my grave. I have to tell you though I know it's going to be hard for you to hear. You'll know what to do."

"Right now?" Her heart was thumping.

"As soon as we have a cup of coffee. I'm sorry, Mom, I can't be the only one who knows. Not anymore."

Eleanor poured coffee and moved to the end of the table. They both put cream and sugar in their coffee and slurped it, leaning on their elbows. Eleanor wondered what it would be like to wake up and know everything was right with the world. Part of her wanted to reach for Nick, clasp his hands or touch his cheek. Part of her wanted to go to bed and put her head under her pillow.

He said, "It's a problem, it's bad, and it needs to be solved. It's about Karin."

She pushed against the back of her chair. Karin was dead and his life was still about her. She had left him with some terrible conundrum and he wanted his mother to solve it. He would pass the muddle to Eleanor and then he would never have to think about it again. She sighed.

"It's about Peter, Mom. Karin was sick when he was born. She couldn't think straight."

Eleanor held her hand up like a crossing guard. "I know, darling. Remember, I was there afterwards. And Helve told me how difficult it was for all of you. You don't have to." She wanted to put her hands on her ears. She didn't understand why Nick was pulling up that terrible memory now. "That was long ago, love."

He said, "Karin never let Juni forget it. Out of the blue she would say the most oblique thing and Juni would know. Like, 'If only Peter had had time to cry it out.' Then she would call Juni to her and hold her close and murmur that she loved her *anyway*. Months would go by and then she would say something to Juni again, year after year. I didn't know what to do."

Eleanor could feel anger burbling in her chest. At Karin. At Nick. At herself, for assuming Juni was obstinate, when she was carrying such a weight of pain.

Nick said, "I wish when Helve took Juni when she was a baby, she had kept her. Or if only she had taken her when Peter died. I was a coward. I didn't say to Karin, you are hurting Juni with your sly reminders. The baby is dead! That's what I should have said. But I was always afraid Karin would disappear into herself, into madness. I loved her, Mom. I loved her more than I loved Juni.

"Sometimes she would turn to the girls and make paper dolls and cookies, and streamers to hang over the windows. She would kiss them and call them her darlings. She draped their necks with jewelry, braided their hair, painted their nails."

Eleanor wanted Nick to stop talking. Her chest burned with outrage at the enormity of his neglect.

She said, "I don't want to hear anymore."

"But Mom, that's not all."

Eleanor put her hand up like a traffic cop. "I need a break, Nick. I need to breathe." She left the room and stepped out of the house. Someone was in Velma's house, looking out the side door.

Her "wasteful love" was being sorely tested! Where had they gone wrong, she and Walter? How had their smart good son grown up to be a coward? Of course he wanted to live in the bungalow; he would be alone to wallow in grief about his dead Karin. Maybe she should make it requisite—for him to live in the bungalow—that he get psychological help. His stew of guilt and blame was far too murky for her to deal with. But she knew help was no help if you didn't want it, and Nick wasn't ready to let go of Karin.

She had calmed down by the time she got back to Nick. He was sitting at the table. His hands were flat on the table, his cup between them, his coffee cold. He looked as if he meant to get up but hadn't quite got to it. She said his name and he startled.

"Mom," he said. "Mom."

"I'm going to make a pie. I have frozen peaches—"

"*Mom.* Please sit down."

She held onto the back of a chair. "I'm sorry, Son. I'm sorry for your grief and shame, but I'm sorrier for your girls and I'm angry on their behalf. It's good—for you—that you told me all this, because you said it out loud, but it's disturbing for me. I can't do anything to make the past better, you know. You have to pull yourself together."

"*Mom*. I haven't told you the worst thing."

Tears welled up in Eleanor's eyes so fast she was blinded. She picked up a kitchen towel and wiped her eyes. "Christ, Nick, can you make it quick?"

"It was all a lie. Juni and the baby—it was all Karin's invention. Mom, don't look away. I am going to tell you this. I didn't know. Not for years. Karin finally told me the truth. We were smoking, sitting on the back step. It was a nice day. I remember I was admiring the clouds. And out of the blue, she said, 'It wasn't Juni, it was me.' I knew immediately what she meant. 'How?' I asked her. She had been smoking that night, she had been—she called it dreamy—and the sound of Peter's crying woke her. She took him to bed with her. She meant to comfort him. She fell asleep and rolled over on him. It was a terrible accident, only it was her, not Juni, who did it. When she had waked up, she put him in bed with Juni, because she didn't want to tell me that she had killed our son. Mom, she put it on me, didn't she?"

Eleanor thought she would faint. She gasped for air. Nick reached for her hand and she pulled away. She stepped back until she hit the stove with her hip. She was looking at her son, but she couldn't focus. She pressed her closed eyes with the heels of her hands, then looked at him again.

"Get your things and move into the bungalow now." She fumbled in a drawer and came up with a key. "You have to tell Juni, Nicky. If you don't know how, talk to someone who can help you. You have to tell Juni, because her whole life is marred by Karin's lie. And by yours."

He was weeping. "But if I tell her the truth—don't you see, Mom? She'll know her mother lied to put the blame on her. She'll know I knew and didn't say. Won't that be worse for her? Isn't it the most awful thing ever, what my Karin did? To Juni, and to me?" He made a terrible gargling sound.

Eleanor rubbed her arms. She felt dizzy. She thought the most awful thing ever was what her son had done and was doing now, and it made her sick that he acknowledged Karin's guilt *to get out of his own responsibility.*

"Don't ask me to decide what Juni should know," she said.

"I just did."

"You are her father." She left the room, went to her own, and shut the door hard.

Some time that night, Nick put a check for a thousand dollars on the kitchen table and moved into the bungalow. Eleanor saw the check the next morning. She snatched the check and put it in her purse to deposit on her way to work.

That evening, Eleanor and Walter sat in the back yard and tried to catch up on what was going on with the family. They agreed it was as if a storm had come through the house: Alison and her fraying marriage; Juni and Brian's accident; Helve's plan to go back to Sweden; and worst of all, Nick's account of Karin's duplicity and his collusion. Walter said he was going to tell Nick that he needed to see a psychologist, but there wasn't any way to make him do so.

Eleanor said, "I'm so angry with him, I don't want to see him, but he can't just walk away from Tilde, he has to show up now and then. How can we explain any of this to her? We need help. I'm going to offer her the option of talking with a counselor. I've been so absorbed with Juni, I've ignored Tilde. She seems self-sufficient. But she is twelve years old, with the same burden of grief and displacement that Juni has, and who does she have to talk to about it? Certainly not Nick. I don't think she wants that kind of intimacy with me, and I don't want it, either. I'm going to call that woman Juni wouldn't talk to, Meghan Lewis. I'll ask Tilde first."

"But you're all right with Nick in the bungalow?"

"It's a great arrangement for him, isn't it, out from under our gaze? He can show up for meals a couple times a week; he doesn't actually have to do anything to be a father. And he can pay me more than I would have rented it to a stranger for."

"Be kind, Eleanor, he's our son."

"I don't want to be kind. I want not to know about his life with Karin. I don't think I love him anymore."

"I love him, Eleanor. He's suffering. I'm going to help him if I can."

"How!"

"He's not so intimate with me as with you. We can spend time together in neutral ways. He has to connect with the present world, I think I can help with that."

"And Alison, too? It's a good thing you went out of business."

"She's so impetuous, it's hard to pin her down. This on-off marriage is destabilizing. I don't want to say that Ben smells blood in the water, but there's no question that Alison is vulnerable to his claims of insecurity in her living situation, and to top it off, she says she is going to move in with her friend Charlotte."

"You don't think—she can't be giving up yet. And Steve—we haven't even heard what he thinks. They just got married!

"I am trying not to draw conclusions. Right now I'm concerned about Ben. It's hard to know what he's actually thinking and what is Alison's hysteria. I think she's using Ben as an excuse to back out of her marriage, and she might be making things worse. I asked her if she would talk to someone, and she said yes, a lawyer. So we'll do that. She will have to do better than bunking with a friend, if she comes up against Ben. I wish they had never left our house."

"Can you stay friends with Steve if they separate?"

"Of course I can. I will. I've already talked to Alison about it. She doesn't care."

Eleanor said, "Thank you for stepping up with Alison. I don't have it in me to deal with her hysteria. And I'm so relieved to not feel I'm battling Helve anymore. A few hours of talk, a bottle of wine, and something shifted. Opened. We have more in common than just Juni. She is very good with her, you know. She calms and reassures her. But when she told me she was moving to Sweden, she said at the end of the summer she would put Juni on the plane, or I could come and get her. I was surprised."

"Let it unfold, honey," Walter said. "And right now—could you just be with me?"

Eleanor felt something slip in her chest; a kind of settling. It was a relief.

They went to bed. Walter slipped his arm under her. He said, "I think it's great that you are going back to school."

"You'll have to be the majordomo of the household."

"I'm up for that."

"I had no idea we were rich. I suppose not *so* rich, but we're lucky."

"I'm sorry. I wasn't keeping it secret. I always thought of the money as my father's, and mostly ignored it. The funds have done well, we pay taxes, and after almost thirty years since my folks died, here we are. Any decisions to be made going forward, we'll make together."

She turned on her side and laid her arm across his chest. "I'm sorry we lost ourselves for a while."

"I didn't want to explain myself, though that's all it would have taken. I'm sorry, too."

Eleanor straddled him and bent close to whisper, "Remember what I told you about the sermon? About wasteful love? Do you think that includes sex? Do you think passion is bottomless?"

Both of them began to laugh hysterically.

Walter said, "Is there any other kind?"

42

"I hoped there might be a happy ending to this," Walter said to Alison the day before Steve was due home. She scowled, and he didn't state the obvious—that he had hoped she and Steve would work something out. They had just moved Fiona's Princess bed and some boxes into the front bedroom, across from Juni's bed. Now they were taking Fiona's and Alison's clothes to Charlotte's house, where they were settling in for the time being. Steve was due back the next morning, but Alison wouldn't be at home.

Complaint papers had been delivered to Alison at school, with a summons to appear in court in June to review custody. Alison had promptly taken off a day from work and filed for divorce, a step that was logical only to her. Steve would be served as soon as he returned from Texas. It didn't make sense to act so rashly, but Walter didn't argue. He did try to get Alison to wait to talk to Steve. He tried to make the case that Steve would have had a hard time in Texas, and it wasn't fair to ambush him. She said nothing would change her mind. She said she would text Steve to tell him the papers were coming.

"Don't you think this is horrible for me, too?" she asked her father. "Don't you think I wanted to be married to Steve?"

Walter asked her to talk to a counselor, but the only advisor she wanted to see was a lawyer. She told Walter, "I don't love Steve enough to be his wife and take on his burdens. I'm not a big enough person. I thought I loved him, because we had good times. I thought if I got married I would be happier and Ben would realize that Fiona had a good family life with me. But I don't like being married. I don't want to be someone's wife. When we spent every other weekend together while Fiona was at Ben's—that was perfect. I wish we could go back to that, but we can't. I've hurt him too much. And he has his sons. And I—I don't really like him anymore. He's too *guy* for me, Dad."

Walter sighed. "Oh, honey. Don't try to sum it all up. You don't have to defend yourself to me. I don't want to see you and Steve bitter toward each other, though. I'm sure it's a shock to him, you up and leaving, but he's going to be busy with his boys, and that's a good thing. I hope you don't expect me to cut ties with him, because I like him a lot, and we have things going on."

"All I care about is Fiona."

"I know, I know."

When the papers had been served on Alison, she called Ben and he told her he wouldn't talk to her on the phone anymore. They shouldn't talk without lawyers present. He said they could text about visitation. He said he didn't think Alison was a bad mother, he just thought it was his turn. He didn't say anything about Steve and his sons.

Fiona didn't know what was going on. She was thrilled when she heard they were moving to Charlotte's, whose daughter, Daphne, was her best friend.

Alison took another day off from school and she and Walter went to see a lawyer Walter had chosen after talking to half a dozen friends. He was an older man; Alison hoped that meant he was experienced and wise.

He said that Ben had no grounds to challenge Alison's custody. What he did have was an increasingly common argument that a child didn't necessarily belong with her mother if the father was a good parent.

"Perhaps he will claim he has a better environment for her, but any judge will understand that you are merely in transition from your marriage, and, I think, will not hold that against you, because you have a good job and ample support from your extended family. If he tries to say his home would be better because he has a wife and more children and a beautiful environment, well, I don't think a judge will go for it."

Alison had been holding her breath; she exhaled noisily in relief.

"However," the lawyer went on, "A judge could entertain Mr. Corry's request for primary custody on the grounds that Fiona is no longer a small child, and he, her parent, has as much to offer her as the mother does. His case, I must tell you, could be as simple as, turnabout is fair play. I'm not saying he will win. Fiona has always been with you, and there is sound reason for continuing what she knows as her life just the way it is, at her age. But year to year, there has been growing sympathy for fathers. When both parents are competent and loving, how do you make a choice? Does Fiona stay with you because that is what she has always known? Or does she go to her father because she has not had the benefit of his full-time love and company? There is no case law to answer that, so it comes down to the bias of the judge."

By then, Alison was sobbing, clutching Walter's handkerchief with one hand and his arm with the other.

"I urge you to take this to a mediator," the lawyer said. He laid a piece of paper between them on his desk. "Here are several I know well enough to recommend. I urge you to work something out you can live with. You and Mr. Corry have had a contentious relationship, but he sounds like a good father, and he certainly has standing in the community, as do you. Court is a gamble, an expensive one. Judges aren't really trained for family issues. You would be up against a judge's own experience and prejudices. I would do my very best to represent your interests as your daughter's best interests, but I can't promise you you will win."

Alison and Ben had been to arbitration years before. They hadn't been able to agree what day it was.

Walter said he was going to talk to Ben. Alison said he shouldn't waste his time. Ben took Walter's call and was civil, but he said it was better for a judge to hear the issue. School was out and he got a temporary court order allowing him every other full week with Fiona, pending a hearing, starting on the next Saturday. Alison broke out in hives. That was when Walter realized what had to be done.

He took Alison to Venti's coffee shop and found a corner table. He reached for her hands and squeezed them gently. "Here's what we are going to do," he said.

"If you go to court, I will help you with the lawyer's bills, but it is money down a rathole, Alison. You are a good mother, but there's nothing to say Ben isn't a good father. You will have the luck of the draw, like the attorney said. Has the judge been divorced? Has one of his or her daughters or sons gone through what you are suffering? You shouldn't fight Ben for custody."

"Dad!"

"You should share custody. Even-steven."

Alison scoffed. "We don't even live in the same town!"

"Exactly. You just put your finger on the central problem. So you are going to move to Wellen and share custody with Ben."

Alison's iced coffee had gone watery. She took a deep drink of it, burped, and shoved the cup to the edge of the table. A dare. Walter picked it up along with his own empty cup and set them on the neighboring table. He leaned on his elbows, his face close to Alison.

"You can't fight him for sole custody. It's too big a gamble. And I'm not sure it's fair. He's a decent guy. He loves Fiona, he has a stable home."

"Thanks a lot, Dad."

"Fiona loves both of you. Look, Alison, the timing is perfect. We can start looking for a house for you. We'll help you buy it, sweetheart. Please."

"What does shared mean? Every other night? Every other month?"

"You think about what feels right for you and offer that. You're making the big move, maybe Ben will give you grace points on scheduling."

"I have a job in Lupine."

"So you commute."

"That's a big burden."

"Listen, Alison. Ben left a prestigious job to move to Wellen, and his wife left her extended family, all so Ben could see Fiona every other weekend. It's your turn to give."

Alison sagged in her chair. In a little while, she asked, "Do you think this will be enough for him? Do you think this will end the war?"

"Let's call him and find out."

Before Walter could explain himself, Ben said again they shouldn't talk without their lawyers. He was high on having the upper hand. Walter calmly suggested that Ben and Alison meet soon with a marriage and family therapist in a formal setting to discuss how joint custody—now a given, as far as Alison was concerned—might work out to make Fiona happy. Alison was willing to move to Wellen. Nobody would be bound to anything, they would just test the waters. Of joint custody.

"Joint custody? With Fiona and Alison in *Wellen?*" Ben said. Walter said yes.

The following Sunday, Alison and Walter spent an hour driving around the neighborhood where Ben and his family lived. It was an area with older houses on large lots with trees and gardens. They would need to find something smaller or a little farther away, for Alison to afford it, but Walter thought they could buy a house no more than ten minutes from the Corrys by car, and an easy route to the freeway entrance. There was a house for sale every few blocks and Alison would have a big advantage: Walter and Eleanor were going to give her the cash to buy a house outright; they would carry a mortgage at market rate, discounting their substantial contribution. It was a good investment for them. It was a godsend to Alison. Walter told Eleanor he thought he saw a spark of enthusiasm in Alison: her own home; an end to fighting with Ben.

Alison applied for a position in the Wellen School District in case something opened up for fall, and if it didn't, it would eventually. She would miss her school, but kids were kids, and maybe John Kenyanjui could replace her. She was being awfully optimistic, but sometimes miracles happened, didn't they?

JUNE

43

Helve believed in routine. If your life had a framework—the things you did every day, the times you did them—you could do those things instead of breaking down when you might otherwise. She respected Eleanor's sincere attempt to establish a routine with Juni, but so many things had been out of their control at school, and their home had felt alien to the girl despite the family's good intentions. Perhaps there had simply been too much: too many people talking too much; too much love; too many rules. Here, in the quiet of Helve's home, she hoped Juni could let go of what agitated her, whether it was grief or anger or adolescent angst. She would have liked to have both girls with her, but perhaps it was better for Juni this way. Tilde was thriving.

Helve woke Juni at seven-thirty every morning—gently, saying her name, raising a window blind. They had coffee, and bread and jam or cereal; later in the morning, after they took a long walk, they had another cup of coffee or a glass of milk, and slices of meat and cheese, or a boiled egg.

Helve explained her plans to Juni and said she needed her help in getting the house ready for its next owners. Juni was placid, agreeable.

They started in the main room. The front opened onto the porch and the yard. There was a small garage on the south side, with nothing in it. They could move their bags and boxes into it temporarily, until Helve arranged for donations or a transfer to the dump. The church would help. They ran a free store one Saturday a month.

The main room had a porch along the back, a door that led onto it, and two large windows. In the original plans, that had been the front of the house. It faced west and would have made the room very hot in summer if not for the porch, which now had an awning, and there was a long twill curtain that could be pulled across both windows; in the winter, the sun was pleasant. The south wall had the door that led to the bedroom and an alcove, a kind of wide hall structure the length of the bedroom. One end was a linen closet, the other was the bathroom, which was narrow with a tub set in the long way. On the other side of the main room was a wall of deep cupboards for storage; it ended before going under the stairs, where there was a cramped bathroom with a shower, toilet, and small sink.

Helve explained to Juni that they would empty each cupboard into large plastic bags. There were two piles, one with things to be donated, the other to be discarded. Everything was already neatly folded, so it was easy enough with the two of them working together. There were blankets, pillows, tablecloths, baby clothes, forgotten jackets, boxes of stationery, a sewing machine and its paraphanelia, winter boots and gloves, manuals for tools and machines and appliances. And books, piles of them—these were put into boxes. There were atlases, boxes of receipts, a set of good dishes, skeins of knitting yarn, several first aid kits, a tempera painting set—never opened, a box of discarded eyeglasses, some old frames with nothing in them, seven photo albums, a pile of report cards, large casserole dishes and platters; dog leashes, a back scratcher, board games, two old radios, a portable typewriter, an old record player and a dozen vinyl records.

At first Juni would wonder about something, and rather than ask a question, she would hold an object up in front of her, maybe shake it or extend it. Helve patiently but briefly answered, glad for Juni's curiosity, though she was eager to be rid of all of it as fast as she could.

After the first day the pantomimed inquiries tapered off, and soon Juni handed things to Helve or vice-versa without remarking on anything.

Helve had never eaten lunch—she preferred the two-part breakfast and an early supper—but she stocked snacks in the refrigerator or pantry for Juni. After a few days, Juni chose to eat when Helve ate, and the combination of her diet and their long walks began to tone her legs and reduce the baby fat around her middle

In the late afternoons, they sometimes took a drive to another part of the valley. Juni especially liked to go to the park on the river, where there was a grassy slope, and below it a shallow pool with smooth rocks. Other times they stayed at the house and read. Juni set aside half a dozen novels from the cupboards, ones her mother and aunt had owned. They were old-fashioned—well written, with a nicely elevated language—and they absorbed Juni in the evenings. Helve thought they would last her until they left for Sweden, with one for the plane.

Helve began to teach Juni some basic practical Swedish. She didn't push her to speak. Instead, she combined her own naming of objects with Juni picking things up. So, for example, as she practiced counting one-to-five, they moved spoons around on the table, depending on Helve's announcement of a number. She taught her important words like "come," and "stop," and "don't touch that," "give me," "take," and so on. There was no rush, and Juni didn't seem to be frustrated, though the language was of course very foreign to her. Helve didn't ask her to speak. She didn't understand why Juni didn't want to speak, but she wasn't going to try to make her. She wanted her to be able to follow directions.

They shared Helve's king-sized bed, with Juni on the inside and the bed pushed to the wall. Helve read to her before they went to sleep, or played music on her I-pad. Juni didn't present any real difficulty, though sometimes she would sit down on a couch or a chair and shake her head if Helve suggested that they do something or go somewhere. The weather was mild and lovely, so if Juni was feeling unsociable and Helve had nothing she had to do, she went out onto the back porch and sat on the step with a book, and eventually Juni came and joined her in the nice air. Then Helve would talk. She liked to tell Juni about the people in the family whom she would be meeting, and Juni seemed to enjoy hearing what she had to say.

Helve had thought about what traveling with Juni would be like if she didn't snap out of her strange state, and she decided that it would be easier to speak for her, saying that she was mute, rather than have Juni become scared about speaking. They definitely didn't want to have any scenes at customs. Helve couldn't think of any reason to pressure Juni. She would explain about check-in and customs, and give her the choice: speech or silence. Perhaps what wasn't spoken didn't matter, or mattered too much to say; or maybe Juni didn't have words for what she felt. Whatever the reason, she functioned for now in silence. When Juni wanted to speak, Helve would listen. Until then, Helve wasn't going to disturb the peace.

The passports arrived.

Eleanor drove over after work to give Juni's passport to Helve. As soon as she stepped in the house, she realized that much of it had been emptied. There was nothing on any wall, not a clock or a calendar or a picture. The floor was gleaming. A cupboard door in the main room was open, and she could see there was nothing left inside.

Helve made tea for them and they sat at the kitchen table. The window was open wide and a light breeze blew across them. Helve said, "Juni is asleep upstairs. We're going to clear out that space tomorrow, and today is her last chance to choose anything to keep. Otherwise, everything is going to the church or Goodwill. The house sale has gone through, though of course I can stay until the day of my flight. Collin and Lily are in Collin's old room next door for now."

"Here is Juni's passport." Eleanor handed the document to Helve. "There's also a notarized letter authorizing you to travel with Juni, signed by Nick and me. It is valid June fifteenth, and is good for ninety days, which is the length of a regular tourist visa. For longer— you will have to look into all that and tell me what you need from us. I also bought travel insurance for medical emergencies for her, for that same time frame; all the information is in the documents. Tilde and I will come in early August. We can sort things out then if Juni wants to—to stay longer."

Helve held the documents in her lap. "You don't have to worry about where you will stay, I'll arrange everything for you and Tilde. Juni and I will plan the sightseeing. We can get around by train, mostly. I'm so pleased that you will come with Tilde."

Eleanor said quietly, "I thought it was essential for the girls to be together and to be with their father, but now I don't know if it matters. Nick is a ghost; I don't think he'll ever change. He has moved into our bungalow. He goes to work. He's under the care of a doctor, at least. The girls don't seem to have any expectations of him."

"There is stability now. That means a lot to a child," Helve said.

"Oh, and these." Eleanor took out Juni's I-phone, which Juni had left in Lupine. "Do you understand Facetime? The girls can talk on their phones on Facetime for free, either audio only or with pictures.

Someone there will be able to explain it. Do you have one of these phones, Helve?"

"Yes. Karl and Ivy gave me one last Christmas, I've not used any of its features except the phone."

"I'm going to get one, too. Then you and I can talk or text on wifi. We have to figure out the time difference."

Helve took the phone. "I bet Lily would help us with the phones."

"Juni can text if she doesn't want to talk."

"I'll make more tea. Or coffee, would you prefer coffee? Would you like some cheese and crackers? I have a sliver of lemon cake, too."

"I don't need anything, thank you. I have more to tell you. I'm so sorry, but for Juni's sake, there is something you must know."

As Eleanor succinctly explained Karin's lie about Peter's death, Helve's head fell forward, frightening Eleanor. Eleanor touched her arm. "Helve? Helve?"

Helve was crying.

"You have to tell Juni," Eleanor said. "No one else can do it."

"I know." Helve wiped her tears and straightened her posture.

Eleanor said, "I have given up trying to understand either of them, Karin or Nick. What matters is that Juni is—as you once told me—a wounded child. It's not our fault that she is troubled, Helve."

"No, it's not. What matters is, it isn't Juni's fault, either." Helve reached for a napkin and wiped her eyes and cheeks. "I'll tell her in Sweden. Is that all right with you?"

"I think you are the best person to decide what to do. She loves and trusts you. Is it better for her to continue to think she accidentally killed her brother, or to know the blame was a lie? You don't think she would eventually get over the guilt she feels for an accident, but she might not get over her mother's lie?"

"I can't maintain a lie of such magnitude, Eleanor. Peter's death is more important to Juni than her mother's. Karin was sick, but she was responsible, and as it was horribly wrong of her to blame Juni, it would also be wrong for us to elaborate the lie. Truth is better than deception. And I believe in the resilience of youth."

Eleanor said, "I'm going to tell Tilde soon, you should know. She is seeing a counselor now."

Helve said, "I think the trip will be good for Juni. She will hear a strange language around her, but everyone we meet will speak English. There will be interesting and beautiful things to see. Maybe the past, even her mother, will seem distant. There will a day when I can talk to her and clear that lie away like heavy dust."

"Helve, if Juni wanted to stay with you for a while, would you keep her? Would your family welcome her? Is it possible, legally?"

"Yes. There are many relatives younger than I. My sister has a large home on the outskirts of Stockholm; she has grandchildren Juni's age. Elin will love having Juni at her home. Juni can get a resident visa as Elin's guest, or as mine, I suppose. I am after all a citizen and will be a resident again; and I am her grandmother. She could extend her visit, perhaps spend a whole year. Many young people from all over the world do so. More than that, how can we know? A lot would depend on Juni's response to the language—whether she is too intimidated to learn it. And as much as I love Juni, I hope her strongest bond will be with Tilde."

"We would be glad to have her back," Eleanor said, "if she wants that."

Helve squeezed Eleanor's hand. "Nothing has to be decided today."

"Thank you," Eleanor said on the porch. "Thank you," Helve said in return.

Going home, Eleanor felt lighter. Helve wanted Juni, Juni wanted Helve. She didn't think expect that to change; the trip would strengthen their attachment. There you go. She expected that in the end, Juni would stay in Sweden and be Helve's responsibility. Eleanor didn't know why she had fought so hard for authority over Juni. It was only right that she finally be free of the weight of worry of the girl.

Helve realized that she needed to explain to Juni what the plans were for the summer. One morning at breakfast, she took Juni's tourist guide and opened it to a map of the country. She pointed out Stockholm and Uppsala and a few other places.

"We'll visit some of the places tourists go to, but we will spend most of our time with our relatives, especially my sister, Anna, and my daughter Elin. Swedes are very happy in the summer, you will see them outdoors everywhere. You will like the folks. We can sit down one day soon and look at the guidebook and you can pick out a few things you want to see. When I was a girl, I was mad for all things Viking." She smiled, remembering. "There is a wonderful museum in Stockholm."

"Eleanor and Tilde will come in August, after Tilde's school is over. By then you will know if you like Sweden and want to stay, or if you would rather come back with them."

Juni opened her eyes wide.

"Now," Helve said, after a deep breath. "I think we should visit Ivy. I haven't seen her in a while, and I know the chickens will be glad to see you."

To Helve's relief, Karl was nowhere in sight when she and Juni showed up at the house. Ivy held Helve a long time, until her tears dripped onto Helve's shoulder. They couldn't talk much with Juni there—a relief to Helve—but it was good to clear the air.

That evening, after Juni went to bed, Helve called Otto. He came over the next afternoon, and she told him about the sale of her house, and a little about her summer plans. She patted the couch for him to sit beside her. She got out her map of Sweden and showed him where she had grown up, and where her daughter lived, and a few famous sites.

"What is the best season for a person to visit Sweden?" he asked.

"Oh, every season has its merit," Helve said.

"I suppose you will be very busy after you arrive."

"I plan to do things in my good time."

"I've never been out of the country."

Both of them smiled. Helve said, "Do you understand Facetime?"

One day after class, Eleanor picked up Tilde and took her to Frost Valley to see Juni. Tilde wanted to visit the chickens. The hens remembered Juni, and liked for her to sit in the coop while they gathered around her. Tilde giggled when Juni held the red one on her lap. It put its head close to Juni and chirped. Other hens clustered at Juni's feet. Tilde asked if she could pick one up, and Juni nodded.

Helve and Ivy stood on the porch and watched.

"Will the girls be sad to be separated?" Ivy asked.

Helve said, "I don't think so. It's only a little over a month. They like different things and they seem to respect that about one another. They can text on their phones and think about what they'll do together in August."

"I don't know how I'll bear it without you," Ivy said, a catch in her throat. "These past weeks have been hard enough."

Helve reached for her hand. "I know. I'm so sorry, Ivy."

"Well, it's going to be nice having Collin and Ivy close by. She's a good girl."

"You could come for a visit. I would love that." Helve squeezed Ivy's hand. She didn't think a visit would ever happen.

The girls came running in for drinks of water. Ivy took them to see the baby chicks in the cage in the warm bathroom. Ivy had ordered them, as she did every year, because she loved them so much; she would eventually give all but one or two away.

The girls sat down on the floor and Ivy gave each of them a peeping chick to hold in her palm. When they put them back and washed their hands, Ivy brought out a pan of brownies and everyone had one. They stayed to have soup. While Ivy was at the stove, the girls sat across the room from one another and texted and waved into their cameras.

One day, Helve asked Collin and Lily to come to the house. It was spotless. The furniture was arranged neatly. Helve had scrubbed the old brown couch and it had dried bright and glossy. Helve showed them the bedroom, the linen closet that held towels and blankets; in the kitchen, pots and pans and containers in the cupboard.

She explained that there were boxes and sacks of clothes and other things in the garage that were to be given away. Someone from the church would come to pick them up. Upstairs had been cleared of everything but twin beds and a small bureau.

"What I need to know is if you want any of what is left—the furniture, the kitchen goods, and so on. I can leave the house absolutely empty, if you like, but—"

"Oh, leave it just like this!" Lily cried. "We have nothing of our own. It's perfect, truly. We would be honored to use your things. Is that okay?"

"It's perfect," Helve said, touched by Lily's warmth.

"We are going to have our wedding next month," Lily said. "In the field behind the house. Collin's brother is coming from Massachusetts, he'll stay with their parents. Our friends will stay over here. A few will bring tents. There are the beds upstairs, and the couch; we'll borrow pads and quilts. I wish you were going to be here! After the wedding we will go down into Frost, to the park, for the summer classical concert."

Helve kissed the young woman on both cheeks.

On their last night, Helve and Juni ate with Karl's family. Ivy had put her foot down with both of them, Karl and Helve, and it was easier than Helve expected. She and Karl didn't speak to one another directly, but they weren't hostile. After supper Collin played the fiddle and Lily played the flute. Helve and Juni stayed past dark, and Collin drove them home .

Lying in bed later, Helve was hit with a wave of nostalgia and longing. She had never let herself think that Henry might not have been in love with her when they married, but in their own way they had rescued one another, and they had forged a marriage that suited them, one of companionship and courtesy and teamwork, parenting, church—and Karl and Ivy. She had been cheated, but she hadn't known it until Henry was dead, and there was no use in holding on to anger. She would never know if Henry had meant to cheat her or had merely done what seemed practical at the time, or perhaps, as the pompous lawyer had intimated, Henry hadn't known what he was doing when some functionary pushed a piece of paper to him to sign. What bothered her most was he had violated the whole history of how families pass property in Sweden.

She was comforted, thinking that when she settled in Sweden, memories of Henry and Karin would grow dim. Oregon would become a myth. She would be a Swede again.

44

The two student guests were vegetarians—not vegans, they were quick to say—and Tilde said she would eat what they ate. Eleanor told them not to worry, she would be able to accommodate them, but the redheaded girl, Violet, had it all figured out. The three girls made a shopping list for Eleanor and went with her to the store. Greens and other fresh vegetables, frozen peas and water chestnuts, rice, noodles, soy sauce, eggs, parmesan cheese, flat bread and bean dip, fruit. They cleaned and prepped the food themselves and stored it in special cloth bags (everything from the Good Food Store) in the refrigerator. Their suggestion, which was agreeable to Eleanor, was that they would make their own meals about five each evening, eat and clean up and leave the kitchen to Eleanor and Walter. Would that be all right? Eleanor was floored, and amused. The sounds coming from the kitchen were delightful, and when the girls were out, Eleanor made big salads for her and Walter and added pasta or a piece of fish. Over the six weeks, both of them would lose several pounds and enjoy their meals immensely. They always finished with a piece of chocolate, and then sat and drank one more glass of wine. Often it was nine o'clock before they got out of the kitchen.

The girls got on famously. The second Eugene girl, Janna, was plump—like a rock. Her sport, she said, was baseball, and Walter took them down to the field with him sometimes to play. Several times they went to his Little League Games. They also shot basketballs, watched movies, listened to music, read, and talked a lot. They huddled behind closed doors. They walked to and from school. They seemed to enjoy the company of adults, in this case their hosts, and liked to talk politics. "Why do we have to pay for internet, when it is a free utility in many European countries? Why shouldn't transgender people have the right to be in the military? Do you know the rate at which we are exterminating animal species in the world?"

There seemed to be no end to what they knew and what they cared about.

Eleanor remarked to Walter that she was sorry that Juni wasn't there; surely the joy and camaraderie of the girls would have rubbed off on her. But who was to say Juni wasn't going through a renewal all her own?

On the weekend, Walter or Eleanor or both of them took Tilde to Frost Valley for a few hours. While the girls hiked or went to Ivy's to check on the chickens, they visited with Helve. On the last visit, Walter hosted an exceptionally good meal at a restaurant in Frost Valley, and Karl and Ivy joined them.

On other weekend nights, Walter and Eleanor got together with Jim and Patricia or Barbara and Tom for dinner while Tilde went to the Kenyanjuis, or they hosted the Kenyanjuis—little to give after the Kenyanjuis' generosity to Tilde. It was that wonderful time of year when the gardens were in bloom and the fierce heat had not yet rolled in.

Alison found a modest, well-cared-for house a mile from the Corrys. She wanted to update the bathroom and add a new back porch and a new fence, and sand the nice wood floors downstairs, but all in all, the house was fine the way it was, and Walter suggested that she settle for redoing the bath and sanding the floor for now. The sellers had put in new kitchen appliances, and had resurfaced the long driveway. There were two bedrooms and a good-sized bath upstairs, large closets; and a toilet and lavatory downstairs. The previous owners had opened up the living room space nicely. The light was good. Walter paid cash for the house, deducted a large sum as a gift, and had a mortgage drawn up for the rest, at low market rate. She could not have rented as nice a house for what her payment would be. If Eleanor and Walter both died before it was paid off, the mortgage would be forgiven as part of her inheritance.

At Alison's invitation, Ben came over with his daughter Polly to see the house one afternoon when Walter was there working in the yard, and he congratulated Alison on finding it. He seemed very happy about Alison's and Fiona's move; indeed, he was so friendly and calm, Walter could see something of what Alison must have fallen in love with years ago. They had been rotating weeks with Fiona for the time being, although they had an appointment to meet with a counselor to talk about a calendar. Fiona was going to spend three weeks of July in Lake Oswego at Ben's inlaws, with Jacqueline and their children. Ben had said, "What would you think—" and Alison had said, "I don't see why not." They had agreed to draw up a schedule a year at a time, and to be flexible for unforeseen circumstances. Ben had readily agreed to continue his child support payments with no reduction; in fact, he had offered the concession. And Fiona would spend one Saturday a month with the Beckers.

45

Helve and Juni left on the first Saturday of July. Walter, Eleanor, and Tilde were there to see them off. Nick was back in the bungalow, asleep after his Friday overnight shift. He had seen them in Frost a few nights earlier. The family met at Denny's for breakfast. Ivy was there without Karl, her eyes red-rimmed from crying. And Otto came, at Helve's invitation.

Juni looked well. She had cut her hair to shoulder length. She was wearing navy-blue linen pants and a cream colored T-shirt with B E R R I E S spelled out on the front in red. She and Tilde sat together in the booth and texted one another all through the meal, giggling. Helve was relaxed; she was going home.

Ivy left as soon as breakfast was cleared, and Otto shortly after. The others went to the airport. Helve checked herself and Juni in, and they stood near the place where they would pass through security. Juni and Tilde hugged and swayed. Eleanor and Helve clasped, and touched one another on their cheeks, and smiled at how far they had come.

Then they were gone. Juni didn't look back.

As the Beckers turned to leave, someone called out Tilde's name. It was Jamila. She and her mother had just arrived. The families met and Amy explained that the refugees were due any minute now. As she said it, they did arrive—a jumble of long skirts and headdresses, shabby suits and polished shoes, wide-eyed children and solemn adults. On and on they came. A small crowd had gathered and everyone stood still and quiet, as if it were a parade of VIPS, deserving of a quiet reception.

Then someone called out, "Welcome!" and there was applause and a few whistles.

In the car, as Walter backed out of their parking place, Eleanor and Tilde started crying. They looked at one another and laughed, too.

"I told Juni I will see her in a month," Tilde said.

"You will. That's quite soon. I'm really excited about it."

"Didn't she look pretty?"

"She did. I loved her T-shirt."

There was silence as Walter maneuvered the car out of the lot and onto the road to the freeway and into the stream of fast-moving cars.

"Do you think the refugees will be happy here?" Tilde asked.

Eleanor turned around to answer. "They are safe now. Their children will go to school. They must be sad to leave their homeland and families behind, but here they can make a new life and in time, be happy."

It took half an hour to drive home, but no one spoke again. It was a pretty day, and Juni and Helve were gone.

There was a moving van in their driveway. Walter parked on the street and they walked up the drive. There were posts—the start of a fence—along the back of the property. There were lights on in the far side of the house, where the bedrooms were.

Tilde cried, "Oh look, a dog!" Sure enough, a greyhound had its nose pressed against the glass in the sliding door. They saw a woman walk briskly across the kitchen. They had new neighbors.

"Wait until tomorrow," Walter said. He could read Eleanor's mind. "We'll have lots of time to meet them."

Inside, they all got drinks of water in the kitchen. Eleanor said she would lie down for a bit. Walter put his arm around her.

Tilde said, "The other day, Meghan asked me what I call my grandparents. And I realized, I don't call you anything."

Eleanor and Walter stared at her. She was right.

"So she said I should talk to you about your names."

"Whatever you want is okay," Eleanor said.

"Would it would be okay if I didn't call you Grandma or like that? If I called you Ellie and Walter. Would that be all right with you?"

Eleanor, blinking back tears, nodded yes. Walter said, "That's just fine."

Tilde said, "I hope the refugees will be happy here. And Juni in Sweden."

"Me too," Eleanor whispered.

"I'm already happy," Tilde said. "I am."

END

ACKNOWLEDGMENTS

I am grateful to Margaret Sutherland Brown for her perspicacious and sensitive reading of an early draft, and for her efforts on behalf of the manuscript.

The book might have died on the vine without the support of my friends who read it and cheered me on. They know who they are. I'm especially beholden to Rebecca Gabriel, who has been relentlessly enthusiastic and optimistic; blessings on her for her sweet spirit.

Of course there is family: my husband, Bill, daughter, Jessica, and granddaughter, Edie, are my stalwarts and I thank them for their faith in my work and patience with my self-centeredness when I am writing. Jonah Bornstein brought his professional acumen to my endeavor. I can't thank him enough.

I would like to add that being able to teach and mentor writers has been a privilege and a nourishment to me for nearly thirty years, and has certainly affected my own writing. I deeply thank Amy Margolis (Iowa Summer Writing Festival) and Meg Kearney (Solstice MFA Program at Lasell University) for the opportunities they have given me to be a part of writing communities.

ABOUT SANDRA SCOFIELD

Sandra Scofield was born and raised in West Texas. As a child, she was educated by the Sisters of St. Mary of Namur. She studied at the University of Texas in Austin, Northern Illinois University, Cornell University, and the University of Oregon, where she earned a PhD. She has taught at grade school, high school, and university levels.

After travels in the US and abroad, she lived for thirty years in Southern Oregon. She now lives in Missoula, Montana in a multi-generational household that includes four dogs and a cat. Her literary awards include a nomination (one of four finalists) for the National Book Award (1991); an American Book Award; a Fiction Award from the Texas Institute of Letters; a Fiction Award from the American Academy of Arts and Letters; and the American Book Award. She has also received a fellowship from the National Endowment for the Arts; a New American Writing Award; and a fellowship from the Oregon Arts Council. Her book *Mysteries of Love and Grief* was a runner-up for the Willa Cather Writing the West Award (2016). Scofield has been on the faculty of the University of Iowa Summer Writing Festival for thirty years, and that of the Solstice MFA Program at Lasell University since its 2006 inception.

She is also an avid traveler, and a painter.